Freshwater Fishes of Connecticut

By Walter R. Whitworth

STATE GEOLOGICAL AND NATURAL HISTORY SURVEY
OF CONNECTICUT

DEPARTMENT OF ENVIRONMENTAL PROTECTION

Second Edition • 1996
Bulletin 114

Originally Published 1968
Reprinted 1976, 1988

Additional copies may be purchased from:
DEP Maps and Publications Office
79 Elm Street
Hartford, Connecticut 06106
(860) 424-3555

ISBN 0-942081-08-0 (paper)
ISBN 0-942081-07-2 (cloth)

STATE GEOLOGICAL AND NATURAL HISTORY SURVEY
OF CONNECTICUT

DEPARTMENT OF ENVIRONMENTAL PROTECTION

The Honorable John G. Rowland
Governor of Connecticut

Sidney J. Holbrook
*Commissioner of the
Department of Environmental Protection*

Richard C. Hyde
Director, Natural Resource Center

Leslie J. Mehrhoff
*Supervising Biologist
State Geological and Natural History
Survey of Connecticut*

Allan N. Williams
Publisher, Technical Publications Program

Book Design by Mary Crombie, Acorn Studio

Cover Art by Duncan Somerville

Scientific Editing by Michael Oliver, Ph.D.
Text Editing by Julie Tamarkin
Indexing by Molly Brennan

Published by the DEP Technical Publications Program
79 Elm Street, Store Level
Hartford, Connecticut 06106-5127
(860) 424-3555

FRONTISPIECE: Photographic reproduction of an oil on canvas painted by Gurdon Trumbull in 1872, entitled "Black bass." Courtesy of the Fine Arts Collection of the Hartford Steam Boiler Inspection and Insurance Company, Hartford, Connecticut.

SHIRLEY

We have followed the stream
of life together,
and have enjoyed many wonderful
and rewarding experiences.
Because we were comrades,
we have passed through the few dark
days without losing heart.
This ichthyologist could have had
no better luck, than to have
"collected" you years ago.

Table of Contents

SCIENTIFIC NAME	COMMON NAME	NUMBER OF SPECIES	
Acipenseridae	sturgeons	2	84
Amiidae	bowfins	1	85
Ammodytidae	sand lances	1	86
Anabantidae	gouramies	1	87
Anguillidae	freshwater eels	1	87
Ariidae	sea catfishes	1	88
Atherinidae	silversides	2	89
Batrachoididae	toadfishes	1	90
Belonidae	needlefishes	1	91
Bothidae	lefteye flounders	5	91
Carangidae	jacks	2	95
Carcharhinidae	requiem sharks	1	98
Catostomidae	suckers	3	98
Centrarchidae	sunfishes	10	102
Characidae	characins	2	110
Cichlidae	cichlids	1	111
Clariidae	labyrinth catfishes	1	112
Clupeidae	herrings	7	113
Cottidae	sculpins	3	119
Cyclopteridae	snailfishes	2	121
Cyprinidae	carps and minnows	22	123

List of Tables

List of Figures

Preface

The purpose of this book is to document the distribution of all fish that were reported in the freshwaters of Connecticut. The intended audience is both the professional and the amateur ichthyologist, *i.e.*, manager, fisherman, naturalist, aquarist, and conservationist. The historical documentation of the ichthyofauna is summarized first, followed by a listing of six groups of fish that may be found within the freshwaters of Connecticut. The first group contains twenty-three species that must spend their entire lives in freshwaters and probably migrated to the freshwaters of this state through a freshwater route. The second group has twenty-five species that must spend their entire lives in freshwaters. They were probably moved to Connecticut by humans and have at least one recently verified viable population. The third group contains twenty-nine species that have the same origin as the second group except that there are no recently verified viable populations. The fourth group has populations of two species that must live in freshwaters, one probably evolved from an anadromous species and one probably evolved from a saltwater species, both within the last 14,000 years. The fifth group contains ten species that must spend part of their lives in the freshwaters of Connecticut and part in saltwaters. The sixth group contains seventy-two species that must spend all or part of their lives in saltwaters and either occasionally, or regularly, enter the freshwaters of Connecticut for purposes other than to spawn. The two species that are contained in the fourth group are not included in the total count of species since both are listed in other groups. Two other species are removed from the total species list also. One, *Arius felis* (hardhead catfish), is listed in the sixth group and should be collected in freshwaters near saltwaters. The other, *Scardinius erythrophthalmus* (rudd), is listed in the third group. It is a European cyprinid that has been recently introduced in all of the contiguous states and, although it has not yet, it will undoubtedly be collected in one of the freshwaters of Connecticut. Therefore, although 159 species are included, a total of 157 species of fish live in or have been captured in the freshwaters of Connecticut.

The factors influencing the distribution of fishes within the freshwaters of Connecticut are then discussed. This is followed by a section on how to identify fish and an illustrated key to the families of fishes that may be found within the freshwaters of Connecticut. Next, there is a section on each family that contains an illustrated key to the species, if more than one species is found in Connecticut, and documentation of the distribution of each species within the freshwaters of Connecticut. Technical terms are explained in the glossary and illustrated in both the keys and the text. Finally, a literature cited section is included for those who wish more information.

This is the second edition, and has profited from both comments to the first edition (Whitworth *et al.* 1968), and twenty-five years of additional collecting in the freshwaters of Connecticut. New information and comments are welcome and should be sent to the State Geological and Natural History Survey of Connecticut and to the Fisheries Division of the Connecticut Department of Environmental Protection.

Acknowledgements

The contributions of those who helped in the first edition are deeply appreciated, especially those of Lou Page, the editor. I am sincerely grateful for the helpful editorial comments of Dr. Michael Oliver, Allan Williams and Mary Crombie. The University of Connecticut Research Foundation provided financial support for some of the travel to historical collections in Connecticut. The University of Connecticut Computer Center provided support for the writing of this manuscript. I am deeply grateful to the many artists who created the illustrations that are included; credit is given to the publications that contained the illustrations. Don Flescher, the National Marine Fisheries Service, helped me locate some of the illustrations. Hildy Cummings, the University of Connecticut, helped me locate the oil painting by Gurdon Trumbull used on the cover. Judith Lefebvre and Randi Brandt, The Hartford Steam Boiler Inspection and Insurance Company, graciously provided a photograph of the painting.

I sincerely appreciate the assistance of six friends and colleagues. R. Jack Schultz, the University of Connecticut, provided a thoughtful review of the keying section and a slide of *Poeciliopsis monacha-lucida*. Douglas Lee, the University of Connecticut, offered constructive comments on the first three chapters. Douglas Tolderlund, the United States Coast Guard Academy, Robert Schmidt, Simons Rock College, and Steve Gephard and Rick Jacobson, the Connecticut Department of Environmental Protection, reviewed the entire manuscript and provided many helpful suggestions. I am forever grateful to five friends, colleagues, and former graduate students, David Bennett, Peter Berrien, John Heuer, Walter Keller and Robert Schmidt. They have greatly influenced my career.

Special thanks are extended to all of the other graduate and undergraduate students who have worked with me over the years and have challenged me to learn more about the freshwater ichthyofauna of Connecticut. Particularly, Peter Aarrestad, Peter Auster, Tim Barry, Al Basile, Mike Beauchene, Ernest Beckwith, Jr., Alan Beebe, Chris Belluci, George Benz, Dick Biggins, H. Richard Carlson, Steve Caromile, John Castleman, David Chestnut, Paul Cislo, Chris Clark, Alan Cohen, Victor Crecco, John DeLaurentis, Donald Dorfman, Steve Ells, Ed Enamit, Steve Gephard,

Dave Gibbons, Robert Goldstein, Steve Goodbred, Kurt Gottschall, Neil Hagstrom, Bill Hyatt, Robert Jacobs, Paul Jacobson, Rick Jacobson, Doreen Jezek, Warren Johns, Paul Kaminski, Nick Kaputa, Connie Kelly, George Kissil, Bob Koski, Mark Kowtko, Ed Lesser, Joeffre Levesque, Alan Libby, Joe Loesch, Steve Long, Bart Marcy Jr., Paul Marsh, Tom McManus, Jim Monopoli, Earl Morse, Don Mysling, Bradley Olson, D. Reed Ostrander, Deborah Pacilleo, William Pohley, Steve Reagan, Robert Rocks, Joe Rubertone, Robert Sampson Jr., Greg Sanders, Tom Savoy, Scott Sauter, Jeffery Schmaltz, Louis Sileo, Gary Smith, Al Sonski, Steve Sousa, Tony Spinnelli, Lance Stewart, Charles Suprenant, Ralph Taylor, Ralph Tiner, Scott Thurmond, Joseph Valentine, George Valulius, Al VanDyke, Richard VanNostrand, Richard Voyer, William Walsh, Dennis Walsh, E.A. Wells, Bruce Williams, Stella Williams, Ann Witt, John Wraight, Steven Yeo, and Miro Zyndol.

I sincerely appreciate all of the courtesies extended me by the many helpful librarians I have encountered at the University of Connecticut. Particularly, Roberta Smith, Richard Schimmelpfeng, Randall Jimerson, Pat McGlamery, Tom Jacoby, Valerie Oliver, Nancy Kline, Jane Recchio, Carolyn Stockings, Robert Vrecenak, and Mohini Mundkur. I apologize to the many other librarians at this and other institutions for not remembering their names. All of them have been most helpful at Trinity, Wesleyan, The State Historical Society, Branford Historical Society, Yale University, and Eastern Connecticut State University.

The comments and suggestions made by other colleagues have definitely influenced my studies of the ichthyofauna of Connecticut, and I am deeply grateful to them—especially, William Lund Jr., Robert Thorson, Nickolas Bellatoni, and Marc Banks, the University of Connecticut; Janet Stone, the United States Geological Survey; Ralph Lewis, the Connecticut Department of Environmental Protection; Russel Handsman the American Indian Archaeological Institute, Washington, Connecticut; David Halliwell, formerly of the Massachusetts Department of Fisheries; William Krueger, the University of Rhode Island; Keith Thomson, Daniel Merriman, and Edward Migdalski, formerly of Yale University; Edward Kluck, the Housatonic Fly Fishermen's Association; Vincent Ringrose, Connecticut Fly Fishermen's Association; and Carl Fontneau, Omni Analysis.

Many current and former employees of the Connecticut Department of Environmental Protection have supported and assisted me in my work with the fishes of Connecticut, and I am deeply appreciative of their efforts. Particularly, Ted Bampton, Cole Wilde, Robert Jones, John Woods, David Green Jr., Peter Minta, Penny Howell-Heller, Robert Orciari, Les Mehrhoff, Richard Hames, Charles Phillips, Eric Schluntz, Rick Jacobson, Steve Gephard, Bill Hyatt, Robert Jacobs, Mike Humphries, Eileen O'Donnell, Tony Petrillo, James Bender, Brian Murphy, Neal Hagstrom, Dave Sumner,

Pete and Mike Vernesoni, Joe Holyst, Mathew Bannack, John Orintas, James Moulton, Joseph Piza, John Overturf, Lyle Thorpe, Harding Joray, Louie Baer, and Larry Bandolin.

Our departmental secretaries, Elsie Spoust, Debbie Horton, and Cheryl Bessenet, have provided invaluable advice and assistance in assembling the final manuscript. I sincerely appreciate their collective efforts to keep me on track. Our department head, David Schroeder, expedited the approval of a sabbatical leave during the fall semester, 1992, so that I could complete this publication. I sincerely appreciate his efforts and support over the years. I especially thank A.J.R. Guttay, former departmental head, and E.J. Kersting, former dean of the College, for their support of the fisheries program.

Unfortunately, with age there is a propensity to forget. I sincerely thank all of those who I failed to recognize here.

I owe a great debt to the people who helped shape my career by providing me encouragement, support and love. My parents, Catherine and Floyd Whitworth; my mentors and friends at Oklahoma State University, William Irwin, George Moore, and Roy Jones; and my friend and colleague at this University, Robert D. McDowell. I wish that they could have shared the completion of this publication with me.

Finally, I especially thank my wife, Shirley, and my children, Susan, Sally, William, and Ward. They not only encouraged and supported me throughout my career, but they spent many "vacations" helping me collect fish. They made living a rewarding experience.

CHAPTER ONE

History of ichthyological studies in Connecticut

The colonial period

Virtually nothing is known of the ichthyofauna of Connecticut during the 1600s. Much of the energy of the average settler was devoted to survival, and nature was usually considered an adversary in the quest to obtain food and shelter and to raise a family. Furthermore, the creatures that lived in the deep woods and waters of the state were often viewed in awe and fear. Few of the travelers to southern New England commented on the fish or fisheries of Connecticut; those who did usually reflected their or their sponsors' biases, *e.g.*, Josselyn 1672, Morton 1637, and W. Wood 1634.

The next century brought more settlers, allowing those with the inclination and the financial resources to devote some of their thoughts and energies to topics other than survival. Although many people viewed the natural resources of the state as sources of wealth, few viewed them as objects to be studied, even those associated with Yale University (McKeehan 1947). Most of the people with free time became involved with the political, social, or religious activities associated with the development of the new country, rather than studying and documenting the natural resources of the state. Furthermore, based on comments made in European angling literature, most colonists were considered uncivilized and there were few, if any, "gentlemen" that indulged in the gentle art of angling during this century.

However, a few references were made to the fisheries resources in American literature. For example, Roger Wolcott (1679-1767) wrote a poem about a brief account of the Honourable John Winthrop, Esq., in the court of King Charles II when he obtained the charter of the colony of Connecticut in 1692. Part of the poem concerns the Connecticut River and some of its resources. The following is taken from Wolcott (1898 reprint of 1725).

> *This gallant stream keeps running from the head*
> *Four hundred miles ere it with Neptune bed,*
> *Passing along hundreds of rivolets,*
> *From either bank its christial waves besets,*
> *Freely to pay their tributes to this stream,*
> *As being chief and sovereign unto them,*

It bears no torrent nor impetuous course
As if 'twere driven to the sea by force;
But calmly on a gentle wave doth move;
As if 'twere drawn to Thetis' house by love.
"The waters fresh and sweet, and he that swims
In it, recruits and cures his surfeit limbs,
The fishermen the fry with pleasure gets,
With seins, pots, angles, and his trammel-nets.
In it swim salmon, sturgeon, carp and eels
Above fly cranes, geese, ducks, herons, and teals;
And swans which take such pleasure as they fly,
They sing their hymns oft long before they die.

An examination of many historical perspectives on the relationships between the human and the fisheries resources of Connecticut and an evaluation of British records for the late 1600s and early 1700s offer one explanation for our limited knowledge of the fish and fisheries resources of Connecticut. British records for that period, *e.g.*, Stock (1927 and 1930), listed Connecticut as one of the colonies with large numbers of citizens engaged in both illegal trade and fishing activities. Fisheries, particularly salt water, were very important to the economy either as a direct product or in a series, *e.g.*, fish–rum–slave (Elliot 1857, Hooker 1936, Peters 1781, Savelle 1966). Thus, in the case of fisheries, the less that the Crown knew about those resources, the easier it would be to pay only a small fraction of the tariffs that were required.

The nineteenth century

Relationships that existed between the citizens of Connecticut and their environment changed in the 1800s. Fewer people were involved with the pursuits that utilized the natural resources of the state for food, fiber, and trade, and more became involved with the development of the industrial resources of the state. Now that business was flourishing and the new country was established, more people were able to consider the natural resources of the state as a source of beauty, peace, and intellectual stimulation. Additionally, more people in the arts turned to nature.

Gurdon Trumbull (1841-1903), who was born in Stonington and raised in Hartford, was considered by some to be the best fish artist in North America (French 1879). He was financially independent and apparently only painted when the mood struck him. Although few of his paintings are available, one of them, painted in 1872, entitled "Black bass," is an excellent representation of the smallmouth bass (a photograph of that is shown on the cover). That painting, and another one that I have not seen, were noted for their quality in a leading sporting magazine (Anonymous 1874).

John G.C. Brainard (1796-1828) was a poet who was born and raised in New London, Connecticut. As a youth, he had heard folklore that American shad were guided from the Gulf of Mexico back to Connecticut by a spirit in the form of a bird that was called yankee bogle. Not only was the function of this spirit to guide the fish back, but to alert the fishermen that it was time for them to repair and set their nets. Thus, poetry was used to introduce people to a life history style that we now call anadromy, *i.e.*, the species spawns in freshwater, the newly hatched fry grow there for part of their juvenile stage, then they migrate to the ocean and grow to adulthood, then the cycle repeats as they return to freshwater to spawn. By formalizing knowledge gained from folklore, others were stimulated to study fish. The following version of Brainard's poem, written about 1825, is from Anonymous (1849).

The Shad Spirit

Now drop the bolt, and securely nail
The horse-shoe over the door;
'Tis a wise precaution, and if it should fail,
It never fail'd before.

Know ye the shepherd that gathers his flock,
Where the gales of the Equinox blow,
From each unknown reef, and sunken rock,
In the gulf of Mexico;

While the Monsoons growl, and the trade-winds bark,
And the watch-dogs of the surge
Pursue through the wild waves the ravenous shark,
That prowls around their charge ?

To fair Connecticut's northernmost source,
O'er sand-bars, rapids, and falls,
The Shad Spirit holds his onward course,
With the flocks which his whistle calls.

O how shall he know where he went before ?
Will he wander around for ever ?
The last year's shad-heads shall shine on the shore,
To light him up the river.

And well can he tell the fated time
To undertake his task-
When the pork barrel's low, he sits on the chine,
And drums on the empty cider cask.

The wind is light, and the wave is white,
With the fleece of the flock that's near;
Like the breath of the breeze, he comes to the seas,
And faithfully leads them here.

And now he passed the bolted door,
Where the rusted horse-shoe clings;
So carry the nets to the nearest shore,
And take what the Shad Spirit brings.

The European influence

Until this century, the natural history of North America that had been documented was mostly done by people who were born, educated, and lived in Europe. They depended on travelers and colonists with the interest to supply them with specimens (Gunter 1880, Hindle 1956, Rafinesque 1817, 1818). Apparently none of the travelers in or residents of Connecticut sent any specimens of fish from Connecticut waters back to Europe prior to the 1800s. Now that the new country had been stable for about a quarter of a century and was becoming "civilized," many educated people immigrated to North America, although no one that settled in Connecticut had any interest in studying fish. One individual, Alexander LeSueur, who did travel in Connecticut documented two species of fish that were collected in the Connecticut River near Connecticut, but probably in Massachusetts (LeSueur 1817a and b).

The American influence

Naturalists from both Connecticut and two adjoining states, (Massachusetts and New York,) made the first contributions to our knowledge of the ichthyofauna of Connecticut. David H. Storer (1804-1891), an obstetrician and naturalist, documented the fishes of Massachusetts (Storer 1839). James E. DeKay (1792-1851), an author, medical doctor, and naturalist, documented the ichthyofauna of New York (DeKay 1842). He received some of his schooling in Connecticut, and his medical degree in Scotland. Both commented on the occurrence of some species of fish in the freshwaters of Connecticut in their tomes.

The first substantial contributions to our knowledge of the fishes of Connecticut were from two native-born residents who became interested in the study of natural history while they were students at Yale University. The first was James H. Linsley (1787-1843, shown in Figure 1). He enrolled in the university to study for one of the professions, theology. Although there were no classes in natural history, he attended all of the extra lectures on the subject. He supported himself while attending Yale by teaching school. Upon graduation, in 1817, he was convinced by his doctors and friends not to enter the ministry. They thought that his health was not up to the rigorous physical demands of that profession.

Figure 1. Reverend James H. Linsley, father of Connecticut naturalists. Illustration from the New Englander (1844), number VII, opposite page 43.

He then taught school for a few years and subsequently established a successful school. His health improved and he gave up his school and entered the ministry for five years. He was forced to give up his churches in 1836 after his health again deteriorated and he devoted the rest of his lives to his favorite study, natural history. He obtained large cabinets of not only fish, but birds, mammals, reptiles, and shells; shells were his favorite study. He then compiled and published the first documentation of the fish (1844b), mammals (1842), birds (1843), reptiles (1844a), and shells (1845) of Connecticut; the latter was finished by a friend after his death.

Few people referred to Linsley's work in Connecticut when evaluating ichthyological contributions in North America. Although Gill's (1873) list of the fishes of the east coast of North American referred to Linsley's tome, he made no comments about the work. Subsequently, historical reviews of ichthyologists in the northeast during that time period did not refer to his work, *i.e.*, Gunter (1880), Jordan (1905), H.W. Fowler (1945), and Myers

(1964). Surprisingly, when Garman (1891) from Harvard, evaluated Dr. H. Storer's ichthyological work in Massachusetts, he compared Storer's (1839) tome on the fishes of Massachusetts with Mitchell's (1818) in New York, Thompson's (1842) in Vermont, and works by Kirtland and Rafinesque in Ohio, Baird in New Jersey, and Holbrook in South Carolina. His evaluation of them was that only one or two of those approached, and that none of them surpassed, Storer's work. Linsley's work in the contiguous state of Connecticut was not even mentioned! Since Linsley's documentation of the ichthyofauna of Connecticut was at least equal to Storer's and DeKay's documentations (Massachusetts and New York, respectively), I believe all three should have equal status in the history of ichthyology in the northeast.

The second of the native-born to make substantial contributions to our knowledge of the fishes of Connecticut was William O. Ayres (1817-1887, Yale class of 1837, M.D. from Yale in 1854). He also was drawn to the study of natural history while he was a student. He initially wanted to work with birds and was a friend of John James Audubon. Apparently Audubon influenced him to concentrate on fish. After graduation, he taught at schools in New York and Connecticut, and performed studies of the natural history of the area, particularly fish (1842, 1843a, 1843b, 1845, 1849, 1851-1854).

He moved to California in 1854, after receiving his M.D., and continued his studies in natural history, especially fish, while working at the Tolland Medical School and maintaining a private practice. Besides his own work, he sent specimens to others, e.g., Girard (1856). Additionally, he was one of the founders of the California Academy of Sciences. Gill (1882) listed forty-four ichthyological papers that Ayres published in the *Proceedings of the California Academy of Sciences* from 1854 to 1863, although 71% of them were published in 1854 and 1855. He published no more papers on ichthyology after 1863. He then relocated for a short time in Chicago and Easthampton, Massachusetts, before returning to New Haven and joining the staff of Yale Medical School. Ayres' ichthyological work in California and Connecticut was often cited, in contrast to Linsley, e.g., Agassiz (1855), Fowler (1945), Girard (1852), Hubbs (1964), and Myers (1964). It is interesting that in the National Cyclopedia of American Biography, Ayres was not listed but Linsley was (Anonymous 1897).

The rise of professionalism

Although the beginnings of professionalism were evident in many fields early in the nineteenth century, most of the fields in the natural sciences did not mature until late in the century. Whether or not a person was a professional depended on how one's peers evaluated that person's accomplishments. For example, after Jordan (1905) reviewed the history of ichthyology in North America, he concluded that some facts were contributed by persons with whom ichthyology had been of incidental rather than of central importance. Thus, some, *e.g.*, Ayers and Storer, were recognized for their professional accomplishments, whereas Linsley was not. Technically, all three were amateur ichthyologists, as they were trained and employed in other professions, the first two in medicine and Linsley in theology.

Naturalists, whether professional or amateur, were categorized as either compilers or explorers by Jordan (1905). Compilers were people of extensive learning, methodical ways, sometimes brilliant and of deep insight, but more often, on the whole, dull, plodding, and mechanical. Whereas explorers were people who traveled far and wide, often enduring hardships, who worked with great zeal to describe new species. Linsley was often characterized as a compiler. We shall probably never know why most of the people that documented the accomplishments of professional and amateur scientists in Connecticut rarely recognized the contributions made to our knowledge of zoological resources by Reverend Linsley and Dr. W. O. Ayres (E. Baldwin 1838, S.E. Baldwin 1901-1903, Bottsell 1950, Brewer 1901-1903, Chittenden 1928, W. Lewis 1946).

The people that contributed to our knowledge of the freshwater fishes of the rest of the United States were similarly educated and employed as those in Connecticut. For example, Spencer Baird, while he was associated with both the Smithsonian / United States National Museum and the United States Fish Commission, relied on amateurs to do much of the work accomplished by those agencies during the nineteenth century. Many of the amateurs he utilized during the summers were professional teachers, as opposed to professional medical doctors or theologians. As the professions were maturing, there apparently developed a distinction between the amateur ichthyologists in certain professions (law, medicine, and theology) and all of the natural science professions. The former, that contributed so much to ichthyology until the middle of the 1800s, were now being discriminated against by some of the newer professionals (natural scientists). The conflict between Dr. W.O. Ayres and Dr. T. Gill, *e.g.*, Ayres (1863), Gill (1864a, 1864b, 1864c) could have been the major reason for the sudden withdrawal of Ayres from ichthyology in the mid 1860s.

Only one of the professional naturalists employed as a teacher in Connecticut added to the documentation of the ichthyofauna of the state during the latter half of the 1800s. Dr. A.N. Rice (1845-1928), who taught at Wesleyan University, documented the introduction of one species of fish in the freshwaters of Connecticut (Rice 1887 and 1888). One of his students, G. Brown Goode (1851-1896), made significant contributions to ichthyology while employed at the Smithsonian / United States National Museum (Jordan 1922).

Fish cultivation

During the second half of the 1800s, many entrepreneurs became involved with raising fish, *e.g.*, Anonymous (1871b, 1876, 1878) and Bunker (1870). Most wanted to cultivate fish, like domestic plants and other domestic animals, to provide profit and food. For example, Elijah C. Kellogg (1811-1881), and all or some of his four brothers, had a lithograph firm in Hartford, Connecticut. He experimented in fish culture and published one paper (Kellogg 1857). Kellogg earned a reputation in the state and, in 1860, Colonel Sam Colt, a Hartford gun manufacturer, sent him to obtain information on current fish culture techniques employed in Europe. Colt's ponds were subsequently stocked under Kellogg's direction.

Other entrepreneurs wanted to raise and manipulate wild populations of fishes to encourage species that were perceived to be useful and discourage those that were considered not useful. One of these entrepreneurs published a paper on fish culture and its use in manipulating wild populations (Comstock 1857). Additionally, Comstock was probably one of the citizens who influenced the legislature to form a state agency, in 1866, that would be primarily responsible for the fisheries resources of the state. That agency, currently called the Fisheries Division, Connecticut Department of Environmental Protection (DEP), was subsequently staffed by both amateur and professional ichthyologists. They obtained a great deal of information about the fisheries resources of the state, some of which was published in the annual and biannual reports of the agency, *e.g.*, Anonymous (1896).

One of the entrepreneurs from Connecticut also participated in manipulating fish throughout the country. Reverend William Clift (1817-1890) graduated from Amherst College in 1839 and from Union Theological Seminary in New York City in 1843. He was then pastor of two churches in the Stonington area for about thirty years. During his career he had many business pursuits, some of them agricultural. He organized and operated a fish cultural business in the Mystic area in the early 1870s. Clift was one of the founders of the American Fisheries Society and he served as the first president of that organization from 1870-1874. In this role he was able to play a part in the formation of the United States Fish Commission in 1871. Clift documented some of his work with American shad in Connecticut (Clift 1872), and also participated in some of the activities of the United States Fish Commission. He traveled across the country and stocked American shad from Connecticut in many other drainage basins (Anonymous 1882). His professional work in fish culture ceased during the early 1880s and he embarked on other ventures.

The twentieth century

The 1900s ushered in a civilization in which many people had achieved enough time, education and motivation to devote much of their energies to the study, contemplation and enjoyment of natural resources. Although some of the professional ichthyologists were university trained, most were not. The first university trained ichthyologist (Lyle Thorpe) employed by the Fisheries Division, Connecticut Board of Fisheries and Game, was hired in 1934. Many amateur and professional ichthyologists consulted after they retired, or in addition to their professional responsibilities. For example, J.W. Titcomb worked as a professional ichthyologist for the states of Vermont and New York and the federal government before coming to work for the state of Connecticut. After working three years with this state, he became a professional consultant to anyone who wanted to make hatcheries or natural bodies of water more productive for fish.

The first program at an institution of higher education in Connecticut that developed to train ichthyologists was begun at the University of Connecticut in 1954, by Dr. Russell Hunter, the former director of the Connecticut Board of Fisheries and Game. One of the zoologists / ichthyologists that worked at Yale, wrote two ichthyology books (Migdalski 1958, Migdalski and Fichter 1976). However, those publications did not document the distribution of any fish in the freshwaters of Connecticut. Migdalski's professional responsibilities were, for some time, devoted to collecting biological specimens abroad for Yale. He then developed a strong program in outdoor recreation, including fishing, at Yale. Another ichthyologist at Yale subsequently documented the saltwater ichthyofauna of Connecticut (Thomson *et al.* 1971, 1978).

During this century, the first two compilations of the fishes of Connecticut that were published since Linsley's original documentation were Kendall (1908) and Behnke and Wetzel (1960). It is interesting that Nichols' (1913) listing of fishes reported within fifty miles of New York City made no references to locations in Connecticut. The first systematic surveys of the fishes living in the standing (Webster 1942, Anonymous 1959), and flowing waters (Whitworth *et al.* 1968) were performed about mid-century. Additionally, Marcy (1976a, 1976b) conducted a systematic survey of the fishes of the Connecticut River. The Fisheries Division of the DEP has been systematically surveying both the standing, since 1981, and flowing, since 1988, water bodies of the state (*e.g.*, Jacobs *et al.* 1991, Hagstrom *et al.* 1991).

Many other studies documenting the distribution and functional relationships that exist between the freshwater fishes of Connecticut and their environment were conducted during this century that, along with the above, documented the fishes that were found in the state. For example, Baker 1971;R. Booth 1967; Cadigan and Fell 1985; Collette 1962; Crecco and Savoy 1984, 1985a, 1985b; Crecco *et al.* 1986; Dowhan & Craig 1976; Kissel

1974; Leggett 1976; Leggett and Jones 1971; Loesch and Lund 1977; Marcy 1969, 1972, 1976c; Marcy and Richards 1974; Merriman 1941, 1947; Merriman and Jean 1949; Merriman and Thorpe 1976; O'Leary and Smith 1987; Pearcy and Richards 1962; Steinmetz and Boehm 1980; Steir and Kynard 1986; and Tolderlund 1975. Because I am intimately associated with this period I will leave the evaluation of this time in the ichthyological history of Connecticut to some ichthyologist in the twenty-first century.

CHAPTER TWO

Distribution of fishes in the freshwaters of Connecticut

The drainage basins

Most of the freshwaters that flow from the land area of Connecticut empty into Long Island Sound from three major drainage basins through the Housatonic, Connecticut, and Thames Rivers, and many minor coastal drainage basins through smaller rivers (Figure 2). Additionally, two small drainage basins in western Connecticut drain into the Hudson River, which empties into the Atlantic Ocean directly. However, before the Hudson enters the Atlantic Ocean, there is a connection between that river and the western end of Long Island Sound, the East River and some of its tributaries.

All of the major drainage basins in Connecticut receive waters from land areas outside the state; for example, the Housatonic from New York and Massachusetts, the Connecticut from Quebec, New Hampshire, Vermont, and Massachusetts, and the Thames from Massachusetts and Rhode Island (Figure 3). A few of the minor drainage basins in western Connecticut receive waters from New York, and the last minor drainage basin in eastern Connecticut receives waters from Rhode Island. The drainage basins that I use to document the distribution of fishes in the freshwaters of Connecticut are shown in Figure 2; Thomas (1972) is a good reference to the names of the watercourses in Connecticut.

The fishes

Fish found in these freshwaters are either species that must live (1) their entire lives in freshwaters, or (2) part of their lives in freshwaters and part in saltwaters, or (3) in saltwaters but enter freshwaters either regularly or occasionally at some time in their lives. Some species have been variously classified in different categories over time. Additionally, there are alternative views as to how some of the species in Connecticut should be classified within these categories. I welcome comments of others, and suggest that interested readers consult other studies and make their own evaluations. There is still much to be learned in this area.

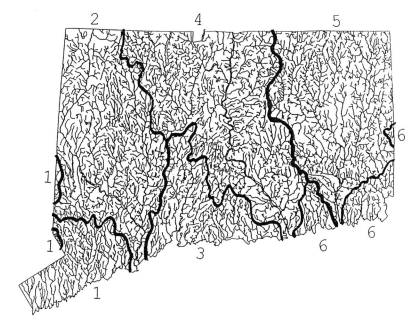

Figure 2. **Drainage basins of Connecticut.** One includes all coastal drainage basins from the New York border to and including the Quinnipiac River and the Hudson River drainage basins in western Connecticut. Two is the Housatonic River drainage basin and three includes all coastal drainage basins from the Quinnipiac River to the Connecticut River. Four and five are the drainage basins of the Connecticut and Thames Rivers, respectively. Six includes all coastal drainage basins from the Connecticut River to the Rhode Island border.

Freshwater species

The species that must live their entire lives in freshwater could be classified into three general groups based on how they migrated to the freshwaters of Connecticut. The first group migrated to the freshwaters of Connecticut through freshwater routes. The second was transported by humans, and the species in the third group became adapted to the freshwaters of Connecticut as the gene pool of either an anadromous (*Morone americana*, white perch), or a saltwater (*Apeltes quadracus*, fourspine stickleback) population evolved during the last 14,000 years. While these two species were evolving populations that were restricted to freshwaters, a freshwater species (*Fundulus diaphanus*, banded killifish) was evolving populations that had to live in saltwaters.

There is no evidence to support transportation of fish into the freshwaters of Connecticut by any organism other than humans. The chance of another vertebrate (bird or mammal) moving either (1) both a mature male and female which then spawned, or (2) enough eggs, that would hatch, grow to sexual maturity, and find a mate, is extremely remote.

***Figure 3.* Major drainage basins of Connecticut in relation to northeastern North America.** Two is the Housatonic, four is the Connecticut, and five is the Thames.

Twenty-three species probably migrated to the freshwaters of Connecticut through freshwater routes (Table 1). Nineteen of those are found in all of the major drainage basins of the state, two are mainly confined to the drainage basins west of the main stem of the Connecticut River, and two are mainly confined to the drainage basins east of the Thames and Quinebaug Rivers.

The minimum number of species that were probably transported to the freshwaters of Connecticut by humans and have at least one recently verified established population is twenty-five (Table 2). However, a minimum of twenty-nine other species have been transported to the freshwaters of Connecticut by humans (Table 3). Twenty-eight species were documented as having had either viable populations for some time period, or specimens deposited in a museum, or verified reports of specimens collected. One of them was recently introduced in all of the contiguous states, probably in this state, and will soon be collected. This is the first time that the collections of "tropical" fish have been formally reported. Although these specimens have probably been introduced for many years, with the increased collecting activity in this state since the early 1960s, more species have been collected. There is little doubt that most, if not all, of those individuals would die before they were able to reproduce. If they were able to spawn, their progeny should not be able to survive to reproduce. Because more collecting is done in the Thames River drainage basin, many of these fish were collected in eastern Connecticut.

It is interesting that not only does the number of species that were moved to the freshwaters of Connecticut by humans outnumber those species that moved to Connecticut by themselves, but most of the larger bodies of water in the state are dominated by introduced species, *e.g.*, Jacobs *et al.* (1991). A similar situation exists in other states. For example, Moyle (1976) reported that about one third of the documented ichthyofauna in California was introduced by humans and that most of the larger bodies of water also were dominated by introduced species.

There is a possibility that two species that I feel were probably moved to the freshwaters of Connecticut by humans, migrated through saltwaters, and then evolved a population that was restricted to freshwater. For example, anadromous populations of *Dorosoma cepedianum* (gizzard shad) were reported in New Jersey in the nineteenth century (Abbott 1871). Additionally, the gene pools of both this species and *Ameiurus catus* (white catfish) in the mid-Atlantic states still produce individuals with a high tolerance for saltwaters. Thus, individuals could migrate northward toward Connecticut one drainage basin at a time during periods of high freshwater flows. However, these species were not reported in the freshwaters of Connecticut until after the 1940s. Considering the documented distribution of both of these species through space and time and the propensity of humans to move fish, the most logical explanation for their movement to Connecticut is transportation by humans!

Two of the species that had been previously classified as having moved to the freshwaters of Connecticut naturally were reclassified as having been moved by humans because of their documented distribution through time. The first is *Lampetra appendix* (American brook lamprey). This species has been known since the middle 1900s to have a viable population in one of the smaller tributaries of the Connecticut River near Windsor Locks (Russell Hunter, formerly of the DEP and the University of Connecticut). This brook was the location of a fish hatchery in the early 1900s. Although Linsley (1844b) reported this species in the Housatonic River, those specimens were probably *Petromyzon marinus* (sea lamprey). If this species gained entry to the freshwaters of Connecticut from a refugium to the south, it would have entered from Long Island Sound, as did the other freshwater species that returned naturally. There are many water bodies that have reasonable habitat for this species between refugia to the south of Connecticut and the location of this population. Many electrofishing collections have failed to document other populations in drainage basins between Long Island Sound and the known population over the last five years. Since no specimens have been obtained, the most reasonable explanation for how this species moved to the freshwaters of Connecticut is transportation by humans. If the type of area for this species was around Providence, Rhode Island, then the populations in the Blackstone drainage basin in Massachusetts and Rhode Island may be native.

The second species is *Lota lota* (burbot). The specimen reported by LeSueur (1817a) was obtained by a sportsman, and was probably captured in the Connecticut River in southern Massachusetts. The first verifiable report from Connecticut was by Linsley (1844b). He obtained specimens from a fisherman. The fisherman thought that they were a cross between an eel and a trout and also remarked that they were strangers to that stream in northwestern Connecticut. The next specimens were obtained from Middlesex Quarry, Portland, in the early 1900s. These were initially deposited in the Museum at Wesleyan University and later transferred to the American Museum of Natural History and the National Museum of Natural History. The next specimen was caught by a fisherman in the Farmington River in the 1960s (John Orintas, DEP, personal communication). Consultants working for the Hollenbeck Club obtained the next specimens in 1988, in the Hollenbeck River (Doug Smith, University of Massachusetts, reported that population a few years earlier). The next specimens were captured in the mouth of a tributary of the Connecticut River near Glastonbury in 1989 (Hagstrom *et al.* 1990). It is not known if those specimens represent a viable population. The spotty distribution through space and time of this species in Connecticut, as well as North America, is not consistent with natural movement to Connecticut through freshwaters from any of the possible refugia.

Two species have populations that are restricted to freshwaters that I feel evolved from the gene pools of forms that migrated to the freshwaters of Connecticut through saltwaters. This modification could have taken place at any time during the postglacial period prior to the physical isolation of that area. The freshwater stock of the first species, *Apeltes quadracus* (fourspine stickleback), has many populations that live in the saltwaters of Connecticut. A few freshwater populations were documented in the mid-nineteenth century in a few coastal drainage basins. Therefore, based on the current and historical distributions of this species, it seems more probable that these freshwater populations evolved from one of the saltwater populations.

The other species is *Morone americana* (white perch). The first report of this species in the freshwaters of Connecticut (Anonymous 1896) stated that its natural habitat rarely extended beyond tide water, although specimens could be raised in freshwater. Since then, many populations have been introduced in the waters of all of the drainage basins of the state. Therefore, based on the current and historical distribution of this species overall, it seems reasonable to assume that the freshwater populations in Connecticut were derived from an anadromous population that entered its freshwaters after deglaciation. This species, with the help of humans, is now found in all drainage basins of the state. Because few saltwater populations have been documented, I feel that those populations also developed from the original anadromous stock that migrated to Connecticut.

Maintaining a gene pool of individuals that are able to live in only one environment would seem to be more easily accomplished for an anadromous species. *Morone americana* (white perch) has the advantage that large numbers of either young-of-the-year or adult fish could have been restricted to freshwaters by mechanical blockages to the watercourse 13,500 to 11,000 years ago. These specimens had (1) to survive long enough in freshwater to reproduce and (2) to have the potential in their genetic makeup to produce some offspring that had the ability to osmoregulate and excrete efficiently in freshwater. If enough of those individuals hatched, grew, and reproduced to maintain that freshwater gene pool, the freshwater stock was formed. The conversion to a saltwater stock would be accomplished similarly, except that the individuals that could not enter freshwaters to spawn would have to maintain their gene pool. Both the freshwater stock that was not isolated from saltwaters and the saltwater stocks would have possible problems because of dilution from some of the anadromous individuals that could occasionally enter spawning congregations.

The freshwater stock of *Apeltes quadracus* (fourspine stickleback) more likely developed within the last few thousand years. The gene pool of this species, and of the stickleback family in general, undoubtedly still contains the allelic expressions that allow individuals to osmoregulate and excrete in both freshwaters and saltwaters. If enough of those individuals hatched, survived, migrated to the same freshwater area and reproduced, then, over a few generations, a gene pool that produced mostly freshwater stock would be formed. Since only two known populations are isolated from saltwater, this species has apparently not been able to develop a gene pool that is dominated by alleles that produce individuals that are able to survive in freshwater because it is not completely isolated from the saltwater populations.

Diadromous species

Fishes that must spend part of their lives in both fresh and salt waters are collectively termed diadromous and, specifically, either anadromous or catadromous fishes. Ten species of fish that could be found in the freshwaters of Connecticut are in this category (Table 4). They are widely distributed in the drainage basins of all watercourses that have sufficient freshwater habitat below the first barrier (dam or falls) that limits the upstream movement of each species from the sea. This freshwater habitat must be able to support all of their life history requirements in freshwater.

Anadromous fishes are those in which the eggs are laid and develop in freshwaters and the young fish spend part of their early lives in freshwater, e.g., the American shad of Brainard's poem noted earlier. They then must migrate to saltwater and live until they reach sexual maturity. Sexually mature fish must then return to freshwater to spawn. In most of our anadromous species, some of the adults can and do return to saltwater and may subsequently spawn again. In others, e.g., *Petromyzon marinus* (sea lamprey), sexually mature fish die after spawning.

Catadromous fish must lay their eggs and spend part of their early life history in saltwater. They then must migrate to freshwater and grow to sexual maturity. Males of our only catadromous species, *Anguilla rostrata* (American eel), apparently do not have to migrate into freshwater to grow to sexual maturity. After reaching sexual maturity in either fresh or coastal waters, individuals migrate back to the saltwaters of the Sargasso Sea, spawn, and then die.

Saltwater species

The last general category of fishes that are found within the freshwaters of Connecticut are the saltwater species that occasionally or regularly enter freshwaters of the state, but are not required to do so to complete their life history. Seventy-one species have been documented, and one additional species is included as it will probably soon be collected (Table 5). The bulk of these species has been added to the freshwater fauna in the last twenty years as more collections have been obtained, and we have little knowledge of how the use of freshwaters in Connecticut by these species has evolved since the last glaciation. Therefore, the chance of capturing other saltwater fish in freshwaters near saltwaters in Connecticut is very high, and one should not be surprised if a species not previously reported in freshwater is captured.

About twenty-five of these saltwater species regularly enter freshwaters, many of them at predictable times. However, they often enter at other times as well. Myers (1949) used the term amphidromous to describe a regular movement between salt and fresh waters other than for breeding. His usage of the term and later modifications by McDowell (1992) require a regular movement at some life history stage. Rather than coin a new term, I have used amphidromous to describe a movement that is regularly made by a species at one or many life history stages other than spawning. All individuals in the population in this life history stage do not have to enter freshwaters, *i.e.*, *Pomatomus saltatrix* (bluefish), *Morone saxatilis* (striped bass), *Menidia beryllina* (inland silverside), and *Apeltes quadracus* (fourspine stickleback). Although there could be many reasons for this movement, more favorable temperature and food supplies along with less competition and predation would appear to be logical forces (Warner and Kynard 1986, Kynard and Warner 1987). These species would have the potential to develop freshwater populations over time.

Table 1.

Distribution of fishes that must spend their entire lives in freshwater and probably migrated to Connecticut through freshwater routes. Major drainage basins are arranged west to east. Drainage basins are 1, coastal from the New York border to and including the Quinnipiac River and the Hudson River drainage basins; 2, the Housatonic River; 3, coastal basins from the Quinnipiac River to the Connecticut River; 4, the Connecticut River; 5, the Thames River; and 6, coastal basins from the Connecticut River to the Rhode Island border.

Scientific name	Common name	Drainage basins of Connecticut					
		1	2	3	4	5	6
Ameiurus nebulosus	brown bullhead	X	X	X	X	X	X
Catostomus commersoni	white sucker	X	X	X	X	X	X
Erimyzon oblongus	creek chubsucker	X	X	X	X	X	X
Esox americanus	grass pickerel	X	X	X	X	X	X
Esox niger	chain pickerel	X	X	X	X	X	X
Etheostoma olmstedi	tessellated darter	X	X	X	X	X	X
Fundulus diaphanus *	banded killifish	X	X	X	X	X	X
Lepomis auritus	redbreast sunfish	X	X	X	X	X	X
Lepomis gibbosus	pumpkinseed	X	X	X	X	X	X
Luxilus cornutus	common shiner	X	X	X	X	X	X
Notemigonus crysoleucas	golden shiner	X	X	X	X	X	X
Notropis bifrenatus	bridle shiner	X	X	X	X	X	X
Notropis hudsonius	spottail shiner	X	X	X	X	X	X
Perca flavescens	yellow perch	X	X	X	X	X	X
Rhinichthys atratulus	blacknose dace	X	X	X	X	X	X
Rhinichthys cataractae	longnose dace	X	X	X	X	X	X
Salvelinus fontinalis	brook trout	X	X	X	X	X	X
Semotilus corporalis	fallfish	X	X	X	X	X	X
Cottus cognatus	slimy sculpin		X		X	X	
Semotilus atromaculatus	creek chub	X	X	X	X	X	
Exoglossum maxillingua	cutlips minnow	X	X		X		
Enneacanthus obesus	banded sunfish				X	X	X
Etheostoma fusiforme	swamp darter					X	X

* Saltwater populations were also derived from this stock.

Table 2.

Fishes that must spend their entire lives in freshwater, were probably transported to the freshwaters of Connecticut by humans, and have at least one recently verified established population.

Scientific name	Common name	Distribution in Connecticut	
		Populations	Basins
Ambloplites rupestris	rock bass	many	most
*Ameiurus catus**	white catfish	many	most
Ameiurus natalis	yellow bullhead	some	all major
Amia calva	bowfin	few	Housatonic
Carassius auratus	goldfish	some	most
Cyprinus carpio	common carp	many	all
Dorosoma cepedianum[†]	gizzard shad	some	all major & central coastal
Esox lucius	northern pike	few	all major
Ictalurus punctatus	channel catfish	few	Connecticut &Housatonic
Lampetra appendix	American brook lamprey	one	Connecticut
Lepomis cyanellus	green sunfish	some	all
Lepomis macrochirus	bluegill	many	all
Lota lota	burbot	one	Housatonic
Micropterus dolomieu	smallmouth bass	some	all
Micropterus salmoides	largemouth bass	many	all
Oncorhynchus mykiss	rainbow trout	two	Housatonic & Connecticut
Oncorhynchus nerka	sockeye salmon	one	Housatonic
Pimephales notatus	bluntnose minnow	few	Housatonic
Pimephales promelas	fathead minnow	few	Connecticut & Housatonic
Pomoxis annularis	white crappie	few	Connecticut
Pomoxis nigromaculatus	black crappie	some	all
Prosopium cylindraceum	round whitefish	one	Housatonic
Salmo trutta [‡]	brown trout	some	all
Stizostedion vitreum	walleye	few	Connecticut & Housatonic
Umbra limi	central mudminnow	few	Connecticut

° Since some individuals in this species have a high salt tolerance, the original movement to the larger rivers of Connecticut could have been a natural range extension.

† This species could have moved to the freshwaters of Connecticut as described in °1, or from an anadromous stock that extended its range northward from the mid-Atlantic coast.

‡ Some populations produce some anadromous specimens.

Table 3.
Fishes that must spend their entire lives, or part of their lives, in freshwaters, were probably transported to the freshwaters of Connecticut by humans, and do not have at least one recently verified established population.

Scientific name	Common Name	Drainage basin
Ameiurus melas	black bullhead	Housatonic
Betta splendens	Siamese fightingfish	Thames
Campostoma anomalum	central stoneroller	western coastal
Catostomus catostomus	longnose sucker	Housatonic
Cichlasoma octofasciatum	Jack Dempsey	all major
Clarias batrachus	walking catfish	all major
Ctenopharyngodon idella	grass carp	most
Culaea inconstans	brook stickleback	Connecticut
Danio rerio	zebra danio	Thames
Esox masquinongy	muskellunge	Connecticut and Thames
Gambusia affinis	western mosquitofish	western coastal
Hypostomus sp	"suckermouth catfishes"	Thames
Leuciscus idus	ide	eastern coastal
Margariscus margarita	pearl dace	western coastal
Notropis amblops	bigeye chub	Hudson
Notropis rubellus	rosyface shiner	Connecticut
Oncorhynchus clarki	cutthroat trout	Connecticut and Housatonic
Oncorhynchus kisutch	coho salmon	all major
Oncorhynchus tshawytscha	chinook salmon	all major
Percopsis omiscomaycus	trout-perch	Housatonic
Poecilia reticulata	guppy	Thames
Poeciliopsis sp	"livebearers"	Thames
Pygocentrus sp	"piranhas"	Thames
Salvelinus alpinus	Arctic char	Housatonic
Salvelinus namaycush	lake trout	all major
Scardinius erythrophthalmus	rudd	no verified records
Serrasalmus sp	"piranhas"	Thames
Thymallus arcticus	Arctic grayling	Housatonic
Tinca tinca	tench	Housatonic

Table 4.

Fishes that must spend part of their lives in freshwaters and migrate to Connecticut through a saltwater route. All are anadromous, except *Anguilla rostrata* which is catadromous.

Scientific name	Common name	Distribution in drainage basins
Acipenser brevirostrum	shortnose sturgeon	Connecticut
Acipenser oxyrhynchus	Atlantic sturgeon	Connecticut
Alosa aestivalis	blueback herring	most
Alosa pseudoharengus*	alewife	most
Alosa sapidissima	American shad	all major
Anguilla rostrata	American eel	all
Morone americana[†]	white perch	Thames
Osmerus mordax *	rainbow smelt	all major
Petromyzon marinus	sea lamprey	Connecticut and west
Salmo salar[‡]	Atlantic salmon	Connecticut

° Freshwater populations have been derived from this stock and introduced into some lakes by humans.

† Both freshwater and saltwater populations have been derived and freshwater populations spread throughout the state by humans.

‡ Extirpated from all of the major drainage basins by the middle 1800s. Present populations have evolved from a variety of introduced stocks.

Table 5.

Fishes that must spend their lives in saltwaters and might be found in the freshwaters of Connecticut. Amphidromous species typically have some individuals of one or more life history stages other than spawning adults that are present in freshwaters during some time period. However, all individuals of that life history stage do not have to enter freshwater.

Scientific name	Common name	Status in freshwaters
Alosa mediocris	hickory shad	Amphidromous
Ammodytes americanus	American sand lance	Visitor
Anchoa mitchilli	bay anchovy	Amphidromous
Apeltes quadracus*	fourspine stickleback	Amphidromous
Archosargus probatocephalus	sheepshead	Visitor
Arius felis	hardhead catfish	Not verified
Bairdiella chrysoura	silver perch	Visitor
Brevoortia tyrannus	Atlantic menhaden	Amphidromous
Caranx hippos	crevalle jack	Amphidromous

° Some freshwater populations were derived from this stock.

Table 5. cont.

Scientific name	Common name	Status in freshwaters
Centropristis striata	black sea bass	Visitor
Chilomycterus schoepfi	striped burrfish	Visitor
Citharichthys arctifrons	Gulf Stream flounder	Visitor
Clupea harengus	Atlantic herring	Visitor
Cyclopterus lumpus	lumpfish	Visitor
Cynoscion regalis	weakfish	Amphidromous
Cyprinodon variegatus	sheepshead minnow	Amphidromous
Enchelyopus cimbrius	fourbeard rockling	Visitor
Etropus microstomus	smallmouth flounder	Visitor
Fistularia petimba	red cornetfish	Visitor
Fundulus heteroclitus	mummichog	Amphidromous
Fundulus luciae	spotfin killifish	Visitor
Fundulus majalis	striped killifish	Amphidromous
Gasterosteus aculeatus	threespine stickleback	Amphidromous
Gasterosteus wheatlandi	blackspotted stickleback	Visitor
Gobiosoma bosc	naked goby	Amphidromous
Hippocampus erectus	lined seahorse	Visitor
Leiostomus xanthurus	spot	Amphidromous
Liparis inquilinus	inquiline snailfish	Visitor
Lophius americanus	goosefish	Visitor
Lucania parva	rainwater killifish	Visitor
Menidia beryllina	inland silverside	Amphidromous
Menidia menidia	Atlantic silverside	Amphidromous
Menticirrhus saxatilis	northern kingfish	Amphidromous
Merluccius bilinearis	silver hake	Visitor
Microgadus tomcod	Atlantic tomcod	Amphidromous
Micropogonias undulatus	Atlantic croaker	Visitor
Morone saxatilis	striped bass	Amphidromous
Mugil cephalus	striped mullet	Visitor
Mugil curema	white mullet	Visitor
Mustelus canis	smooth dogfish	Visitor
Myoxocephalus aenaeus	grubby	Visitor
Myoxocephalus octodecemspinosus	longhorn sculpin	Visitor
Ophidion marginatum	striped cusk-eel	Visitor
Opsanus tau	oyster toadfish	Visitor
Paralichthys dentatus	summer flounder	Amphidromous
Paralichthys oblongus	fourspot flounder	Visitor
Peprilus triacanthus	butterfish	Visitor
Pholis gunnellus	rock gunnel	Visitor
Pleuronectes americanus	winter flounder	Amphidromous
Pleuronectes ferrugineus	yellowtail flounder	Visitor

Table 5. cont.

Scientific name	Common name	Status in freshwaters
Pomatomus saltatrix	bluefish	Amphidromous
Prionotus carolinus	northern searobin	Amphidromous
Prionotus evolans	striped searobin	Amphidromous
Pungitius pungitius	ninespine stickleback	Amphidromous
Raja erinacea	little skate	Visitor
Scomber scombrus	Atlantic mackerel	Visitor
Scomberomorus maculatus	Spanish mackerel	Visitor
Scophthalmus aquosus	windowpane	Visitor
Selene vomer	lookdown	Visitor
Sphoeroides maculatus	northern puffer	Visitor
Squalus acanthias	spiny dogfish	Visitor
Stenotomus chrysops	scup	Visitor
Strongylura marina	Atlantic needlefish	Visitor
Syngnathus fuscus	northern pipefish	Amphidromous
Synodus foetens	inshore lizardfish	Visitor
Tautoga onitis	tautog	Visitor
Tautogolabrus adspersus	cunner	Visitor
Trinectes maculatus	hogchoker	Amphidromous
Ulvaria subbifurcata	radiated shanny	Visitor
Urophycis chuss	red hake	Visitor
Urophycis regia	spotted hake	Visitor
Urophycis tenuis	white hake	Visitor

CHAPTER THREE

Factors influencing the distribution of fishes in the freshwaters of Connecticut

Origin of populations

We will first consider the fish that must live their entire lives in freshwater. The land area that is now Connecticut has had freshwater environments available for fish populations for discontinuous time periods since fish evolved. During the Quaternary, glaciers covered Connecticut during four major periods. Each glaciation lasted about 100,000 years and was followed by a period of about 100,000 to 125,000 years when freshwater fish could ·successfully live and evolve. The fish that lived in the freshwaters of Connecticut before the last glaciation migrated into those waters about 270,000 years ago as the third major glacier, the Illinoian, was receding. These populations then evolved (expanding and contracting their ranges) for over 100,000 years. With the formation of the new, and last major glacial advance, the Wisconsinan, these species either perished or migrated to freshwaters south of the advancing ice edge about 120,000 years ago. The populations that moved south then continued evolving either (1) themselves, or (2) with the indigenous populations of the same species that lived there.

Therefore, the origin of the fish that presently live in the freshwaters of Connecticut was either by (1) migration through freshwater routes of some segments of those populations living in areas that were not covered by the glacier, (2) evolution from one of those populations that returned, (3) transportation by some outside factor, or (4) changes in the gene pool of either an anadromous, catadromous, or saltwater species so that a population restricted to freshwater was formed. The probability that a new species evolved from a species that migrated to the freshwaters of Connecticut after the glacier exposed the land and before saltwaters flooded Long Island Sound (between 17,000 and 12,000 years ago) is so small, we will eliminate the second option.

Glacial considerations

The following discussion of the deglaciation of Connecticut is based on my evaluations of (1) conversations with Janet Stone (United States

Geological Survey) and Ralph Lewis (Connecticut Department of Environmental Protection), and (2) the published literature (J.T. Andrews 1987; Bailey and Smith 1981; Black 1982; Bloom and Stuiver 1963; Borns 1963 and 1973; Bothner and Spiker 1980; Connally and Sirkin 1973; Davis 1965 and 1969; Davis *et al.* 1975 and 1980; Deevey 1939, 1948 and 1949; Edwards and Merrill 1977; Emery *et al.* 1965; Flint 1930, 1933, 1953, 1955, 1956 and 1971; Goldsmith 1982; Hughes 1987; Jacobson *et al.* 1987; Jordan 1888; Lagler and Vallentyne 1956; Larson and Hartshorn 1982; Lougee 1939; Mickleson *et al.* 1983; Miller 1965; Newman 1977; Newman *et al.* 1969; Oldale and Eskenasy 1983; Prest 1970 and 1984; Schaefer and Hartshorn 1965; Schmidt 1986; Sirkin 1982; Stone and Peper 1982; Teller 1987 and 1989; Urry 1948; and Wright 1971 and 1987). It should be noted that there are alternative interpretations of the deglaciation of Connecticut.

The southern extreme of the last glacier approximated the south shore of Long Island, New York, and the shoreline was about 90 km further south. The glacier began to retreat about 21,200 years ago and the north shore of Long Island was exposed about 19,500 years ago. The current shoreline of Connecticut was more or less exposed by glacial retreat about 17,500 years ago, and the northern state boundary was exposed about 14,000 years ago.

While the glacier was receding, all of the meltwaters from the land area of Connecticut flowed south into a giant freshwater lake (glacial Lake Connecticut) that is now known as Long Island Sound. There were two major rivers that carried most of the glacial meltwaters into this giant freshwater lake, the Hudson and Connecticut Rivers. The Hudson River carried meltwaters not only from its present drainage basin, but from parts of the Great Lakes and Saint Lawrence River drainage basin. Glacial Lake Hudson occupied the lower Hudson River from the Harbor Hill Moraine north to the highlands. There was another blockage north of the Highlands that formed glacial Lake Albany. Most of the discharge from the Hudson River probably flowed into glacial Lake Connecticut through what is now called the East River until the blockage that formed glacial lake Hudson, the Harbor Hill moraine, disappeared about 12,500 ago.

The Connecticut River probably only transported meltwaters of the glacier from its present drainage basin. Glacial Lake Hitchcock occupied the Connecticut River from a blockage in the Connecticut River south of Hartford north about 175 miles into Vermont and New Hampshire until about 12,300 to 12,200 years ago. Its spillway, the present site of Dividend Brook, flowed south into the Mattabesset River.

Most of the discharge from glacial Lake Connecticut was through a river that flowed south into the ocean from the eastern end of the lake in the area that is now known as the "Race." The level of the ocean began to rise slowly about 14,000 years ago and about 12,000 years ago saltwaters began to enter the eastern end of glacial Lake Connecticut through the major outlet river.

Glacial Lake Connecticut was completely filled with saltwaters by about 11,000 years ago.

The volume of freshwater flow, primarily glacial meltwaters, into glacial Lake Connecticut was very large. Based on trends calculated by Teller (1989), this flow was reduced about one-third between 13,500 and 13,000 years ago and even more between 12,500 and 12,000 years ago. The ability of fish to successfully establish populations probably increased as the volume of flow decreased because populations of food organisms increased. These organisms increased because water temperatures and the quantity of nutrients available both increased as the volume of flow decreased and the land weathered. Therefore, the best time for fish to repopulate all drainage basins of Connecticut was between 13,500 and 11,000 years ago. The fall line in each drainage basin, which represents a significant change in elevation, probably became a barrier to the upstream movement of some fish between 14,000 and 12,000 years ago as the volume of meltwaters was reduced.

Possible refugia

Fish could have entered any of the drainage basins of Connecticut after deglaciation from glacial Lake Connecticut. They could have migrated to this lake from five possible refugia, *i.e.*, (1) immediately south of the glacier in Connecticut, Rhode Island, and New York in the unglaciated area adjacent to the shoreline of the Atlantic Ocean at that time, (2) further south and east between the current shorelines of the states of New Jersey south to North Carolina and the edge of the Atlantic Ocean at that time, (3) west in any watercourse that flowed into or had connections with the Hudson River, (4) north in any watercourse that flowed into or had connections with the Hudson River, or (5) east in unglaciated areas that are now in Georges Bank. There were probably no refugia under or within the glacier. Not only was all of New England covered by a deep ice mass, but no species have been reported in any of the deep lakes that might have provided such a refugium. Thus, there were no glacial "relics."

Additionally, fish could have migrated from any drainage basin that was adjacent to a drainage basin in Connecticut by either lowland or headwater stream transfer. These exchanges were only possible after fish repopulated the adjacent basins and during a time when there was sufficient water exchanges between basins for the movement to occur. For example, while the glacier was first melting in two adjoining basins, there was probably some water spillage from one basin to another. Furthermore, if an ice blockage occurred in one drainage basin water may have spilled into the next. Not only was timing crucial and these routes available for only a relatively short period of time, but there were probably few species that could have entered freshwaters, survived and reproduced during this period when the meltwaters of the glacier were so cold and the volume was so large.

This type of exchange was thought by some to be an important route for fish migrating into drainage basins in the northeast. McCabe (1942) theorized that some species that entered the St. Lawrence drainage basin, probably from refugia in unglaciated areas between the glacier and the level of the Atlantic Ocean at that time, then moved into the Hudson River, and then gained access to streams in the Housatonic River in western and northern Massachusetts by this type of headwater transfer. C.L. Smith (1985), although he did not provide particulars, theorized that headwater transfer was an important means for fish to distribute themselves throughout the freshwaters of New York. However, I do not believe the overall distribution of any species indicates that this process had a major influence on the distribution of fishes in Connecticut. Although there are many areas in this state in which water from one drainage basin can still flow to an adjacent drainage basin at times of high surface water runoffs, there are no species of fish that require this explanation to account for their present distribution within the state.

It is interesting that there is at least one known documented case of humans effecting a headwater transfer between two drainage basins in New England in the early 1800s. S. Dwight (1826) described the disastrous effects of the rushing water when colonists in Vermont caused a lake that normally flowed into the Connecticut River basin to flow into the St. Lawrence basin in 1810. Therefore, those fishes present in that area would have been introduced into the St. Lawrence drainage basin.

Previous workers in Connecticut (Whitworth *et al.* 1968, Schmidt and Whitworth 1979, and Schmidt 1986) favored the theory that refugia were south and west of Connecticut, in coastal plain streams off of what is now New Jersey to North Carolina. Fish from these refugia could have migrated from drainage basin to drainage basin by lowland stream transfer or low salinity bridges along the ocean next to the shoreline until they gained access to either the eastern or western entrance to glacial Lake Connecticut. Regardless of when they started moving north, they had to enter glacial Lake Connecticut between 17,000 and 11,000 years ago, before Long Island Sound was formed.

Probable refugia and migration routes

After reevaluating all data, I now favor refugia directly south of Connecticut as the source of the freshwater fishes that migrated to our state utilizing freshwater routes (see Figure 4). If refugia were further south, as we previously favored, or west, there should be more species that are present in those areas found in the freshwaters of Connecticut. Closer refugia would have two advantages. First, there would be a shorter distance to travel. Second, as immigrants migrated into new areas, there would be a longer time period to grow, reproduce, and expand their populations prior to their next move further inland. The present distributions of all of the twenty-three species (Table 1) that probably migrated to the freshwaters of Connecticut through freshwater routes are logically explained by having refugia south and possibly east of the state.

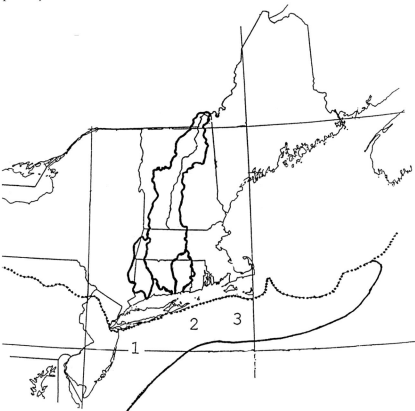

Figure 4. Probable refugia and migration routes of fishes into the freshwaters of Connecticut. One is the southwestern refugia, two is the southern refugia, and three is the southeastern refugia.

Refugia in drainage basins directly south of the eastern third of Connecticut (created as the shoreline retreated some 90 km south in advance of the glacier) are the logical sources for nineteen of the twenty-three species that returned to the waters of Connecticut through freshwater routes (Figure 4, refugium 2). They could either migrate directly into the eastern river that drained glacial Lake Connecticut or gain access to that river by lowland or headwater stream transfer from refugia east or west of that drainage basin.

They could then utilize either the drainage basin of this river, or the lake itself, to live and grow until the watercourses of Connecticut that were carrying the meltwaters of the receding glacier provided them favorable conditions to migrate, grow, and reproduce. This could have been accomplished any time between the initial exposure of the land area of Connecticut (about 17,500 years ago) to the time saltwaters flooded glacial Lake Connecticut and Long Island Sound was formed (about 11,000 years ago). However, as noted earlier, because of unfavorable volume and temperatures of the meltwaters, this return migration into the freshwaters of Connecticut was more likely during the period of 13,500 to 11,000 years ago.

Refugia directly south of the southwestern third of Connecticut account for the distribution of two more of those twenty-three species that returned to the freshwaters of Connecticut through freshwater routes (Figure 4, refugium 1). *Semotilus atromaculatus* (creek chub) and *Exoglossum maxillingua* (cutlips minnow) are both distributed mainly in drainage basins in the western half of the state. An entrance to glacial Lake Connecticut from this refugium would be possible during the time that the moraine blocking the current outlet for the Hudson River was about the same height above sea level as was the glacial outlet of the Hudson River into glacial Lake Connecticut. Both of these species could then migrate through glacial Lake Connecticut through the still existing original outlet (presently called the East River). Since this had to happen between the time the Hudson River outlet changed (about 12,500 years ago) and saltwaters flooded glacial Lake Connecticut (about 11,000 years ago) the limit of their eastward movement through the lake and into eastern drainage basins is consistent with the constraints of this refugium.

Semotilus atromaculatus (creek chub) probably entered glacial Lake Connecticut close to 12,500 years ago and was able to spread east to the Quinnipiac River drainage basin. Because it entered the Housatonic River when water flows were reasonably high, it was able to cross the fall line at Falls Village and enter Massachusetts. Furthermore, when the Farmington Canal connected part of the Quinnipiac and Connecticut River drainage basins in the mid 1800s, it was able to spread into most of the Farmington River drainage basin and contiguous basins in the Connecticut River drainage basin. The few isolated populations of this species in parts of the lower Connecticut River and in the Thames River drainage basins, were undoubtedly due to movement by humans. Otherwise, this species would be distributed in all drainage basins of the state as nineteen of the twenty-three native species are.

Exoglossum maxillingua (cutlips minnow), on the other hand, probably did not enter the freshwaters of Connecticut until closer to 11,000 years ago, because no populations were established above the fall line of the Housatonic River, or in drainage basins east of the Housatonic River. One individual, probably recently stocked, was collected in one location in a small drainage basin of the Farmington River.

The distributions of the final two species are best explained by refugia south of Rhode Island (Figure 4, refugium 3). *Etheostoma fusiforme* (swamp darter) is restricted to drainage basins east of the Thames and Quinebaug Rivers, and in a few coastal lakes a little west of the lower Thames River. This species probably entered glacial Lake Connecticut from that refugium just before saltwaters began flooding the lake about 12,000 years ago. Because flows from the Thames River were still reasonably high, this species probably was not able to migrate up the main stem of the Thames River System, and was able to move into only a few areas near the coast in eastern Connecticut. Based on its overall distribution, this species probably utilized both lowland and headwater transfers from the east, through the Pawcatuck River drainage basin to migrate into the upper Quinebaug River drainage basin.

The other species, *Enneacanthus obesus* (banded sunfish), is found in a few coastal lakes west of the Thames River and extending into the lower Connecticut River drainage basin east of the Connecticut River, with most populations in the Thames Basin or further east. Therefore, this species probably migrated from that same refugium (Figure 4, refugium 3) into glacial Lake Connecticut a few hundred years prior to *Etheostoma fusiforme* (swamp darter), and moved further west in the lake before the penetration of saltwaters forced them into freshwaters. Based on its overall distribution, this species probably also utilized both headwater and lowland transfers to obtain access to the upper Quinebaug River drainage basin from the basin of the Pawcatuck River in Rhode Island and Connecticut.

Evolution of the fish communities

Regardless of how a species got into a freshwater drainage basin in Connecticut, its distribution within that basin was determined by the ability of that species to successfully grow and reproduce as the physical, chemical, and biological features of the drainage basin evolved. All features of the drainage basins of Connecticut were undoubtedly greatly influenced by the climatic changes associated with deglaciation of Connecticut between 19,000 and 11,000 years ago.

The ranges of most species probably continued to enlarge and recede many times after the land area of Connecticut was established as the physical, chemical, and biological features of the state continued to evolve. For example, an increase in the temperature would reduce the habitat suitable for *Cottus cognatus* (slimy sculpin) and *Salvelinus fontinalis* (brook trout), and increase the habitat for *Luxilus cornutus* (common shiner) and *Etheostoma olmstedi* (tessellated darter). Slower flows and increased areas of vegetation would increase suitable habitats for *Notropis bifrenatus* (bridle shiner) and *Notemigonus crysoleucas* (golden shiner) and reduce habitats for

Rhinichthys atratulus (blacknose dace) and *R. cataractae* (longnose dace). Changes in the water volume would also change the range dramatically. For example, Linsley (1844b) noted that populations of *Rhinichthys atratulus* (blacknose dace), one of the species often found in small streams throughout the state, were often left high and dry in some areas during the years in which water flow was reduced. I have also seen the distribution of this species within a stream expand and contract for the same reasons since the 1960s.

Human impacts on the evolution of fish communities

My interpretation of the effects of humans on the evolution of fish communities in the freshwaters of Connecticut is based on my evaluation of the works of archaeologists, historians, and naturalists, *i.e.*, Adams 1926; Agassiz 1850 and 1854; Andrews 1924 and 1934; Anonymous 1867, 1868, 1893 and 1939; Atkins 1874; Avery 1901; Bacan 1911; Bailey and Oliver 1939; Baird 1874; Bayles 1889; Beetham and Niering 1961; Bell 1985; Bonnichsen *et. al.* 1987; Booth 1881; Boyd 1873; Boyle 1969; Brennan 1974 and 1981; Bromley 1935 and 1945; Brugam 1978; Butler 1948; Butzer 1971; Byers 1946; Camp 1917; Caulkins 1866 and 1895; Ceci 1975; Chapin 1853; Church 1851; Coffin 1947; Cole 1888; Cronon 1983; Davis 1969; Day 1953; Decker 1970; Deevey 1939; DeForest 1852; Dincauze and Mulholland 1977; T. Dwight 1821; Eaton 1831; Elliot 1857; Ellsworth 1935; Engelhardt 1937; Fitting 1968; Ford 1981; R.H. Fowler 1967; Galligan 1960; Glick 1980; Goode 1880, 1881 and 1882; Goodkin 1674; Griffin 1965; Haime 1874; Hallock 1894; Hard 1947; Harte 1933 and 1938; Harwood 1932; H.W. Haynes 1889; W. Haynes 1949; Hoffman 1980; Hollister 1857; Hubbs and Potter 1971; Jenkins 1925; P. Johnson 1987; Judd 1905; Larned 1874 and 1880; Lavine 1988; Leopold 1956; T.R. Lewis 1981; Mather 1896; McDonald 1887; Moeller 1980; Nicholas 1987; Olson 1935; Orcutt 1882; Orcutt and Beardsley 1880; Pease and Niles 1819; Peters 1781; Pfeiffer 1952; Pope 1952; Porter 1841; Powell 1965; Pracus 1945; Rand 1968; Rau 1884; Ritchie 1965; Rostlund 1952; Russell 1942; Savelle 1966; Sears 1948 and 1963; C.P. Smith 1946; J.W. Smith 1887; Springman and Giunan 1983; Starr 1926; B.W. Stone 1974; Swigart 1973, 1974, 1977 and 1987; Taylor 1979; P.A. Thomas 1976; Trumbull 1818; Turner and Jacobus 1989; Vallentyne 1960; Vallentyne and Swabey 1955; Warner 1972; Waters 1962, 1965 and 1967; Wheeler 1966; White 1920; Wiegand 1983; Williams 1643; Withington 1935; Wolcott 1759; and G.I. Wood 1850.

Archaeologists have had many problems evaluating the relationships between humans and the fisheries resources of Connecticut. First, the bones and scales of fish did not preserve well in the acidic soils often found in the state. Second, until recently, the techniques used in excavation often did not obtain fish bones and scales. Finally, the most logical locations where early inhabitants would have utilized fish, *i.e.*, at falls and junctions of water courses, were settled and disturbed early by the European colonists. Only a few of these sites have been evaluated, and few fish remains have been found. This lack of documentation, in spite of historical evidence, led one archaeologist (Carlson 1988) to speculate that *Salmo salar* (Atlantic salmon), a large anadromous species that entered the freshwaters of Connecticut and New England, was not important to the early inhabitants of the region.

Herbs became established shortly after deglaciation, about 14,000 to 12,500 years ago. Herds of large, gregarious mammals then migrated to the area in search of food and humans probably followed them for the same reason. As evolution progressed, many of the herbs were replaced by boreal and hardwood forests. Humans periodically burned parts of these forests to provide food for those large mammals. Eventually, the larger mammals disappeared and humans probably began to utilize the larger anadromous and catadromous species of fish for food about 10,000 years ago. About 350 years ago populations of European settlers immigrated to Connecticut. Fishing techniques utilized in freshwaters did not change much nor did the use of those fish for food, trade, or fertilizer. However, the new people did utilize these anadromous fish for animal food. Because the population of humans increased greatly after the European immigrants arrived, the evolution of those communities frequented by these anadromous fish had to be affected because the fishing mortality was increased and population levels were reduced.

Another characteristic of human populations that affected anadromous and catadromous species of fish was the propensity of those European settlers to place mechanical barriers in watercourses. This allowed them to impound water to use for drinking and irrigation during the low water flow seasons. Additionally, it allowed them to obtain enough water to provide mechanical power to mills that would cut wood and grind corn and grain. Thus, evolution of all of the involved fish communities had to be affected (*e.g.*, flowing waters were changed to standing waters and some species were denied access to areas upstream of the barrier).

All of the species of fish that utilized the freshwaters of the state were affected by the land use practices associated with human populations as they evolved in Connecticut. Much land was cleared to provide wood for home building and fuel, to raise food, and to raise large herds of cattle, horses, and hogs. These imported domestic animals not only caused problems among colonists, but also with the Indians. Most livestock were not confined in pastures. Thus they competed with game animals for food and often ate the corn and other domestic plants being raised by the Indians. Additionally, land was occupied by dwellings, industries, and transportation systems. Industries, especially those associated with the industrialization of the Housatonic River drainage basin in the late 1700s and early 1800s, and with the Connecticut and Thames River drainage basins in the 1800s, undoubtedly discharged large volumes of effluents that probably contained numerous toxicants that directly destroyed large numbers of fish. Again, evolution of all the fish communities was affected (*e.g.*, increased siltation and dramatic changes in the timing and the volume of stream flow).

Transportation systems were often associated with the large rivers and some of them definitely affected the evolution of fish communities. For example, construction on the Farmington Canal was begun in 1825. This linked New Haven, on the Quinnipiac River, with Northhampton, Massachusetts, on the Connecticut River. It covered about eighty miles and functioned, in whole or in part, from about 1827 to about 1846. Because of water problems, this canal had to remove and add water at various points along the route. Thus, the timing and volume of flow in the environments, where water was removed would be modified. Anonymous (1858) commented that since the canal began adding water to the Quinnipiac River, salmonids (trout) were replaced by *Esox niger* (chain pickerel) and the water was less aesthetically pleasing. As noted earlier, this was probably the route that *Semotilus atromaculatus* (creek chub) followed to gain access from the Quinnipiac River drainage basin to the Farmington River drainage basin.

Railroads were constructed, beginning in the early 1830s, along most of the major watercourses in Connecticut. Not only did this construction change the volume and timing of the stream flow, rate of siltation and temperature, but the operation of the trains had great impacts. Often wood was cut close to the tracks, thus changing the movement of water into the watercourses. Additionally, in close proximity to transportation systems and major watercourses, industrial uses of land and water developed. These uses not only could directly affect the evolution of fish communities by destroying certain species or life history stages, but could also alter the temperature and the timing and volume of stream flow. The role of railroads in allowing humans to transport live fish and then to introduce them into freshwaters throughout the state has not been documented in Connecticut. There are references in popular literature to passengers and conductors moving fish into other areas (*e.g.*, Anonymous 1870), and I believe that railroads contributed greatly to the introduction of fish into the freshwaters of western Connecticut from the 183's to the 1880s.

Human impacts on diadromous species

Although the effects of all characteristics of human populations on the evolution of fish communities cannot be documented in most species, we can make a reasonable case for certain characteristics of human populations on the evolution of many of the anadromous species.

Both species of *Acipenser* (sturgeons), *i.e.*, *A. brevirostrum* (shortnose sturgeon) and *A. oxyrhynchus* (Atlantic sturgeon), were probably not affected

by the construction of mechanical barriers until these barriers were constructed near the influence of saltwater on the three main rivers. Populations
of both species were probably always low in the Thames River drainage basin
because the fall line (near Norwich) since deglaciation is near saltwater. That
limited area was drastically reduced in 1825, with the building of a dam on
the Quinebaug /Shetucket River at Greenville and there have probably been
no spawning populations in that river since the middle nineteenth century.

Populations of both species in the Housatonic River had a large area available to them between saltwater and the falls at New Milford until a dam was
constructed at Derby in 1870. Note that the fall line for most species was further north at Falls Village. However, in the case of this river, three other factors
probably contributed to the elimination of the spawning populations of both
species. First, both the timing and volume of stream flow were changed
because of the many small dams constructed in the 1600s and 1700s that might
have adversely affected either movement or spawning of adults or growth of
the young. Second, many industrial and municipal effluents, associated with
the industrial revolution that was centered in this basin in the late 1700s and
early 1800s, were introduced and probably killed many young fish. Third, overfishing. Both species require approximately seven to eleven years to reach sexual maturity. Because of this, they were easy to overfish and there was a large
fishing industry for them in this drainage basin. There have probably been no
spawning populations in this river since the early twentieth century.

The Connecticut River was the only major river in Connecticut that did
not have any mechanical barriers constructed on it prior to the fall line at
Holoyke Massachusetts. The small falls at Enfield, Connecticut, normally
would not be a barrier to movement. Overfishing was the probable cause of
the decline of the populations in this drainage basin. One of these species,
Acipenser brevirostrum (shortnose sturgeon), evolved both estuarine and
freshwater populations from an anadromous population over the years.
Dadswell (1979) reported a similar pattern of evolution in the population in
the St. John's River Estuary, New Brunswick. These estuarine and freshwater
components are probably what has kept the population of this species in the
Connecticut River viable. The other species, *A. oxyrhynchus* (Atlantic sturgeon) probably does not have a spawning population in this river at this time.
Acipenser brevirostrum (shortnose sturgeon) is on both the state and federal
lists of endangered species. Unfortunately, *A. oxyrhynchus* (Atlantic sturgeon), is listed only as threatened in Connecticut.

Salmo salar (Atlantic salmon) was well known to Europeans, although
most colonists had not had the opportunity either to fish for them or eat
them there. Like all anadromous species, harvest was relatively easy during
the spawning season in a few areas on each of the major rivers. Most of the
small streams in the Housatonic River drainage basin had mechanical barriers constructed on them prior to the middle 1700s. Since those streams were

probably the major spawning areas, this species was eliminated from the Housatonic River drainage basin well before 1800. The only documentation of this species are a few references, *i.e.*, Anonymous 1870, Atkins 1874, and a stream named Salmon Creek that is located below the fall line of the Housatonic at Falls Village.

Both the Connecticut and Thames River drainage basins have more available spawning habitat, and it was not until dams were constructed on the larger tributaries and the mainstem that *S. salar* (Atlantic salmon) populations were affected in those drainage basins. The mainstem of the Connecticut was dammed in northern Massachusetts in 1798. This denied the greater number of spawning populations of *S. salar* (Atlantic salmon) access to their spawning habitats. Overharvesting, coupled with further construction of dams on the principal tributaries of the Connecticut and Thames Rivers, eliminated all populations of this species in these rivers by the mid 1800s.

The largest anadromous alosine (herring), *Alosa sapidissima* (American shad), probably also experienced fluctuations in population numbers as mechanical barriers were constructed on the principal tributaries and mainstems of the three large rivers of Connecticut. Additionally, overfishing and pollution have also affected them in each of the major rivers during the last 200 years. Because of the very limited areas of freshwaters available to them in the Thames River, these populations are the smallest of the three rivers. While populations in the Housatonic are much larger, recurring pollution problems often influence those populations. The construction of fish ladders over the first few dams on the mainstem of the Connecticut River in the last twenty years has substantially increased the freshwater habitat available, and the populations of *Alosa sapidissima* (American shad) in that river are increasing. Populations in the Thames River should increase also as efforts are underway to construct fish ladders over the first few dams in that drainage basin.

Another species has also been helped by the construction of fish ladders over the dams on the Connecticut River. *Petromyzon marinus* (sea lamprey) is our only anadromous species that spends its adult life in the ocean as a parasite. Populations of this species in the Connecticut River and its tributaries have been greatly increased by the fishways allowing access to upstream spawning and rearing areas, *e.g.*, Aarrestad (1992), Gephard *et al.* (1992). However, this species has not done well in the other major drainage basins. No populations have apparently been established in the Thames River drainage basin, probably because there was not adequate spawning habitat below the fall line. Although there were populations in the Housatonic River drainage basin below the fall line, there seems to be only one tributary that has a viable population since the construction of the dam at Derby.

Impact of introduced species

Concomitant with all of these factors associated with human populations was the deliberate introduction of fish to freshwaters by humans. Most amateur and professional ichthyologists felt, as did most citizens of the state, that the prime effort of the state fisheries agency was to introduce and manipulate useful fishes and that nonuseful fishes should be removed. This was apparently the attitude at the national level also. Although the United States Fish Commission was formed in 1871 to do work in three areas, the introduction and manipulation of useful fishes was the area that expended the most money and effort. Furthermore, mirroring the attitude of most of the citizens of Connecticut, many respected ichthyologists, *e.g.*, Goode (1880) and Jordan (1888), agreed that the introduction and manipulation of fish must be a leading role of the United States Fish Commission.

Although the professionals working for the state introduced and manipulated fish statewide, much of the amateur activity continued to be centered in the western part of the state. The first report of many species of fish introduced into Connecticut in the 1800s were from western Connecticut (see Tables 2 and 3), e.g., *Ambloplites rupestris* (rock bass), *Lota lota* (burbot), *Micropterus dolomieu* (smallmouth bass), *M. salmoides* (largemouth bass), *Oncorhynchus nerka* (sockeye salmon), *Percopsis omiscomaycus* (trout-perch), *Prosopium cylindraceum* (round whitefish), *Salmo trutta* (brown trout), *Salvelinus namaycush* (lake trout), and *Thymallus arcticus* (Arctic grayling). In addition, the first reports of native fish being manipulated were from western Connecticut, *e.g.*, *Esox niger* (chain pickerel) were moved from Bantam Lake to an area in the upper Housatonic River drainage basin in 1812. This activity has continued, and many of the fish that were introduced in the 1900s by humans were first introduced into the freshwaters of western Connecticut (see Tables 2 and 3), e.g., *Ameiurus melas* (black bullhead), *A. natalis* (yellow bullhead), *Campostoma anomalum* (central stoneroller), *Catostomus catostomus* (longnose sucker), *Ctenopharyngodon idella* (grass carp), *Margariscus margarita* (pearl dace), *Notropis amblops* (bigeye chub), *Pimephales notatus* (bluntnose minnow), and *Pimephales promelas* (fathead minnow).

Just as it is impossible to separate the effects of the existing physical, chemical, and biological factors on the evolution of fish communities, so is it impossible to separate the effects of these introduced fishes. However, there is no doubt that some of the fish introduced in the middle to late 1800s have strongly influenced the evolution of fish communities in the larger bodies of water. For example, many centrarchids (sunfishes), *e.g.*, *Ambloplites rupestris* (rock bass), *Lepomis macrochirus* (bluegill), *Micropterus dolomieu* (smallmouth bass), *M. salmoides* (largemouth bass), *Pomoxis nigromaculatus* (black crappie), and a cyprinid (minnow), *Cyprinus carpio* (common carp), dominate most of those bodies of water (Table 2).

We have always manipulated our environment, and we probably always will, to achieve some social benefit. Theoretical ecologists have long postulated that we can obtain greater benefits by intelligent manipulations (Smellie 1832, Forbes 1925, Evans *et al.* 1987). Once we accept the premise that evolution of a fish community, or any community, is the interaction of all the physical, chemical, and biological characteristics, and is an ongoing process, we have two options to consider. The first is to try to quantify the effects of changes of any particular characteristic with some aspect of the human population. We have attempted to isolate the effects of humans on the evolution of fish communities by assigning values of good or bad to certain combinations of species. We have done this by assuming that there is a "balance of nature" that does not include changes in species combinations due to expansion and contraction of ranges or extinction and birth of species due to changes in the community (physical, chemical, or biological).

The second option, and more appealing to me, is to accept that all fish communities will change in response to interactions between the physical, chemical, and biological characteristics of the drainage basins. Unfortunately, natural selection during these periods of change is so harsh in most aquatic environments that the fish communities often change dramatically. It would seem much more instructive to me to attempt to govern our interactions with other humans by using criteria for a happy, healthy human population living in an aesthetically pleasing environment in which both are continually changing (evolving), rather than attempting to document a process that by definition is changing randomly by the combination of fishes present.

CHAPTER FOUR

Identification of the freshwater fishes of Connecticut

Taxonomic considerations

The basic "kind" of fish considered in this book is the species, a population of morphologically and physiologically similar individuals that do not normally exchange hereditary materials with other related populations. The name bearer of a species is that single specimen (holotype) that the original author designated and deposited in a reputable repository, *i.e.*, one with permanence, close to a good library and having a sound policy concerning loans. Examples of other types used are the paratype (used by the author, along with the holotype, in the original description), syntype (one of several specimens on which the species was described if none was designated as holotype), lectotype (member of a syntypic series later selected to serve as the holotype), neotype (specimen selected to replace a lost type), and topotype (any specimen, other than the original types, from the type locality), hypotype (a described, figured or listed specimen), homeotype (specimen compared by a competent observer with the holotype, lectotype or other primary type and found to be conspecific), and plastotype (cast of a type, used to distribute facsimiles of rare specimens).

Species of similar general appearances that appear to be distinct from closely related species are presumed to be of a common origin and placed in the same genus. The author of that genus designates a type species for the genus. Genera, or a genus, that have common features quite distinct from other genera are then assigned to the same family. The family name is the stem of the type genus (designated by the author who formed the family) with an "idae" appended. When the type genus name is changed, the family name is changed. All types should be representative of the taxa (singular, taxon, term used when referring to a taxonomic entity without reference to its rank, *ie.g.*, phylum, class, order, family or genus), have known geographic and geologic ranges, and have known and established taxonomic relationships.

Scientific names

All described species of fish have accepted scientific (Latin or latinized) names that are composed of two terms (written in italics or underlined) followed by the name of the individual or individuals who described the species, *e.g.*, *Amia calva* Linnaeus. The author's name is placed in parentheses if the fish was first described as being in a different genus, *e.g.*, *Luxilus cornutus* (Mitchill) was originally described as *Cyprinus cornutus* Mitchill. The starting date for this double-name system (binominal nomenclature) is the tenth edition of *Systema Naturae*, 1758, by Linnaeus.

The generic name is a noun in the nominative singular and is capitalized. The species name is a (1) noun in apposition, (2) adjective agreeing in number and gender or (3) noun in the genitive agreeing in number and gender, and is not capitalized. Names can be descriptive, geographic, geologic, barbaric, coined, nonsensical, or patronymic. Rules governing the naming of species have been established by the International Commission on Zoological Nomenclature.

Scientific names are changed occasionally because more intensive study may show that more than one species is contained within the range of variation presently defined as one species (splitting) or that several presently defined species should be combined into one species (lumping). When a taxon is divided into one or more groups, its valid name must be retained by one of the new groups. When taxa are united, the oldest valid name is selected; if more than one name has the same date, the name selected by the first reviser shall stand. Scientific names may also be changed to comply with the Rules of Zoological Nomenclature.

Common names vary dramatically throughout and within the area in which a species is found. A joint committee of the American Fisheries Society and the American Society of Ichthyologists and Herpetologists was established that publishes a list of recommended common and scientific names of fishes in North America (most recently, Robins *et al.* 1991), in order to avoid misunderstanding between similar common names for different species of fish and to help provide stability. However, the names selected by the committee (both scientific and common) may not be accepted by all amateur or professional ichthyologists.

Pronunciation of scientific names also varies. Generally, species names are not accented, whereas, in the family name the syllable before the family suffix (idae) is accented. However, common usage and interpretations of different classical linguists vary. A good discussion of the rules of zoological nomenclature can be found in Stoll *et al.* (1961) and Mayr and Ashlock (1991).

Collecting fishes

Specimens can be collected by various active (*e.g.* sport fishing, trawling, seining, electrofishing) and passive (*e.g.* gill and trap nets) techniques. Check with the Fisheries Division of the DEP if you wish to utilize one of these techniques so that you can obtain a permit and learn the regulations that apply to holders of that license. Additionally, you should check the state

(Anonymous 1992) and federal (Williams *et al.* 1989) list of endangered species so that you can recognize those species before you collect. Specimens are preserved in 10% formalin (the initial concentration of formaldehye gas dissolved in water is about 40%), which can be purchased at a drug store. A 10% formalin solution is obtained by adding one part of the formalin you purchased to nine parts of tap water. Incisions are usually made on the abdomen of large specimens to ensure preservation of the viscera before placing in the formalin solution. After they are hardened (preserved), a few days to a few weeks depending on the size of the specimens, they are stored in a mixture of 70% ethyl or 40% isopropyl alcohol. Living fish can often be identified in aquaria, but some counts require preserved specimens and magnification. Page and Burr (1991) have good colored illustrations of living species, many of which are found in the freshwaters of Connecticut.

Keying techniques

Identification of an unknown fish is accomplished by systematically reducing the number of possible species. "Good" taxonomic characteristics should be observable and quantifiable and should vary among the taxa. If the character is not genetically controlled, we must be able to estimate the effects of the environment. For example, during the development of fish, many characters are additionally influenced by environmental factors, *e.g.*, water temperature and pH. Both meristic (countable) and morphometric (measurable) characteristics can be utilized and should be little influenced by age or sex, or defined by age and sex classes. Examples of meristic characters are the number of (1) supporting elements (spines or rays) of fins, (2) scales (lateral line, mid-lateral and above and below the lateral line), (3) gill rakers, and (4) pharyngeal teeth. Examples of morphometric characters are (1) eye diameter in snout length, (2) snout length in standard length, and (3) snout to dorsal origin length in dorsal origin to base of caudal peduncle.

Some of the standard meristic and morphometric characteristics commonly used are shown in Figure 5, and defined as follows.

Anal and dorsal fin counts — all spines and rays are counted beginning at the dorsal origin if they grade gradually from the smallest to the largest. One or two small rudimentary rays that precede much longer rays are not counted. The last ray is not counted if it is much closer to the preceding ray than the space between the other rays because is has the same base. Spines are usually expressed by Roman numerals and rays by Arabic numerals. See Figure 6 to differentiate between spines and rays. If there is more than one distinct dorsal or anal fin, *i.e.*, the two portions are not connected by a membrane, a dash is used between the counts for each fin. If there is one fin, but it contains both spines and rays, a comma is used to separate the spines and rays. For example, II-14 signifies that there are two fins, the first with two spines and the second with fourteen rays. A formula with III,9 would signify one fin with three spines and nine rays. If there are two dorsal fins, and the first dorsal fin is supported only by spines, it is often called the spinous dorsal and the second fin is called the soft dorsal. Both dorsal and anal fin support counts should be done having the light source behind the fin.

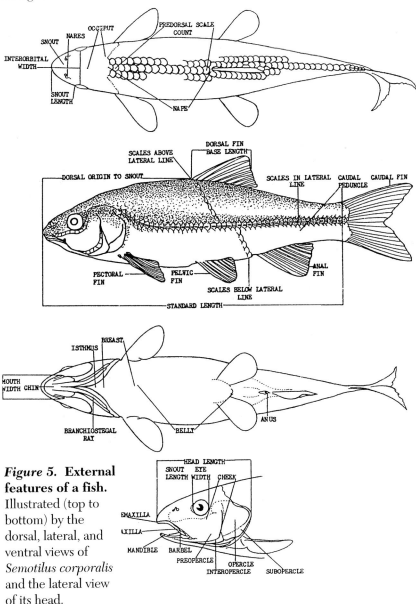

Figure 5. External features of a fish. Illustrated (top to bottom) by the dorsal, lateral, and ventral views of *Semotilus corporalis* and the lateral view of its head.

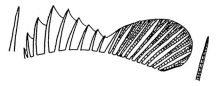

Figure 6. **Front and side views of spines (left) and rays (right).**

Head length — most anterior part of the head to the most posterior part of the opercular membrane.

Interorbital width — least distance across the top of the head between the bony margins of the eyes.

Mouth width — greatest horizontal distance across the mouth.

Predorsal scale count — all scales that touch the mid-dorsal line from the occiput to the origin of the dorsal fin.

Scales in lateral line — count all scales from the first scale in the lateral line that touches the shoulder girdle to the structural base of the caudal peduncle (scale over the middle of the curve produced when the caudal fin is moved laterally). If no lateral line is visible the mid-lateral row of scales is counted.

Scales above lateral line — scales from the origin of the dorsal fin diagonally downward and backward to the lateral line (lateral line scale not counted).

Scales below lateral line — scales from the origin of the anal fin diagonally upward and forward to the lateral line (lateral line scale not counted).

Snout length — most anterior part of the middle of the upper lip to the anterior rim of the orbit.

Standard length — most anterior part of the head to the structural base of the caudal peduncle (base located by bending caudal fin laterally).

Total length — most anterior part of the head to the most posterior part of the caudal fin when the caudal rays are squeezed together.

Body proportions are obtained by measuring the straight line distance (not around the natural curves) between the appropriate points with dividers, determining the length with a millimeter rule, and performing the division indicated.

The number and shape of the gill rakers on the first gill arch are evaluated by lifting the operculum with the thumb of one hand. The count of rakers on the lower limb is obtained by beginning at the angle of the arch and counting anteriorly (see Figure 7). A raker in the angle is included in the count. If two rakers are fused, they are counted as one.

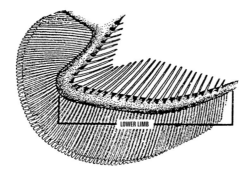

Figure 7. Area included in a count of the number of gill rakers on the lower limb of the first gill arch. The right arch is shown.

When you have a collection of unknown fish, the first step is to separate them into similar looking groups. There is a definite advantage in having several individuals of each group (species). Although the "typical" member of a species has defined characteristics, there is a small percentage of individuals that do not have the characteristic used to separate them in the key. Additionally, many individuals of some populations may not have the typical characteristic. Thus, having more specimens will provide you with a better documentation of "typical" key characteristics or encourage you to resort your "species" groups. Additionally, you may find that one group is males, one is females, and a third is juveniles. Differences between the sexes show up in some species only during the breeding season, whereas some, *e.g.*, cyprinidonts (killifishes), have differences all the time. Once you learn these groups, you will not have so many unknown "species."

The next step is to proceed to the "Key to the families of fishes found within the freshwaters of Connecticut" on page 74. Keys are used by selecting the alternative between couplets that better describes your unknown specimens. If both choices partially describe your specimens, follow both choices until you reach a family. The characteristics used in the keys are those that separate most of the individuals in each family however, your single specimen or the average specimen in your population may not be typical. Some families are diagnosed more than once in the key because there is considerable variation among the species in the family.

After you have determined the family, or families, that contain your unknown specimens, consult the description of each family. Many of the species found within the freshwaters of Connecticut are the sole representative of their family and your unknown specimen is immediately identified in those cases. If there is more than one species in the family, you proceed to the key to species within the family and continue selecting alternatives as you did in the key to the families. Remember to follow both species alternatives to completion when both are partially correct, as you did in the family key. Then, compare the illustration with your unknown species. Consider the listed distribution in Connecticut.

There are occasions when an unknown specimen does not quite fit any of the options. You may have either a specimen that represents (1) the extreme range for the characteristics of the species that is found in Connecticut, (2) a species that has not been reported in Connecticut, or (3) a hybrid of two or more species that are found in Connecticut. Whenever you obtain specimens that you are unable to identify, please preserve them, as described in the previous section on collecting fishes, and call the Fisheries Division of the DEP or the Ichthyologist at the University of Connecticut.

Many meristic and life history characteristics of fish are influenced by polygenes, multiple-alleles, or both. Additionally, these characteristics may be directly influenced by some factor in the environment. Polygenic traits are controlled by genes that are located on more than one chromosome. Their expression may be additive.

Multiple-allelic traits have a series of expressions, *e.g.*, A, a1, a2, and a3, that could be located at any one allele, although only two could be there at one time. For example, a fish could have A and a1, or A and a2, or A and a3, or a1 and a2, or a1 and a3, or a2 and a3. The series of expressions may be ranked in terms of dominance and recessiveness or they could be additive.

A characteristic that is controlled by polygenes, multiple alleles, or both, has the genetic potential to produce a range of expressions of that character in the population. Even if alternative responses for a trait are not noted at one time, some traits are carried in a recessive condition and are expressed in future generations as a result of new gene combinations. Therefore, the range of variation in any characteristic for many of our species can be, and probably is, very large.

Hybrids between species within a family are occasionally captured in any watercourse in the state, rarely in large numbers. Typical hybrids have characteristics intermediate between the two parent species and are usually not fertile. Sometimes hybrids are found that are the result of an F1 hybrid with one of the two parental species; these usually have characteristics closer to one parental species than the other. Sometimes, the F1 hybrid mates with a third species, resulting in a trihybrid with characteristics reflecting all three parental species. Many times it is not possible to definitely identify a hybrid.

The chance for hybridization could occur whenever two or more species are spawning at the same time in the same place. Normally, behavior patterns would prevent sperms and eggs from coming in contact. Additionally, the differences between the different species in the shape and size of the chromosomes, as well as the location and arrangement of the genes on each chromosome, would prevent fertilization and development of the egg.

The typical reasons for two reproductively active individuals, a male of one species and a female of another, coming in contact with each other are (1) spawning populations of one species are so large that the only way for the less aggressive members of that species to spawn is to migrate to another area and spawn with another species, and (2) when an individual of one species becomes reproductively active when no other members of that species are active. In either case, the species in the wrong place at the wrong time may participate in the spawning activities of a male and a female of a different species. This may result in spawning between different species due to either actual mating or coincidental meeting of sperm and egg.

The ability to use keys comes only with practice and beginners should not be discouraged. After one becomes proficient, only selected portions of the keys need be used. Some salient features are illustrated in keys however, the glossary or a standard ichthyology text should be used frequently when there is doubt as to the meaning of a feature in either a key couplet or a description. When special techniques are needed to identify the species found in a family, explanations required to perform the techniques are included.

Glossary

Abdomen — lower surface of the body between the pectoral fins and anus

Acuminate — tapering to a point

Acute — sharp

Adipose eyelid — transparent tissue around margin of eye

Adipose fin — fleshy, rayless fin on the back between the dorsal and caudal fins

Adnate — grown together

Air bladder — gas-filled sac in the dorsal portion of the abdominal cavity, consisting of one to three chambers; also called swim bladder

Allopatric — living in geographically separated areas

Ammocoete — larval form of lampreys

Anadromous — ascending rivers from the sea to spawn

Anal fin — unpaired median fin between the caudal fin and the anus

Anal papilla — an appendage in front of the genital pore and behind anus

Anal plate — bony plate surrounding anus

Anterior — toward the front

Antrorse — turned forward

Anus — posterior opening of the digestive tract, also known as the vent

Articulate — joined

Asymmetrical — the two sides (halves) differ

Attenuate — long and slender

Axillary process — membranous flap at origin of pectoral or pelvic fins

Barbel — fleshy protuberance in the form of a thread, flap, or cone usually found around the mouth or chin

Basibranchials — three median bones on the floor of the buccal cavity, joined by the ventral ends of the gill arches posteriorly and by the basihyal (or tongue) anteriorly

Basihyal — anterior median bone (tongue) on the floor of the buccal cavity

Basicaudal — pertaining to the area at the base of the caudal fin

Belly — region on the ventral side immediately behind the pectoral fin and extending to the anus

Bicuspid tooth — one with two tips

Bifurcate — divided into two branches

Body depth — depth of body at deepest part

Body width — width of body at widest part

Branchiocranium — the bony skeleton supporting the gill arches

Branchiostegal rays — elongated bones supporting the gill membranes

Breast — region on ventral side between the isthmus and a point immediately behind and below the pectoral fins

Buccal — pertaining to the mouth

Caecum (plural *caeca*) — sac-like pouch connected to the digestive tract between the stomach and the intestine

Canine teeth — elongated conical teeth

Cardiform teeth — slender teeth of uniform length, in brush-like bands or patches

Catadromous — going from freshwaters to the sea to spawn

Caudal fin — tail fin

Caudal peduncle — region behind the anal fin extending to the structural base of the caudal fin

Cheek — region between the eye and the preopercle

Chin — region between the halves (sides) of the lower jaw

Circumferential scale rows — the number of scale rows around the body at the greatest depth of the body

Circumoral teeth — innermost teeth, lateral to the mouth, in lampreys

Cirri — fleshy extensions, single or divided, of the skin

Compressed — flattened laterally

Concave — curved inward

Confluent — flowing together, *i.e.,* dorsal anal and caudal fins flow together and are indistinguishable

Conjoined — joined, at least in part

Convex — curved outward

Ctenoid scale — one having tiny prickles (cteni) on its posterior edge

Cycloid scale — one having a smooth posterior edge

Deciduous — said of scales that are easily removed

Decurved — bent downward

Dentaries — paired anterior bones of the lower jaw

Dentary nipple — a protuberance at the tip of the lower jaw

Depressed — flattened from top to bottom

Depressed fin length — length of the fin when rays or spines are pressed against the body

Diadromous — fishes that must spend part of their lives in both fresh and saltwater

Distal — farthest from the point of attachment

Dorsal — upper surface

Dorsal fin(s) — median unpaired fin(s) on the back

Dorsum — pertaining to the upper part of the body

Emarginate — said of fins having the distal margin notched or indented

Entire — smooth, as opposed to emarginate

Eye diameter — horizontal diameter of the eyeball

Falcate — sickle shaped

Filament — threadlike fin rays that are appreciably longer than the other rays

Fimbriate — fringed at the margin

Fin base — area where the fin is attached to the body

Fin membrane — membrane connecting spines or rays

Finlets — a series of small individual fins between the dorsal fin and caudal fin or between the anal fin and caudal fin

Focus — center of a scale, around which growth proceeds

Fontanel — an unossified space on top of the head between the parietals

Fork length — distance from the anteriormost point of the fish (mouth closed) to the tip of the middle ray of the caudal fin

Frenum — a bridge of tissue that connects the upper lip and the snout

Fusiform — spindle-shaped and slightly, or not at all compressed

Gape — length of gape is the distance from the median anterior part of the mouth to the angle of the mouth; width of gape is the horizontal distance between the two angles of the mouth when mouth is closed

Genital papilla — a protuberance at the genital opening, just anterior to the anal fin

Gill arch — a bony support for a gill

Gill cover — bony covering of the gill cavity, usually composed of four bones; also called operculum

Gill filaments — paired structures on the posterior face of the gill arch

Gill membrane — membrane, supported by the branchiostegal rays, that encloses the bottom and lower sides of the gill chamber

Gill rakers — structures on the anterior face of the gill arch

Gonopodium — modified anterior rays of the anal fin that function as a sex organ in male poeciliid fishes

Gular plate — bony plate between the halves of the lower jaw

Head length — distance from the anteriormost part of the head to the posterior edge of the opercle

Heterocercal — vertebral column arches upward posteriorly, supporting caudal fin dorsally and ventrally; lobes of caudal fin usually unequal

Homocercal — vertebral column terminates posteriorly in a series of bones (hypural plate) that support the entire caudal fin; lobes of caudal fin usually equal

Humeral — region just behind the gill opening and above the pectoral fin

Hyoid apparatus — a series of bones supporting the tongue

Hyoid teeth — teeth on the tongue

Hypural plate — modified last vertebrae which support the caudal fin

Imbricate — overlapping in shingle fashion

Immaculate — without spots or pigment

Inferior mouth — mouth is located on lower side of the head and the upper jaw is overhung by the snout

Infraoral teeth — teeth immediately below oesophageal opening in lampreys

Infraorbital — region immediately below eye

Intermuscular bones — branched bones that are isolated in the connective tissue between myomeres

Interopercle — bone in the opercular series anterior to the subopercle

Interorbital — area between the eyes on the top of the head

Interradial membrane — membrane connecting the fin rays or spines

Isthmus — region anterior to the breast and lying between gill chambers

Jugular — pertaining to the throat (the isthmus region)

Keel — scales or tissue forming a sharp edge

Larva (plural *larvae*) — young fish before they change in appearance and assume the adult form(s)

Lateral — pertaining to the sides

Lateral band — pigment stripes along the sides, often extending along the head

Lateral-line scale count — scales bearing the lateral-line pores and tubes are counted from the shoulder girdle to the structural base of the tail fin

Lateral-line system — a series of pores and tubes branching on the head and extending along the sides of the body

Lateral series scale count — mid-lateral scale row from the shoulder girdle to the structural base of the tail fin

Leptocephalus — larvae of eels

Lingual — pertaining to the tongue

Mandible — the lower jaw

Mandibular knob — a knob-like protuberance on the tip of the lower jaw where the two halves unite

Mandibular pore — small sensory opening in the undersurface of the bones of the lower jaw

Maxilla or *maxillary* — bone on each half of the upper jaw immediately behind the premaxillae

Melanophore — black pigment cell

Middorsal stripe — a pigmented line lying along the median of the back

Multiserial — said of teeth that are in more than one row

Myomere — muscular segment or impression

Nape — region from the occiput to the origin of the dorsal fin

Nares — paired nostrils, each with two openings, usually located dorsally in front of the eyes

Nonprotractile — upper jaw is firmly bound to the snout and no groove separates the jaw from the snout

Nuptial tubercle — temporary cornification (hardened protuberance) of the skin of adult male, and sometimes female, which usually appears just before or during the breeding season

Occiput — dorsal surface of the head from above or immediately behind the eyes to the nape; in many species it separates the scaled and scaleless regions anterior to the dorsal fin

Ocellus — an eyelike spot

Opercle — uppermost, large bone of the gill cover

Opercular flap — membranous or bony flap at the posterior edge of opercle

Operculum — the bony covering of the gill cavity, also called gill cover

Oral disc — expanded mouth of a lamprey

Oral valve — thin membranes attached behind the jaws that prevent water from escaping through the mouth during respiratory movements

Orbit — eyesocket

Origin of fins — anterior end of dorsal or anal fin base

Paired fins — pelvic and pectoral fins

Palatine teeth — teeth on the paired palatine bones located on the roof of the mouth adjacent to the median vomer

Papilla (plural *papillae*) — a small fleshy protuberance on the skin

Papillose — having many papillae, usually referring to the lips

Parietals — paired bones on the dorsal surface of the skull

Parr — young salmonids that have not attained the adult color pattern

Parr marks — dark vertical marks on the sides

Pectoral fins — the more anterior or dorsal set of paired fins

Pelvic fins — the more posterior or ventral set of paired fins

Peritoneum — membranous lining of the abdominal cavity

Pharyngeal teeth — teeth on the pharyngeal bones (representing the 5th nonfunctional gill arch) located immediately posterior to the last functional gill arch

Physoclistous — having the swim bladder isolated from the digestive tract

Physostomous — having the swim bladder connected with the digestive tract

Plicate — having grooves formed by parallel or transverse folds of skin, referring to the lips

Posterior — toward the rear

Postorbital length — greatest distance between the posterior edge of the orbit and the posterior edge of the opercular membrane

Predorsal length — distance from the origin of the dorsal fin to the anterior edge of the snout

Predorsal scales — scales lying along the dorsal ridge between the occiput and the origin of the dorsal fin

Predorsal stripe — a pigmented line lying along the median between the occiput and the origin of the dorsal fin

Premaxilla — anterior bone of each half of the upper jaw

Preopercle — most anterior bone of the opercular series; bone of cheek

Preoperculomandibular canal — a cephalic portion of the lateral-line system which extends along the preopercle and the mandible

Prickles — small, fine, sometimes curved spines, on or in place of scales

Protractile — upper jaw not firmly bound to the snout and capable of being projected; separated from snout by a groove

Proximal — nearest the point of attachment

Pseudobranch — gill-like structure on the inner surface of the opercle

Pyloric caeca — fingerlike projections from the digestive tract in the region of the stomach and the intestine

Ray — support for the fins, usually segmented, and branched; flexible and paired when viewed from the front

Ray count — all are counted if they grade gradually from smallest to the largest; one or two small rudimentary rays preceding the remainder of the longer rays are not counted; the last ray is not counted if it has the same base as the second to the last ray

Radii — grooves that radiate out from the center of a scale

Refugia — freshwater habitats supporting fishes displaced during glaciation

Retrorse — turned backward

Rudimentary ray — poorly developed ray, or one that is appreciably shorter than the others

Saddle — rectangular or linear bars or bands which cross the back and extend downward on the sides

Scales above lateral line — number of scale rows from the dorsal fin origin diagonally downward and backward to, but not including the lateral line

Scales around caudal peduncle — number of scale rows counted in a zigzag manner around the slenderest part of the caudal peduncle

Scales below lateral line — number of scale rows from the origin of the anal fin diagonally upward and forward to, but not including the lateral line

Scapular bar — a pigmented area above the pectoral fin

Serrae — saw-like extensions of spines

Serrate — notched or toothed on the edge

Snout length — distance from anteriormost part of fish to anterior margin of the orbit

Soft dorsal — posterior portion of the dorsal fin when supported by rays

Spatulate — spoon shaped

Spine — support for the fins; in most cases not segmented, stiff, not branched and not paired when viewed from the front

Spinous dorsal — anterior portion of the dorsal fin when supported by spines

Standard length — anteriormost part of the head to the structural base of the caudal fin (base located by bending the caudal fin laterally)

Stellate — resembling a star

Striations — grooves or streaks

Subopercle — lower, posteriormost bone of the gill cover

Subterminal mouth — located below the anteriormost point of the fish, but not quite ventral

Supramaxilla — bone of the upper jaw attached to the dorso-posterior end of the maxilla

Supraoral teeth — paired teeth just above the throat of lampreys

Supraorbital canal — a paired branch of the lateral line system that extends along the top of the head between the eyes and forward onto the snout

Supratemporal canal — a branch of the lateral line system that extends across the occiput and connects the lateral canals

Swim bladder — gas-filled sac in the dorsal portion of the abdominal cavity, consisting of one to three chambers; also called air bladder

Sympatric — living in overlapping ranges

Teardrop — dark bar below the eye

Terete — cylindrical and tapering

Terminal mouth — located at the anteriormost part of the body and neither the upper nor lower jaw projects beyond the other

Tessellated — a squared or checkered pattern

Thoracic — pertaining to the breast

Total length — most anterior part of the head, mouth closed, to the most posterior part of the caudal fin, when caudal rays are squeezed together

Tuberculate — having nuptial tubercles

Tricuspid tooth — one with three tips

Unicuspid tooth — one with one tip

Uniserial — said of teeth that are in one row

Variegated — an irregular pattern of stripes, bars or blotches, often with interconnected components

Vent — external opening of the digestive tract, also called anus

Ventral — pertaining to the lower surface

Vermiculations — worm-like markings

Villiform teeth — slender bands of teeth

Vomer — the median bone on the roof of the mouth

Weberian apparatus — the modified anterior four vertebrae and the small bones and ligaments connecting the air bladder and the inner ear in minnows, characins, catfishes and their relatives

Key to the families of fishes found in the freshwaters of Connecticut

1. No paired fins   Petromyzontidae (lampreys), page 175

   One or 2 sets of paired fins   2

2. More than one gill opening on each side   3
   One gill opening on each side   5

3. Gill openings on ventral surface of head   Rajidae (skates), page 183
   Gill openings on lateral surfaces of head   4

4. Anal fin absent   Squalidae (dogfish sharks), page 202

   Anal fin present   Carcharhinidae (requiem sharks), page 98

5. Caudal fin absent   Syngnathidae (pipefishes), in part, page 204

   Caudal fin present   6

6. Heterocercal tail   7
   Homocercal tail   8

Figure 8. Heterocercal tails of *Acipenser* (left) and *Amia* (center) and a typical homocercal tail (right).

7. Mouth ventral, essentially toothless,
   gular plate absent   Acipenseridae (sturgeons),
   page 84

   Mouth terminal, strongly toothed,
   gular plate present   Amiidae (bowfins), page 85

Figure 9. Ventral view of the head of Amia calva, showing the gular plate.

8. Skull asymmetrical, both eyes on
   same side of head   9
   Skull symmetrical, eyes on opposite
   sides of head   11

9. Left pectoral fin rudimentary or absent,
   right pectoral may also be absent,
   posterior margin of preopercle hidden
   by skin or scales   Soleidae (soles), page 199
   Pectoral fins present, posterior
   margin of preopercle exposed   10

10. Eyes on the right side   Pleuronectidae (righteye
    flounders), page 178
    Eyes on left side   Bothidae (lefteye flounders),
    page 91

11. Pelvic fins united to form a suction disc   12
    Pelvic fins, if present,
    not completely united   13

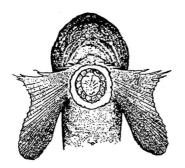

Figure 10. Ventral view of a fish showing the pelvic fins united to form a suction disc.

12. Two dorsal fins   Gobiidae (gobies), page 158
    One dorsal fin   Cyclopteridae (snailfishes), page 121

13. Head encased by bony plates   Triglidae (searobins), page 208
    Head not encased by bony plates   14

14. Five finlets posterior to both the dorsal and anal fins   Scombridae (mackerels), page 197

    Finlets absent posterior to both dorsal and anal fins   15

15. Row of keeled scales on either side of caudal peduncle   Carangidae (jacks), in part, page 95

    No row of keeled scales on either side of caudal peduncle   16

16. Both 2d dorsal and anal ray greatly elongated   Carangidae (jacks), in part, page 95

    Both 2d dorsal and anal ray not greatly elongated   17

17. Pelvic fins absent   18
    Pelvic fins present, may be modified   22

18. Unpaired fins all confluent   Anguillidae (freshwater eels), page 87

    Unpaired fins all, or in part, separated   19
19. Body long and slender   20
    Body shorter and deeper   21

20. Snout tubular, anal fin rudimentary or absent   Syngnathidae (pipefishes), in part, page 204

    Snout not tubular, anal fin well developed   Ammodytidae (sand lances), page 86

21. Row of pores dorsally near dorsal fin   Stromateidae (butterfishes), page 204

No row of pores dorsally near dorsal fin   Tetraodontidae (puffers), page 206

22. Unpaired fins all confluent   Ophidiidae (cusk-eels), page 170
Unpaired fins all, or in part, separated   23

23. Dorsal fin preceded by free spines   24
Dorsal fin not preceded by free spines   25

24. Free spines unconnected   Gasterosteidae (sticklebacks), page 155

Only three spines unconnected, the first modified into a "lure" to attract food   Lophiidae (goosefishes), page 165

25. Adipose fin present   26
Adipose fin absent   32

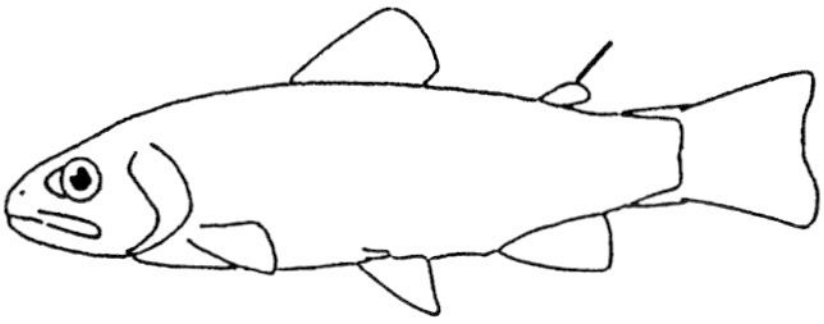

Figure 11. **Location of adipose fin.**

26. Body with 3-5 rows of bony plates on sides   Loricariidae (suckermouth catfishes), page 165
Body scaled, or naked, but not with bony plates on sides   27

27. Three or more pairs of barbels present   28
No paired barbels present   29

28. Nasal barbels present   Ictaluridae (bullhead catfishes), page 159
Nasal barbels absent   Ariidae (sea catfishes), page 88

29. Pelvic axillary processes present   30
Pelvic axillary processes absent   31

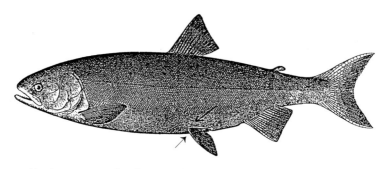

Figure 12. **Location of pelvic axillary process.**

30. Premaxillaries form entire margin of
    upper jaw

    Synodontidae (lizardfishes),
    page 206

    Maxillaries form posterier margins
    of upper jaw

    Salmonidae (trouts), page 183

31. Pectoral fin extends beyond pelvic fin
    base; no or fine teeth on tongue

    Percopsidae (trout-perches),
    page 174

    Pectoral fin does not extend beyond
    pelvic fin base, canine teeth on tongue

    Osmeridae (smelts), page 170

32. One dorsal fin with < 5 spines   33
    One or more dorsal fins, if one,
    > 5 spines   45

33. Head produced into an elongate
    garlike snout   34
    Head not produced into an elongate
    garlike snout   35

34. Small terminal mouth at end of snout   Fistulariidae (cornetfishes),
    page 150
    Mouth makes up much of the snout   Belonidae (needlefishes),
    page 91

35. Three or more pairs of barbels present   Clariidae (labyrinth
    catfishes), page 112

    Two or fewer pairs of barbels present   36
36. Scales present on cheeks or opercles   37
    Scales absent from cheeks or opercles   40

37. Mouth upturned, maxilla not bordering
   upper jaw   38
   Mouth terminal, maxilla forming border
   of upper jaw   39

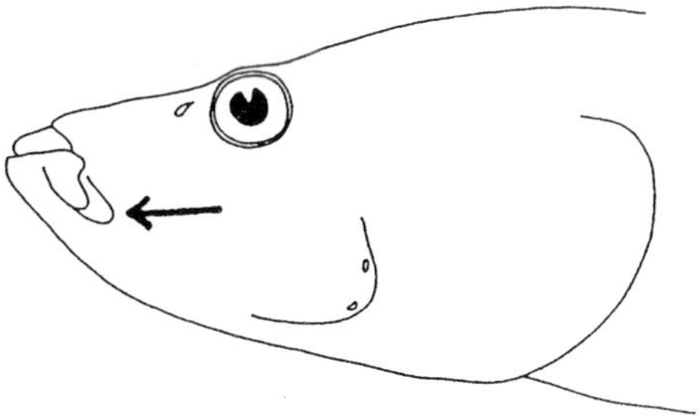

Figure 13. **Mouth upturned, and maxilla does not border upper jaw.**

38. Third anal ray unbranched (this count
   includes the anterior rudimentary rays),
   gonopodium present in males   Poeciliidae (livebearers),
                                            page 180

   Third anal ray branched, males
   lack a gonopodium   Cyprinodontidae (killifishes),
                                            page 140

39. Caudal fin forked, large canine
   teeth present   Esocidae (pikes), page 148
   Caudal fin rounded, no canine teeth   Umbridae (mudminnows),
                                            page 209

40. Gill membranes broadly joined to isthmus 41
   Gill membranes not joined to isthmus,
   or only slightly joined to anterior end   44

41. Dorsal rays usually 8, if 9, lateral
   line present   Cyprinidae (carps and
                                            minnows), in part, page 123

   Dorsal rays usually > 9, if 9,
   lateral line absent   42

42. First major dorsal ray serrated   Cyprinidae (carps and
                                            minnows), in part, page 123

   First major dorsal ray not serrated   43

43. Mouth terminal, < 6 pharyngeal teeth
    in two rows   Cyprinidae (carps and
          minnows), in part, page 123

    Mouth ventral, > 5 pharyngeal teeth
    in one row   Catostomidae (suckers), page 98

44. Maxillary extends well past eye   Engraulidae (anchovies),
          page 147
    Maxillary does not extend past eye   Clupeidae (herrings), page 113

45. Body scaleless   46
    Body with scales   47

46. Dorsal spines > 4   Cottidae (sculpins), page 119
    Dorsal spines < 4   Batrachoididae (toadfishes),
          page 90

47. Chin with one median barbel   48
    Chin without a median barbel   49

48. No spines in anal fin   Gadidae (cods), in part, page 151
    One or two spines in anal fin   Sciaenidae (drums), in part,
          page 194

49. Maxilla covered by preorbital when
    mouth is closed   Sparidae (porgies), page 200
    Maxilla not covered by preorbital
    when mouth is closed   50

50. Two dorsal fins present and space
    between them is > half the first
    dorsal base   51
    One or two dorsal fins, if two,
    space between them is < half
    the first dorsal base   52

51. Anal rays < 13   Mugilidae (mullets), page 168
    Anal rays > 13   Atherinidae (silversides),
          page 89

52. Anal fin rays > 20   53
    Anal fin rays < 20   56

53. More than one dorsal fin 54
  One dorsal fin 55

54. First dorsal fin without spines Gadidae (cods), in part, page 151
  First dorsal fin with spines Pomatomidae (bluefish),
   page 182

55. Dorsal fin with > 60 spines, anal
  fin rays > 35 Pholidae (gunnels), page 178
  Dorsal fin with < 59 spines, anal
  fin rays < 35 Stichaeidae (pricklebacks),
   page 203

56. Anal fin spines > 2 57
  Anal fin spines < 3 62

57. Dorsal spines > 15 Labridae (wrasses), page 163
  Dorsal spines < 16 58

58. Pseudobranchiae small, or absent,
  often concealed by a flap of skin 59
  Pseudobranchiae well developed 61

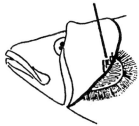

Figure 14. **Well developed
pseudobranchia.**

59. Lateral line pores arranged in a
  single series, 2 pairs of nostrils 60
  Lateral line pores arranged in a
  double series, one pair of nostrils Cichlidae (cichlids), page 111

60. < 9 anal spines Centrarchidae (sunfishes),
   page 102
  > 8 anal spines Anabantidae (gouramies),
   page 87

61. Opercle with 3 spines, dorsal fin
    usually not deeply incised   Serranidae (sea basses),
        page 199

    Opercle with 2 spines, dorsal fin usually
    strongly incised, may be divided into two   Moronidae (temperate basses),
        page 166

62. Length of soft dorsal base < 1.2 times
    in length of spinous dorsal base   Percidae (perches), page 171
    Length of soft dorsal base > 1.2 times
    in length of spinous dorsal base   Sciaenidae (drums), in part,
        page 194

CHAPTER FIVE

Families of fishes found in the freshwaters of Connecticut

Families are listed alphabetically. Within each family, genera are ordered alphabetically and within each genus, species are arranged alphabetically. Often, when annotated lists are presented, families, genera, and sometimes species are listed in phylogenetic order (most primitive to most advanced). Not only does an alphabetical arrangement facilitate finding any specific taxon, but phylogenies do change as more information becomes available or the current knowledge is reevaluated. All species and family names agree with those in Robins *et al.* (1991), except I follow G.O. Johnson (1984) in using Moronidae instead of Percichthyidae.

Information summarized for each family includes the (1) approximate number of genera and species, (2) distribution, and (3) number of species in Connecticut. Special techniques required to identify the species in the family are included if more than one species in the family could be found within the freshwaters of Connecticut. A few of the introduced species are representatives of "tropical" fish often kept in home aquaria. The few species we collected were not included in the keys because you must obtain a key that includes all of the possible species in that family if you obtain a specimen. Alternatively, you could preserve your specimens and send them to an ichthyologist.

Information summarized for most species includes its (1) scientific and common names and date of the original description (Robins *et al.* 1991), (2) status in freshwaters, *e.g.*, native, anadromous, catadromous, introduced, or marine visitor, (3) general distribution and distribution in Connecticut, (4) first report of anadromous, catadromous, and native species, and status of introduced and marine species and (5) selected life history characteristics. Those who are interested in more life history or taxonomic information should consult one of the many general and regional works available. For example, comprehensive general works are those of Berra (1981), Greenwood *et al.* (1966), Lee *et al.* (1980), and Nelson (1984). Regional publications appropriate to Connecticut include those of Massachusetts (Halliwell 1979, Mugford 1969), Maine (Everhart 1966), New Hampshire (Scarola 1973), New York (C.L. Smith 1985), Pennsylvania (Cooper 1983), Canada (Scott and Crossman 1973, Scott and Scott 1988), and Wisconsin

(Becker 1983). Previous studies of the fishes of Connecticut (*e.g.* Linsley 1844b, Webster 1942) would add further information on distribution and life history of fishes in the state.

Family Acipenseridae, sturgeons

Four genera with about 24 species (anadromous and freshwater) are distributed in the waters of the northern hemisphere. Two anadromous species live part or all of their lives in the freshwaters of the three major rivers of Connecticut, although only the Connecticut River has documented spawning populations at this time. Remains of these species found in Indian middens along the entire Connecticut coast (Coffin 1947, Waters 1965 and 1967) reveal that this family was an important source of food and utensils to native peoples. Additionally, many stories were circulated and often appeared in magazines and newspapers in the eighteenth and nineteenth centuries about these fish because of their size and appearance. For example, J. Smith (1833) retold a fish tale reported in the Middletown Gazette, July 1831, in which a 186 pound sturgeon leaped into a rowboat near Rocky Hill, on the Connecticut River, and broke the oars.

Spawning occurs in spring in freshwaters of higher velocities that are usually near the first major change in elevation. In the Housatonic River it was probably near New Milford, in the Thames it was probably below what is now the Taftville and Tunnel Dams, and in the Connecticut it was probably in the Windsor Locks area. Eggs are broadcast and adhere to the substrate; no parental care is afforded either them or the young. The unfertilized eggs of sturgeons are used to prepare the famous "caviar." Both species are associated with the bottom and feed on a variety of invertebrates and fishes.

Key to the species of Acipenseridae

1. Mouth width < 55% of interorbital width, > 23 anal rays   *Acipenser oxyrhynchus*, page 85
   Mouth width > 60% of interorbital width, < 23 anal rays   *A. brevirostrum*, this page

Acipenser brevirostrum Lesueur, 1818, shortnose sturgeon

Figure 15. *Acipenser brevirostrum*, from Goode *et al.* (1884), plate 243.

This is the only species of fish on both the federal (Williams *et al.* 1989) and state (Anonymous 1992) lists of endangered species. Populations of this anadromous species are found along the Atlantic coast from New Brunswick to Florida. First reported in Connecticut by Linsley (1844b) who obtained specimens caught by fishermen at the mouths of both the Connecticut and Housatonic Rivers. Only the Connecticut River has known spawning populations of this species and there is a strong possibility that these populations represent only estuarine and freshwater gene pools and have no anadromous components (Tom Savoy, DEP). Sexual maturity is reached in 7-9 years and lengths in excess of 100 cm are often attained.

Acipenser oxyrhynchus Mitchill, 1814, Atlantic sturgeon

Figure 16. *Acipenser oxyrhynchus*, from DeKay (1842), figure 189.

Although this species is listed as threatened in Connecticut, its population numbers are lower than those of the shortnose sturgeon (Tom Savoy, DEP). This anadromous species is distributed along the east coast of North America from Labrador to Mississippi. First reported in Connecticut by Linsley (1844b) who obtained specimens caught by fishermen at the mouths of both the Connecticut and Housatonic Rivers. Specimens occasionally stray into the Thames and Housatonic Rivers. Recent work in the Connecticut River (Tom Savoy, DEP) suggests that only strays are left of this once viable population. Sexual maturity is reached in 10-12 years and lengths in excess of 200 cm are often reached.

Family Amiidae, bowfins

This primitive family contains only one species that is found in freshwaters, occasionally in brackish waters, of much of the eastern two thirds of North America. Bowfins are found mainly in lakes and slow-moving streams. Males build a nest (a depression in the substrate) in spring–summer. More than one female may lay her adhesive eggs in a nest and females may spawn in more than one nest. Their colors intensify during the spawning season and males develop an orange-edged dark spot at the upper base of the caudal fin. After the eggs hatch the young attach themselves to the nest with an adhesive organ on their snouts. When they leave the nest they travel in dense schools and are guarded by the male until they are 6 to 8 cm long. They feed on a variety of fish and invertebrates.

Amia calva Linnaeus, 1766, bowfin

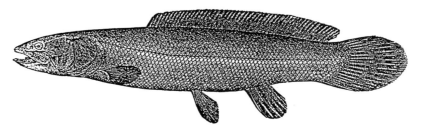

Figure 17. *Amia calva*, from Smith (1890b), plate XXII.

This introduced species was first reported in Connecticut by Webster (1942). Little is known about where or why it was introduced; apparently the specimen was brought to Yale University in the late 1930s. Specimens were later introduced into some lakes as a sporting fish. All of those populations were illegally stocked and most were subsequently eliminated. The only known self-sustaining population is in Scovill Reservoir (Timothy Barry and Robert Orciari, DEP). Sexual maturity is reached in 2-3 years and lengths in excess of 50 cm are often attained.

Family Ammodytidae, sand lances

Three genera containing about 12 species (marine) are distributed in the Atlantic, Indian, and Pacific Oceans. One species has been collected in the freshwaters of Connecticut.

Ammodytes americanus DeKay, 1842, American sand lance

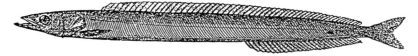

Figure 18. *Ammodytes americanus*, from Bigelow and Welsh (1924), figure 89.

This marine species is found along the Atlantic coast from Labrador to North Carolina. Individuals of any age occasionally enter freshwaters near saltwaters of all watercourses of Connecticut that drain into Long Island Sound (Whitworth *et al.* 1975). Adults reach lengths of about 15-18 cm and feed on a variety of invertebrates.

Family Anabantidae, gouramies

About 14 genera containing 68 species are found in the freshwaters of Africa and southern Asia. Many species have been sold to aquarists, and one species was collected in the freshwaters of Connecticut.

Betta splendens Regan, 1909, Siamese fightingfish

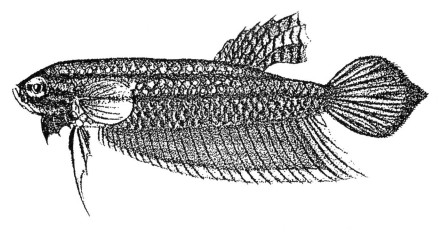

Figure 19. *Betta splendens*, from Cantor (1849), plate II, figure 4. This figure was referenced in the original description by Regan (1909).

This introduced species is found in the freshwaters of Thailand. Many gene pools have been developed by aquarists worldwide and in North America. The specimens that we collected (lengths of 1-3 cm) in a drainage basin of the Thames River would not be able to survive the winter months in the freshwaters of the state and, therefore, would not be able to establish viable populations.

Family Anguillidae, freshwater eels

One genus containing about 16 species (catadromous) is found in the warm and temperate zones of the world. One species lives part of its life in the freshwaters of Connecticut.

Anguilla rostrata (Lesueur, 1817), American eel

Figure 20. *Anguilla rostrata*, from Whitworth *et al.* (1968), page 32.

Populations of our only catadromous fish species are distributed along the eastern and southern coasts of North America and found in the freshwaters of most states in all drainage basins from that of the Mississippi, eastward to the Atlantic Ocean. First reported in Connecticut by Linsley (1844b). Populations are found in most drainage basins of the state, often in large numbers. Because population densities are much lower in the headwaters of watercourses that have many, or high, dams and falls, movement upstream is probably affected by both the number and the height of the obstructions (Levesque & Whitworth 1987).

Adults spawn in the South Atlantic (Sargasso Sea) in spring and die. After hatching the larval fish, called leptocephali, are carried by the ocean currents for 1-2 years. When the leptocephali reach lengths of 4-8 cm they transform into miniature looking adults, called elvers. At this time they are transparent and migrate into freshwater, often called glass eels. Females then migrate inland, whereas most males are thought to remain either in the estuary or in freshwaters near the estuary. Females feed on a wide variety of animal foods, often at night, until they reach sexual maturity, 7-9 years. They then migrate to the ocean and complete the cycle. Males apparently mature sexually in 4-6 years, and then return to the Sargasso Sea. Sexually mature females often reach lengths in excess of 60 cm, males usually less.

Family Ariidae, sea catfishes

Twenty genera containing about 120 species (mostly marine, a few freshwater) are distributed worldwide, mainly in warmer waters. One marine species could enter the freshwaters of Connecticut.

Arius felis (Linnaeus, 1766), hardhead catfish

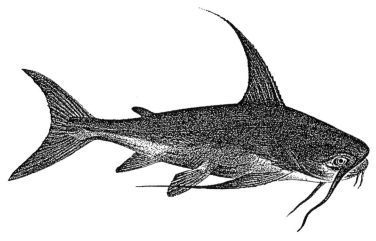

Figure 21. *Arius felis*, from DeKay (1842), figure 118.

This marine species is found along the eastern and southern coasts of North America from Cape Cod to southern Mexico. Although it is not reported in the freshwaters of Connecticut, both Linsley (1844b) and Berra (1981) included it because, in other areas of their range, specimens did enter freshwaters. Thomson *et al.* (1978) did not include this species in the saltwater fauna of Connecticut. Specimens of 20-35 cm would probably be found in freshwaters near saltwaters feeding on invertebrates and fishes during the evening hours.

Family Atherinidae, silversides

Twenty-nine genera with about 160 species (mostly marine, some freshwater) are distributed throughout the warm and temperate areas of the world, mainly in the northern hemisphere. Two marine species are often collected and may live part of their lives in the freshwaters of Connecticut. Both species spawn from spring to early summer and feed on a variety of invertebrates. The relative numbers of these two species vary greatly through space and time in freshwaters. Furthermore, a segment of the populations of both spawn in freshwaters.

Key to the species of Atherinidae

1. Anal fin with > 22 rays, lateral line
   scales modified with tubes   *Menidia menidia*, page 90
   Anal fin with < 22 rays, lateral line
   scales modified with pits   *M. beryllina*, this page

Menidia beryllina (Cope, 1866), inland silverside

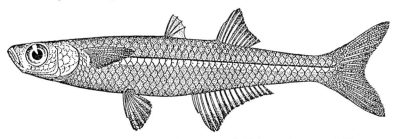

Figure 22. *Menidia beryllina*, from Kendall (1901), page 260.

This marine species is distributed along the eastern and southern coasts of North America from Massachusetts to Veracruz. Populations containing many age classes and often spawning adults are commonly found in freshwaters close to saltwaters from early spring to late fall in all watercourses in Connecticut that empty into Long Island Sound (Whitworth *et al.* 1968). Sexual maturity is often reached in one year and lengths of 6-8 cm attained.

Menidia menidia (Linnaeus, 1766), Atlantic silverside

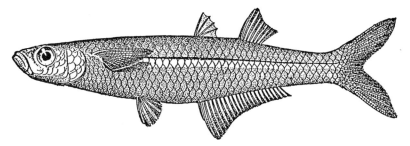

Figure 23. *Menidia menidia*, from Kendall (1901), page 263.

This marine species is distributed along the Atlantic coast from New Brunswick to Florida. Populations containing many age classes and often spawning adults are regularly found in freshwaters close to saltwaters from early spring to early fall in all watercourses in Connecticut that drain into Long Island Sound (Marcy 1976a, Whitworth and Marsh 1980). Sexual maturity is reached in 1-2 years and lengths of 9-11 cm are attained.

Family Batrachoididae, toadfishes

Nineteen genera with about 64 species are found in the Atlantic, Indian, and Pacific oceans. One species has been collected in the freshwaters of Connecticut.

Opsanus tau (Linnaeus, 1766), oyster toadfish

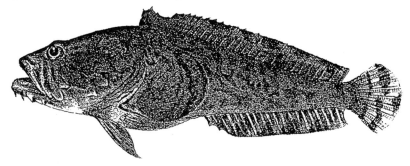

Figure 24. *Opsanus tau*, from DeKay (1842), figure 86.

This marine species is distributed along the east coast of North America from Maine to the West Indies. Adults occasionally enter freshwaters near saltwaters in rivers in Connecticut that drain into Long Island Sound (Penny Howell-Heller, DEP). Adults often attain lengths of 25-35 cm, and feed on invertebrates and small fish.

Family Belonidae, needlefishes

Ten genera with about 32 species (mostly marine, some freshwater) are distributed throughout the temperate and tropical areas of the world; one marine species has been collected in the freshwaters of Connecticut.

Strongylura marina (Walbaum, 1792), Atlantic needlefish

Figure 25. *Strongylura marina*, from Whitworth *et al.* (1968), page 82.

This marine species is distributed along the Atlantic coasts of North and South America from Maine to Brazil. Adults occasionally enter freshwaters near saltwaters in rivers of Connecticut that empty into Long Island Sound (Whitworth *et al.* 1968). Although adults may attain lengths in excess of 40 cm, specimens collected in freshwaters have been only 10-25 cm, and were feeding on invertebrates.

Family Bothidae, lefteye flounders

Thirty-seven genera with about 212 species (marine) are distributed in the Atlantic, Indian, and Pacific Oceans. Five species have been collected in the freshwaters of Connecticut.

Key to the species of Bothidae

1. Left and right pelvics about the same
   size, left not continuous with anal fin   2
   Left pelvic fin larger and
   continuous with anal fin   4

2. Lateral line straight anteriorly   *Citharichthys arctifrons*, page 92
   Lateral line arched anteriorly   3

3. Dorsal fin with > 81 rays   *Paralichthys dentatus*, page 93
   Dorsal fin with < 82 rays   *P. oblongus*, page 94

4. Lateral line arched anteriorly near
   pectoral fin, greatest body depth
   > 0.5 standard length   *Scophthalmus aquosus*, page 95
   Lateral line not arched anteriorly near
   pectoral fin, greatest body
   depth < 0.5 standard length   *Etropus microstomus*, page 93

Citharichthys arctifrons Goode, 1880, Gulf Stream flounder

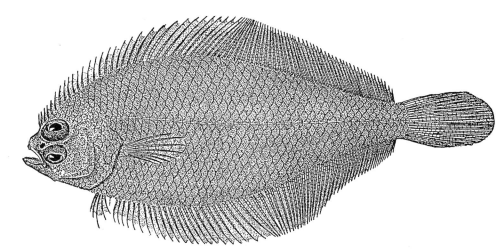

Figure 26. *Citharichthys arctifrons*, from Goode and Bean (1895), figure 366.

This marine species is distributed along the outer edge of the continental shelf from Newfoundland to Florida. Individuals occasionally enter freshwaters near saltwaters in rivers in Connecticut that empty into Long Island Sound (Douglas Tolderlund, U.S. Coast Guard Academy). They feed on invertebrates and attain lengths of about 15 cm.

Etropus microstomus (Gill, 1864), smallmouth flounder

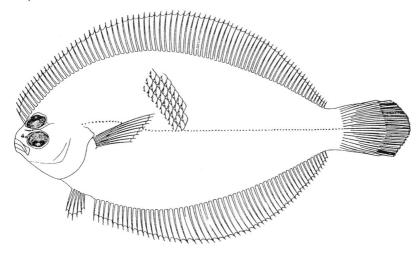

Figure 27. *Etropus microstomus*, from Gutherz (1963), figure 30.

This marine species is distributed along the Atlantic coast from southern New England to Florida. Individuals occasionally enter freshwaters near salt-waters in rivers in Connecticut that empty into Long Island Sound (P. Howell-Heller, DEP). This species feeds on invertebrates and attains lengths of 6-8 cm.

Paralichthys dentatus (Linnaeus, 1766), summer flounder

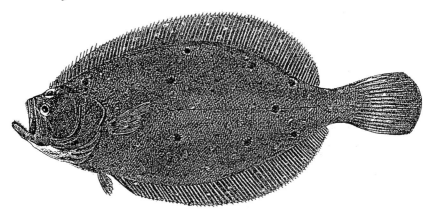

Figure 28. *Paralichthys dentatus*, from DeKay (1842), figure 152.

This marine species is distributed along the Atlantic coast from Maine to South Carolina. Adults often, and young (2-5 cm) typically, during spring and summer, enter freshwaters near saltwaters of rivers of Connecticut that empty into Long Island Sound (Whitworth and Schmidt 1971). They feed on invertebrates and fish and attain lengths of 35-45 cm.

Paralichthys oblongus (Mitchill, 1815), fourspot flounder

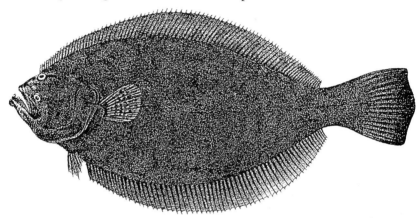

Figure 29. *Paralichthys oblongus*, from DeKay (1842), figure 156.

This marine species is distributed along the Atlantic coast from Newfoundland to South Carolina. Adults occasionally, during summer and fall, enter freshwaters near saltwaters of rivers of Connecticut that empty into Long Island Sound (Whitworth and Marsh 1980). They feed on invertebrates and fish and attain lengths of 30-35 cm.

Scophthalmus aquosus (Mitchill, 1815), windowpane flounder

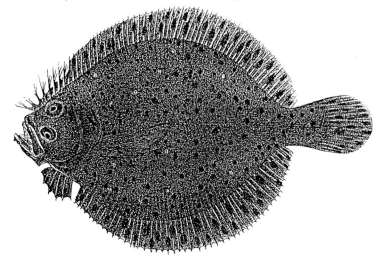

Figure 30. *Scophthalmus aquosus*, from DeKay (1842), figure 151.

This marine species is found along the Atlantic coast from Nova Scotia to South Carolina. Adults occasionally, during winter and spring, enter freshwaters near saltwaters of rivers of Connecticut that empty into Long Island Sound (Whitworth and Schmidt 1971). Adults commonly reach lengths of 30-40 cm, and feed on a variety of fishes and invertebrates.

Family Carangidae, jacks

Twenty-five genera with about 140 species (marine) are distributed throughout the Atlantic, Indian, and Pacific Oceans; two species have been collected in the freshwaters of Connecticut.

Key to the species of Carangidae

1. Row of keeled scales on either side
   of caudal peduncle   *Caranx hippos*, page 96
   No rows of keeled scales on caudal
   peduncle   *Selene vomer*, page 97

Caranx hippos (Linnaeus, 1766), crevalle jack

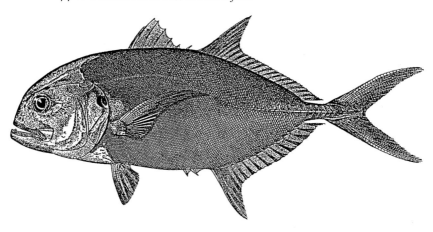

Figure 31. *Caranx hippos*, from H.W. Smith (1891), Plate LII.

This marine species is distributed along the east coasts of North and South America from Nova Scotia to Uruguay. Young (2-5 cm) regularly, and adults occasionally, during summer and fall, enter freshwaters near saltwaters of rivers of Connecticut that empty into Long Island Sound (Whitworth and Schmidt 1971). They feed on a variety of invertebrates and fishes and attain lengths of 25-40 cm.

Selene vomer (Linnaeus, 1758), lookdown

Figure 32. *Selene vomer*, from DeKay (1842), figure 238.

This marine species is distributed along the east coasts of North and South America from Maine to Uruguay. Adults occasionally enter freshwaters near saltwaters in rivers of Connecticut that drain into Long Island Sound (Whitworth, Minta, and Orciari 1980). They feed on invertebrates and fishes and attain lengths of 15-25 cm.

Family Carcharhinidae, requiem sharks

Twenty-four genera with about 91 species are found in all oceans of the world. One species has been collected in the freshwaters of Connecticut.

Mustelus canis (Mitchill, 1815), smooth dogfish

Figure 33. *Mustelus canis*, from DeKay (1842), figure 209.

This marine species is found along the Atlantic coast from Maine to South Carolina. Individuals occasionally enter freshwaters near saltwaters of rivers of Connecticut that drain into Long Island Sound (P. Howell-Heller, DEP). They feed on larger invertebrates and fishes and attain lengths of 90-150 cm.

Family Catostomidae, suckers

Twelve genera with about 65 species (freshwater) are distributed in North America (mainly), China, and northeastern Siberia. Three species have been collected in the freshwaters of Connecticut. These species are bottom-dwelling and feed on a variety of plant and animal foods. Plant materials probably do not furnish much energy to the fish. Spawning usually occurs in shallow riffles in early spring after an upstream movement. There is no nest preparation or care of eggs or young. Adults often migrate downstream to deeper waters after spawning. Young usually remain in the shallow headwater streams, or migrate to the shallows downstream.

Key to the species of Catostomidae
1. Lower lips plicate, modified lateral
   line scales not present   *Erimyzon oblongus*, page 101
   Lower lips papillose, modified lateral
   line scales   2

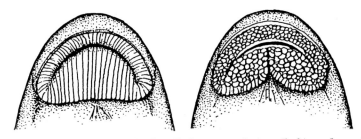

Figure 34. Ventral view of a head showing plicate (left) and papillose (right) lips.

2. Lateral line scales > 85, snout extends
   well beyond mouth, which extends
   beyond nostrils   *Catostomus catostomus*, this page
   Lateral line scales < 86, snout extends
   only slightly beyond mouth, which does
   not or only barely reaches nostrils   *C. commersoni*, page 100

Catostomus catostomus (Forster, 1773), longnose sucker

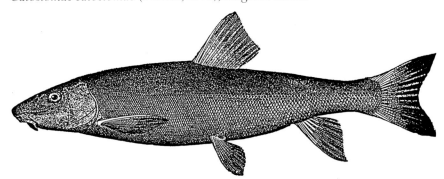

Figure 35. *Catostomus catostomus*, from Smith and Kendall (1921), figure 11.

This introduced species is widely distributed throughout the freshwaters of the northern two thirds of North America. First reported in Connecticut by Hagstrom (DEP) from a tributary of the upper Housatonic River above the fall line in 1992. Sexual maturity is reached in 2-4 years and lengths in excess of 40 cm are often attained.

Catostomus commersoni (Lacepede, 1803), white sucker

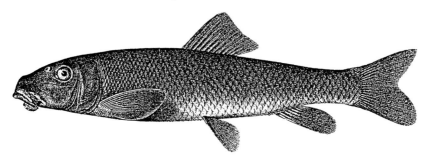

Figure 36. *Catostomus commersoni*, from Storer (1855), figure 3, plate 22.

This native species is distributed in most of the freshwaters of North America east of the Rocky Mountains. First reported in Connecticut by DeKay (1842). Populations, often abundant, are found in all drainage basins of the state. Large adults are usually confined to larger waterbodies except during the spring (spawning season). Sexual maturity is reached in 2-3 years and lengths in excess of 40 cm are attained. Males develop nuptial tubercles on the lower parts of all fins and on the body scales. Additionally, a dusky red band along the sides of spawning males turns brilliant scarlet during the spawning act.

Erimyzon oblongus (Mitchill, 1814), creek chubsucker

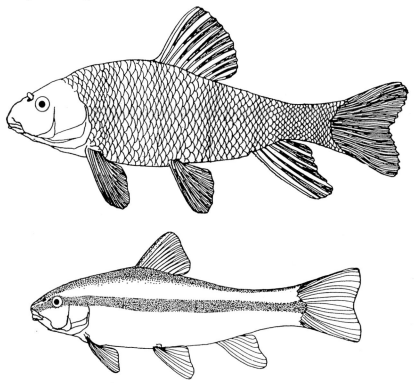

Figure 37. Erimyzon oblongus, from Whitworth *et al.* (1968), page 73. Adult (upper), juvenile (lower).

This native species is distributed in freshwaters throughout North America from the Mississippi River System eastward. First reported in Connecticut by DeKay (1842). Although populations are found in all drainage basins of Connecticut, they are usually small and often widely separated; Linsley (1844b) reported a similar pattern of distribution in the 1800s. Adults are usually found in larger rivers and lakes. They reach sexual maturity in 2-3 years and lengths of 30-40 cm. Males develop nuptial tubercles on the head. Juvenile specimens have a dark lateral band and the mouth is less ventral than in adults.

Family Centrarchidae, sunfishes

Nine genera with about 30 species are distributed in the freshwaters of North America. Ten species live in the freshwaters of Connecticut. Sexual dimorphism is present in most species and males often have intensified colors, especially during the spawning season.

During spring and summer, depending on the species and water temperature, males select a territory over a particular type of substrate in a range of water depths. They then build a nest by clearing a circular depression in the substrate, and will spawn with as many females as they can lure to their nests. Males care for the eggs, sometimes the young. Most centrarchids feed on invertebrates and fishes, depending on the size of their mouths.

Key to the species of Centrarchidae

1. Anal spines usually > 3   2
   Anal spines usually 3   4

2. Dorsal fin with > 9 spines   *Ambloplites rupestris*, page 104
   Dorsal fin with < 9 spines   3

3. Dorsal base < distance from dorsal origin to posterior orbital rim, 6 dorsal spines   *Pomoxis annularis*, page 109
   Dorsal base equal to or > distance from dorsal origin to posterior orbital rim, 7-8 dorsal spines   *P. nigromaculatus*, page 110

4. Caudal fin emarginate   5
   Caudal fin convex   *Enneacanthus obesus*, page 104

5. Lateral line scales > 54   6
   Lateral line scales < 54   7

6. Dorsal fin deeply emarginate, next to last spine < 0.5 of the longest, maxilla usually extends beyond eye   *Micropterus salmoides*, page 108
   Dorsal fin shallowly emarginate, next to last spine > 0.5 of the longest, maxilla usually does not extend beyond eye   *M. dolomieu*, page 108

7. Gill rakers short, when depressed do
   not reach base of 2d raker below, no
   dark spot in posterior membranes
   of soft dorsal fin   8
   Gill rakers long, when depressed reach
   base of 2d or 3rd raker below, dark spot
   in posterior membranes of soft dorsal fin   9

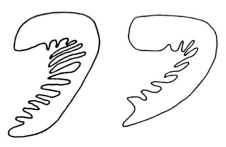

Figure 38. **Gill rakers long (left) and short (right).**

8. Opercle short, a small red semicircular
   spot near margin, not fimbriate,
   pectoral fins < 3.4 in standard length   *Lepomis gibbosus*, page 106
   Opercle long, black to its margin, deeply
   fimbriate, pectoral fins 3.4 in standard
   length   *L. auritus*, page 105

9. Pectoral fins short and rounded and
   < head length   *L. cyanellus*, page 106
   Pectoral fins long and pointed and
   about equal to the head length   *L. macrochirus*, page 107

Figure 39. **Pectoral fins long and pointed (left) and short and rounded (right).**

Ambloplites rupestris (Rafinesque, 1817), rock bass

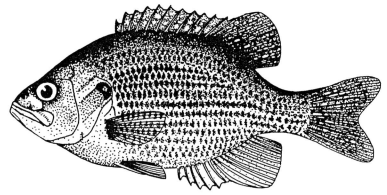

Figure 40. *Ambloplites rupestris*, from Whitworth *et al.* (1968), page 103.

This introduced species is widely distributed in the freshwaters of North America. Although not reported in Connecticut until the early 1900s, populations were probably first introduced into lakes and ponds of western Connecticut during the 1850s. Populations are commonly found in lakes and larger streams of the Connecticut and Housatonic River drainage basins, and we (1991) and Hagstrom (DEP, 1993) found established populations in a few areas of the Thames River drainage basin. Populations will probably soon be found in all suitable habitats in this basin. Sexual maturity is reached in 1-3 years and lengths of 25-35 cm are attained.

Enneacanthus obesus (Girard, 1854), banded sunfish

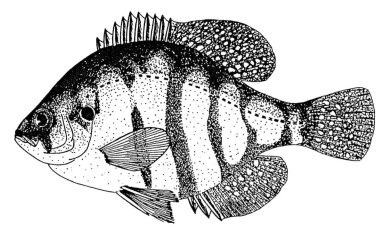

Figure 41. *Enneacanthus obesus*, from Whitworth *et al.* (1968), page 104.

This native species is distributed in coastal freshwaters from New Hampshire to Georgia. The range was first extended to include Connecticut by Jordan (1877). Populations are found only in the lower Connecticut River drainage basin, small coastal drainage basins between the Connecticut River and Thames River, and in eastern tributaries of the Quinebaug River, Thames River drainage basin. Most populations are associated with weedy lowland lakes and streams. Although most populations are small, Cohen (1977) found that the banded sunfish was the most abundant species in Green Falls Reservoir for a few years. Sexual maturity is reached in 1-2 years and lengths of 4-8 cm are attained.

Lepomis auritus (Linnaeus, 1758), redbreast sunfish

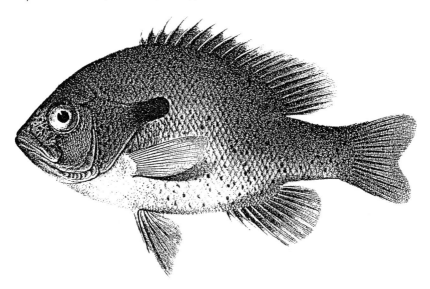

Figure 42. *Lepomis auritus*, from Storer (1853), figure 4, plate 3.

This native species is widely distributed in the freshwaters of eastern North America. First reported in Connecticut by Linsley (1844b). Populations are typically associated with streams and are present in all drainage basins of the state. Sexual maturity is reached in 1-3 years and lengths of 20-30 cm are attained.

Lepomis cyanellus Rafinesque, 1819, green sunfish

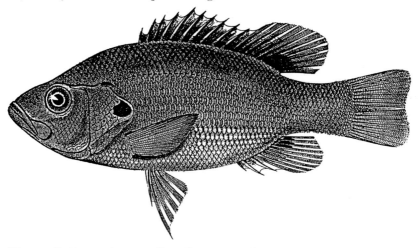

Figure 43. *Lepomis cyanellus*, from Girard (1858), plate IV, figure 1.

This introduced species is widely distributed in the freshwaters of North America. First reported in Connecticut by Webster (1942). Populations are established in most drainage basins of the state; however, they are usually much smaller than those of the other centrarchids present. Sexual maturity is reached in 1-3 years and lengths of 20-30 cm are attained.

Lepomis gibbosus (Linnaeus, 1758), pumpkinseed

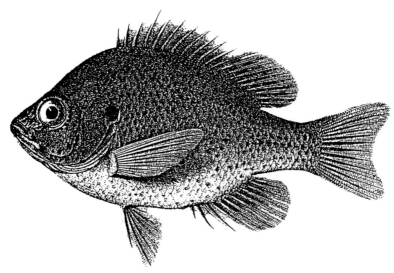

Figure 44. *Lepomis gibbosus*, from Storer (1853), figure 1, plate 3.

This native species is widely distributed in the freshwaters of eastern North America. First reported in Connecticut by Linsley (1844b). Large populations are commonly found in the larger streams and ponds in all drainage basins. However, they may be collected in any watercourse. Since the bluegill was introduced, this species is now the second most abundant sunfish in Connecticut. Sexual maturity is reached in 1-3 years and lengths of 25-35 cm are attained.

Lepomis macrochirus Rafinesque, 1819, bluegill

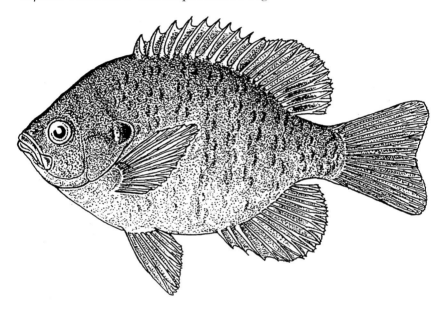

Figure 45. *Lepomis macrochirus*, from Whitworth *et al.* (1968), page 108.

This introduced species is widely distributed in the freshwaters of North America. Although first reported in Connecticut by Webster (1942), populations were probably introduced much earlier. Populations, often abundant, are present in all drainage basins of the state. This species, and another introduced sunfish, the largemouth bass, are probably the most commonly found and abundant centrarchids in all drainage basins of Connecticut. Sexual maturity is reached in 1-3 years and lengths of 25-35 cm are often attained.

Micropterus dolomieu Lacepede, 1802, smallmouth bass

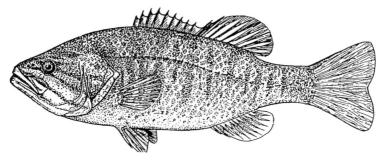

Figure 46. *Micropterus dolomieu*, from Whitworth *et al.* (1968), page 109.

This introduced species is widely distributed in the freshwaters of North America. Populations were first introduced in the 1850s, and reported by Anonymous (1871 and 1878). The stock probably came from Saratoga Lake, New York, via Massachusetts. Although Webster (1942) reported an earlier reference to this species (Linsley 1844b), the species in that report was undoubtedly *Centropristis striata* (Linnaeus), black sea bass. Smallmouth bass are found in lakes and streams in most drainage basins of Connecticut. Although populations are usually larger in lakes, many populations are established in streams. When largemouth bass populations are also present, they are usually more numerous than smallmouth bass. Populations of smallmouth bass in streams seemed much larger than usual in 1991, suggesting that conditions were better for their survival in the previous two years. Sexual maturity is reached in 2-6 years and lengths in excess of 50 cm are attained.

Micropterus salmoides (Lacepede, 1802), largemouth bass

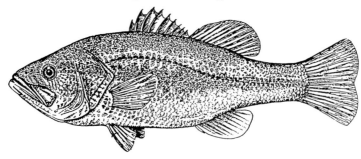

Figure 47. *Micropterus salmoides*, from Whitworth *et al.* (1968), page 110.

This introduced species is widely distributed in the freshwaters of North

America. Populations of this species were probably introduced at about the same time as smallmouth bass (Anonymous 1871a, 1871b, 1878). The stock probably came from Oswego Lake, New York, via Massachusetts. This species is probably one of the most commonly found and abundant fishes in the lakes, ponds and larger streams of all drainage basins of the state. Although specimens are often collected in small streams, they probably came from ponds and will have to migrate to larger watercourses to survive and reproduce. Sexual maturity is reached in 1-6 years and lengths of 50-60 cm are attained.

Pomoxis annularis Rafinesque, 1818, white crappie

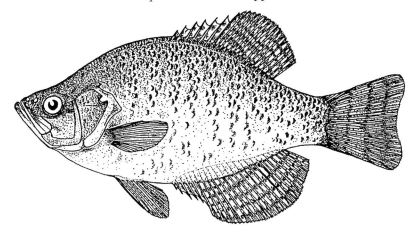

Figure 48. *Pomoxis annularis*, from Whitworth *et al.* (1968), page 111.

This introduced species is widely distributed in the freshwaters of eastern North America. First reported in Connecticut by Behnke and Wetzel (1960). William Kinney (personal communication) reported that this species was found in the Connecticut River in Massachusetts in the middle 1970s. However, the first verified specimens obtained from the Connecticut River were in 1988 (Robert Jacobs, DEP). All known populations are associated with larger watercourses in that drainage basin. Sexual maturity is reached in 2-3 years and lengths of 30-40 cm are attained.

Pomoxis nigromaculatus (Lesueur, 1829), black crappie

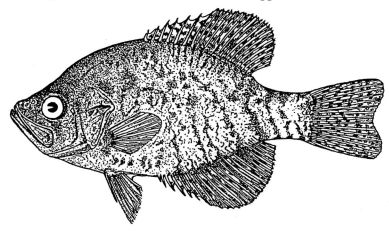

Figure 49. *Pomoxis nigromaculatus*, from Whitworth *et al.* (1968), page 112.

This introduced species is widely distributed in the freshwaters of North America. Although first reported in Connecticut by Webster (1942), populations were probably introduced much earlier. Many lakes and ponds in all drainage basins have established populations. Most of these populations are characterized by extremely large fluctuations in numbers from year to year. This is probably caused by the almost complete failure of some year classes to survive beyond the egg, sac-fry, or first month of life. Sexual maturity is reached in 2-3 years and lengths of 30-40 cm are attained.

Family Characidae, characins

At least 166 genera with a minimum of 841 species are found in the freshwaters of southern North America, Central and South America, and Africa. Although only two species have been caught in the freshwaters of Connecticut, many other have surely been introduced. Most of them have probably been obtained from the freshwaters of Central and South America. The specimens we captured (5-8 cm) in a drainage basin of the Thames River should not be able to establish viable populations in the freshwaters of this state. Illustrations of two species, representative of the genera we captured, follow.

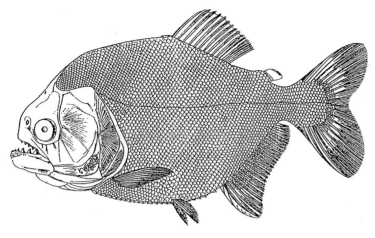

Figure 50. Pygocentrus nattereri (Kner, 1860), red piranha, from Kner (1860), plate 3, figure 8.

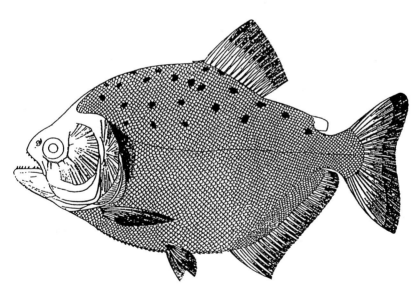

Figure 51. Serrasalmus maculatus Kner, 1860, redeye piranha, from Kner (1860), plate 4, figure 10.

Family Cichlidae, cichlids

About 84 genera containing at least 680 species are found in the warm waters of southern North America, Central America, South America, Africa and coastal India. Although only one species has been documented as being caught in the freshwaters of Connecticut, undoubtedly many have been introduced.

Cichlasoma octofasciatum (Regan, 1903), Jack Dempsey

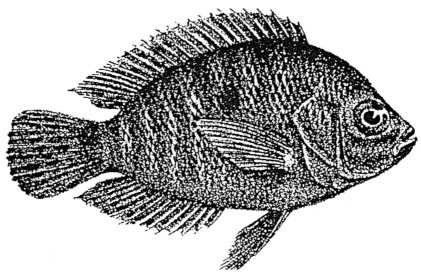

Figure 52. *Cichlasoma octofasciatum*, from Regan (1903), plate 13, figure 1.

This introduced species is found in the freshwaters of the Americas from Mexico to Honduras. The individuals (6-15 cm) that we and Timothy Barry (DEP) obtained (all major drainage basins) should not be able to establish viable populations in the freshwaters of this state.

Family Clariidae, labyrinth catfishes

Thirteen genera with about 100 species are distributed in the freshwaters of Africa and southwestern Asia. One species was widely introduced into the freshwaters of North America and has been collected in the freshwaters of Connecticut.

Clarias batrachus (Linnaeus, 1758), walking catfish

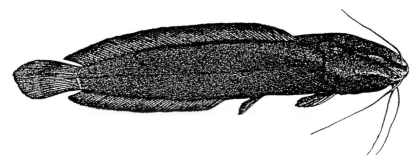

Figure 53. *Clarias batrachus*, from Day (1878), plate CXII, figure 5.

This introduced species is found in the freshwaters of southern Asia and Malaysia. Specimens (5-30 cm) have been occasionally captured in widely separated waterbodies in Connecticut (William Hyatt, DEP). Those individuals were probably recently introduced and, because of their temperature requirements, should not be able to successfully establish viable populations.

Family Clupeidae, herrings

Fifty genera with about 190 species (mostly marine, some freshwater and some anadromous) are distributed worldwide. Seven species, marine, anadromous, and freshwater, have been collected in the freshwaters of Connecticut. Most species are usually found in large schools. Young specimens are often difficult to identify.

Key to the species of Clupeidae

1. Posterior dorsal fin ray greatly
   elongated, jaws not equal (the
   lower included in the upper)   *Dorosoma cepedianum*, page 119
   Posterior dorsal fin ray not greatly
   elongated, jaws equal, or
   the upper included in the lower   2

2. Head length equal to or > 1/3
   standard length   *Brevoortia tyrannus*, page 117
   Head length < 1/3 of standard length   3

3. Dorsal origin about equidistant
   between snout and hypural plate   *Clupea harengus*, page 118
   Dorsal origin nearer snout than
   hypural plate   4

4. Lower jaw outline less abrupt, tongue
   extends well beyond premaxilla when
   mouth is held open, cheek patch
   deeper than wide   5
   Lower jaw outline rises fast, tongue
   does not extend beyond premaxilla
   when mouth is held open,
   cheek patch wider than deep   6

 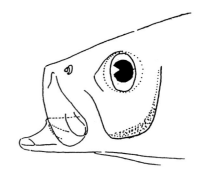

Figure 54. **Lower jaw outline rises abruptly (left) and not so abruptly (right).**

5. Gill rakers on lower limb of first
   gill arch < 25   *Alosa mediocris*, page 115
   Gill rakers on lower limb of first
   gill arch > 24   *A. sapidissima*, page 117

6. Peritoneum black, eye width
   usually < snout length   *A. aestivalis*, page 115
   Peritoneum silvery to dusky, eye width
   usually equal to or > snout length   *A. pseudoharengus*, page 116

Alosa aestivalis (Mitchill, 1814), blueback herring

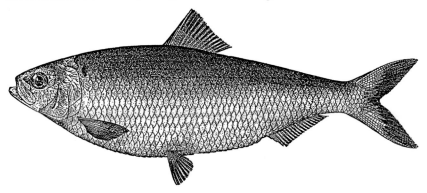

Figure 55. *Alosa aestivalis*, from H.W. Smith (1891), plate XLVIII.

This anadromous species is distributed along the Atlantic coast from Nova Scotia to Florida. First reported in Connecticut by Linsley (1844b). Populations are found in most of the larger streams and some of the smaller streams that have access to Long Island Sound. Since all drainage basins except those in the Connecticut River drainage basin have impassable barriers that deny access to most of the streams that could be utilized, the largest populations of this species are associated with the Connecticut River drainage basin. Sexual maturity is reached in 2-3 years and adults enter freshwaters and spawn in spring to early summer. Eggs are broadcast and no care is given them or the young. Adults leave after spawning. Young-of-the-year remain in freshwaters feeding on invertebrates to middle-fall, and then migrate to saltwaters. Sub-adults (10-15 cm) may be collected at any time in freshwaters near saltwaters. Adults often reach lengths of 20-30 cm, and feed on a variety of planktonic organisms in the ocean.

Alosa mediocris (Mitchill, 1814), hickory shad

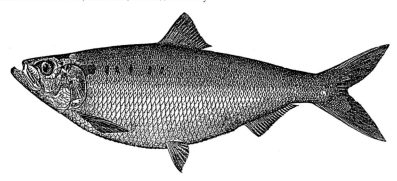

Figure 56. *Alosa mediocris*, from H.W. Smith (1891), plate XLVIII.

This marine species is distributed along the Atlantic coast from New Brunswick to Florida; they are anadromous in the central portion of their range. Seasonally (fall) adults and sub-adults enter freshwaters near saltwaters of the three major rivers of Connecticut (Marcy 1976a, Whitworth *et al.* 1975). Linsley (1844b) reported that subadults were often captured in the Housatonic River in the 1800s. Sexual maturity is reached in 2-4 years and lengths of 30-50 cm are attained. Adults feed on fish and larger invertebrates.

Alosa pseudoharengus (Wilson, 1811), alewife

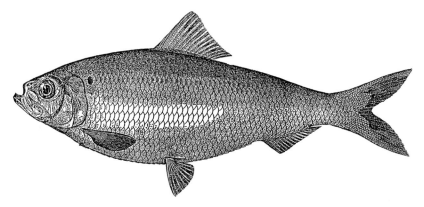

Figure 57. *Alosa pseudoharengus*, from H.W. Smith (1891), plate XLVIII.

This anadromous species is found along the Atlantic coast from Nova Scotia to South Carolina. First reported in Connecticut by Linsley (1844b). Populations are found in most streams in Connecticut that have access to Long Island Sound. Some landlocked populations are present in all major drainage basins. Sexual maturity is reached in 1-3 years and adults enter streams and spawn in spring. Eggs are broadcast and no care is given them or young. Young-of-the-year may stay in freshwaters until middle-fall feeding on invertebrates, then migrate to the ocean. Sub-adults may be collected at any time in freshwaters near saltwaters. Adults often reach lengths of 20-30 cm in saltwaters (freshwater populations usually 10-20 cm), and feed on a variety of plankton organisms in the ocean.

Alosa sapidissima (Wilson, 1811), American shad

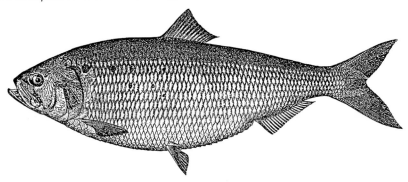

Figure 58. *Alosa sapidissima*, from H.W. Smith (1891), plate LIX.

This anadromous species is found along the Atlantic coast from the St. Lawrence River to Florida; it was introduced on the Pacific coast from California to Alaska. First reported in Connecticut by DeKay (1842) although populations were reported in the popular literature earlier, *i.e.*, Pease and Niles (1819). Populations are found in all the major rivers of the state that have access to Long Island Sound, however, the largest populations are associated with the Connecticut River drainage basin. Sexual maturity is reached in 2-5 years and adults enter freshwaters to spawn during spring and early summer. Eggs are broadcast and no care is given them or the young. Young-of-the-year remain in freshwater until fall feeding on invertebrates. Sub-adults may be collected anytime in freshwaters near saltwaters. Adults often reach lengths of 40-50 cm, and feed on a variety of planktonic organisms in the ocean.

Brevoortia tyrannus (Latrobe, 1802), Atlantic menhaden

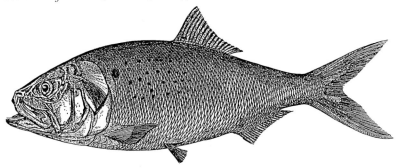

Figure 59. *Brevoortia tyrannus*, from H.W. Smith (1891), plate XLIX.

This marine species is distributed along the Atlantic coast from Nova Scotia to Florida. Young-of-the-year, sub-adults, and adults regularly (spring, summer, and fall) enter the freshwaters near saltwaters of all rivers that empty into Long Island Sound (Marcy 1976a, Whitworth *et al.* 1975). Adults often reach lengths of 45-55 cm and feed on planktonic organisms.

Occasionally large numbers of adults may enter the freshwaters of one river and experience massive mortalities; the last one documented in the state occurred in the Thames River during the summer of 1971. Similar incidents have occurred in other drainage basins along the Atlantic coast. Although many theories have been proposed, two seem more probable. One of them suggests that large populations of predators, *e.g.*, *Pomatomus saltatrix* and *Morone saxatilis*, drive them into freshwaters. Another proposes that a disease or parasite affects them and the school becomes disorientated and migrates into freshwater. Once there, not only is the change in salinity a problem, but the large numbers of fish present in restricted waters of higher temperature, lower oxygen and higher ammonia levels, all contribute to the mass mortalities.

Clupea harengus Linnaeus, 1758, Atlantic herring

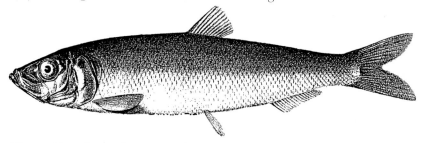

Figure 60. *Clupea harengus*, from Storer (1858), figure 1, plate 26.

This marine species is distributed along the Atlantic coast from Labrador to North Carolina. Adults occasionally, from fall through spring, enter saltwaters of all rivers of Connecticut that empty into Long Island Sound (Whitworth and Schmidt 1971). Adults commonly reach lengths of 25-35 cm, and feed on a variety of invertebrates and fishes.

Dorosoma cepedianum (Lesueur, 1818), gizzard shad

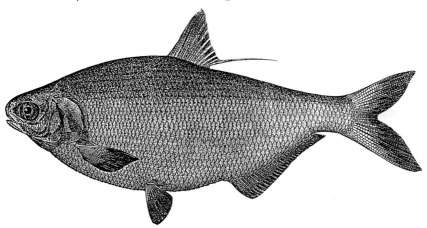

Figure 61. *Dorosoma cepedianum*, from H.W. Smith (1891), plate XLIX.

This species is distributed in freshwaters throughout much of the eastern two thirds of North America; anadromous stocks are found in the middle Atlantic region. Both anadromous and freshwater populations were in northern New Jersey in the 19th century (Abbott 1871). Since this species was first reported at the mouth of the Connecticut River (Whitworth, Minta, and Orciari 1980) spawning populations have been reported above the first dam in Massachussetts (O'Leary and Smith 1987) and both young and adults have been collected in the Connecticut River and its tributaries. Adults have been collected in both the Thames and Housatonic Rivers. Although freshwater populations are definitely established in the major rivers, we have not yet documented an anadromous population. Sexual maturity is reached in 2-3 years and lengths of 40-55 cm are attained. They feed on a variety of invertebrates and small fishes.

Family Cottidae, sculpins

Seventy genera with about 300 species (mostly marine with some freshwater) are distributed worldwide (mainly in the northern hemisphere). One freshwater and two marine species have been collected in the freshwaters of Connecticut.

Key to the species of Cottidae
1. Gill membranes attached to side of
   the wide isthmus   *Cottus cognatus*, page 120
   Gill membranes free from isthmus   2

2. Most dorsal cheek spine < 3 times
    the cheek spine directly below it   *Myoxocephalus aenaeus*, this page
    Most dorsal cheek spine > 3 times
    the cheek spine directly below it   *M. octodecemspinosus*, page 121

Cottus cognatus Richardson, 1836, slimy sculpin

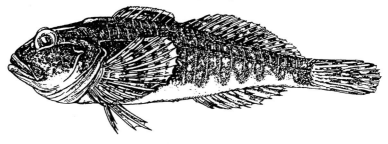

Figure 62. *Cottus cognatus*, from Whitworth *et al.* (1968), page 97.

This native species has a discontinuous distribution from eastern Siberia east throughout much of northern North America. First reported in Connecticut by Linsley (1844b). Populations, often abundant, are found in streams with cooler waters and clean gravel in all of the major drainage basins of Connecticut. Sexual maturity is attained in 1-2 years and lengths of 6-10 cm are reached. Males are usually darker in color during the spawning season and have a broad orange band in the spinous dorsal fin; the band is present all year. Males set up territories under rocks in riffle areas during the spring and early summer. Females lay their eggs on the undersides of rocks and the males guard them until they hatch. A variety of invertebrates are consumed.

Myoxocephalus aenaeus (Mitchill, 1814), grubby

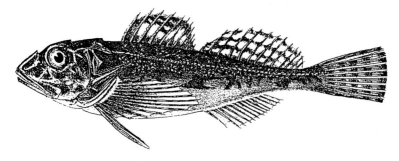

Figure 63. *Myoxocephalus aenaeus*, from DeKay (1842), figure 19.

This marine species is found along the Atlantic coast from the Gulf of St. Lawrence to New Jersey. Individuals occasionally enter freshwaters near saltwaters of all rivers of Connecticut that drain into Long Island Sound (P. Howell-Heller, DEP). Adults often reach lengths of 10-15 cm, and feed on a variety of invertebrates and fishes.

Myoxocephalus octodecemspinosus (Mitchill, 1818), longhorn sculpin

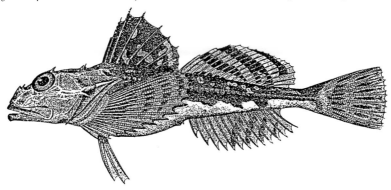

Figure 64. *Myoxocephalus octodecemspinosus*, from Goode *et al.* (1884), plate 73.

This marine species is distributed along the Atlantic coast from Newfoundland to Virginia. Adults often, from fall through spring, enter freshwaters near saltwaters of all rivers of Connecticut that drain into Long Island Sound (Whitworth and Schmidt 1971). These movements may be associated with spawning. Adults often reach lengths of 30-35 cm and feed on a variety of invertebrates and fishes.

Family Cyclopteridae, snailfishes

Approximately 21 genera with about 177 species are distributed in the Antarctic and Arctic Oceans and northern areas of the Atlantic and Pacific Oceans. Two species have been collected in the freshwaters of Connecticut.

Key to the species of Cyclopteridae
1. One dorsal fin, anal rays > 14, body
    elongate   *Liparis inquilinus*, page 122
    Two dorsal fins (body partially covers
    the first), anal rays < 15,
    body thickened around the middle   *Cyclopterus lumpus*, page 122

Cyclopterus lumpus Linnaeus, 1758; lumpfish

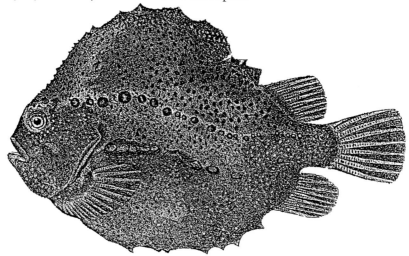

Figure 65. *Cyclopterus lumpus*, from DeKay (1842), figure 175.

This marine species is found along the Atlantic coast from Labrador to Virginia. Individuals occasionally enter freshwaters near saltwaters of all rivers of Connecticut that empty into Long Island Sound (P. Howell-Heller, DEP). Lengths of 20-25 cm are attained and they consume a variety of invertebrates and small fishes.

Liparis inquilinus Able, 1973, inquiline snailfish

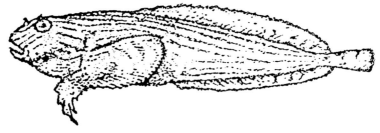

Figure 66. *Liparis inquilinus*, from Garman (1892), plate XVII, fig. 1.

This marine species is distributed along the Atlantic coast of North America from the northern extremities of land to Virginia. Individuals occasionally enter freshwaters near saltwaters of all rivers of the state that drain into Long Island Sound (Carl Fontneau, Omni Analysis). They are usually found within the shells of sea scallops during the day, leaving at night to feed. Adults often reach lengths of 6-10 cm, and feed on small invertebrates.

Family Cyprinidae, carps and minnows

Approximately 194 genera with about 2070 species are distributed throughout the freshwaters of Africa, Asia, Europe, and North America; about 220 species are found in North America. Twenty-one species have been collected in the freshwaters of Connecticut. One other species is included that has been introduced into the freshwaters of all the contiguous states and will undoubtedly be collected in this state.

Species in this family are very diverse. Spawning times vary and extend from early spring to late summer. Eggs may be deposited in nests or broadcast over a variety of substrates and may be demersal or buoyant and adhesive or nonadhesive. Males have no nuptial tubercles or have them in different areas. Although sexual maturity may not be reached until 2-4 years, most species are sexually mature at age 1.

One of the characteristics often used to identify members of this family is the number and shape of the pharyngeal teeth. Although this characteristic is not needed to identify the members of this family that now are found in the freshwaters of this state, instructions for using this characteristic follow. The location of the pharyngeal teeth on the pharyngeal arch is shown in Figure 67. An arch is removed by holding the specimen in one hand while the thumbnail holds the operculum and gill arches forward. Using the other hand, remove the pharyngeal arch with a pair of fine forceps, after cutting the fleshy tendons from the posterior edge of the arch. Place the arch in bleach for 3-5 minutes to facilitate removal of the flesh. If the arch is left in the bleach too long, the arch may dissolve. The whole process is done most efficiently under a dissecting microscope. The first attempts to remove a pharyngeal arch should be done on expendable specimens. Skill will come with a little practice.

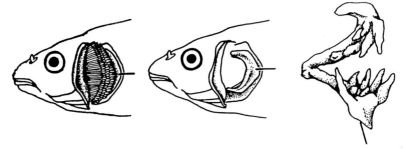

Figure 67. **The pharyngeal bones and teeth of cyprinids (minnows).** At the left is an external view of the head showing the location of the left pharyngeal bone. The center view is the same as the first except that the gill arches are removed. The right view shows the same, except that the head is rotated ventrally and everything removed except the left and right pharyngeal bones so that the pharyngeal teeth are exposed.

Teeth are counted on the left arch first (anterior row to posterior row), and then the right arch (posterior to anterior). For example, the count shown in Figure 67 would be expressed as 2,4-4,2. When counting the number of teeth look for broken teeth, or sockets (teeth that were broken below the arch line), lest you fail to include them in your count.

Key to the species of Cyprinidae

1. Dorsal rays > 11 2
   Dorsal rays < 12 3

2. Barbels present .... *Cyprinus carpio*, page 129
   Barbels absent .... *Carassius auratus*, page 128

3. Lower lip with cartilaginous edge not
   covered by skin, air bladder encircled
   many times by the intestine .... *Campostoma anomalum*, page 127
   Lower lip without cartilaginous edge,
   air bladder not encircled by intestine   4

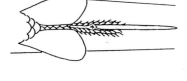

Figure 68. **Ventral views of fishes to show the lower lip with a cartilaginous edge (left) and with thickened posterior lobes (right).**

4. Lower jaw thickened posteriorly
   forming conspicuous lobes .... *Exoglossum maxillingua*,
                                          page 130

   Lower jaw of usual form 5

5. Anal rays > 12 6
   Anal rays < 13 8

6. No fleshy keel between pelvic fins
   and anus .... *Leuciscus idus*, page 131
   A fleshy keel between pelvic fins
   and anus 7

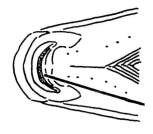

Figure 69. Lateral (lower) and ventral (upper) views of a keel.

7. Dorsal rays > 10, keel scaled,
   pharyngeal teeth 3,5-5,3   *Scardinius erythrophthalmus*,
                                     page 138

   Dorsal rays < 10, keel naked,
   pharyngeal teeth 0,5-5,0   *Notemigonus crysoleucas*, page 133

8. Barbels present, may be terminal on
   maxilla, or hidden in the groove
   above maxilla and a short distance
   towards the midline   9
   Barbels absent   15

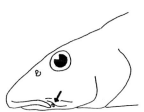
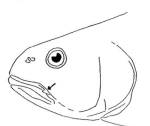

Figure 70. Location of maxillary barbels. Terminal (left) and not terminal (right).

9. Barbels at the terminal end of
   the maxilla   10
   Barbels not at the terminal end of
   the maxilla, usually small, leaflike
   structures in the groove above the
   maxilla and a little in from the
   posterior end of the maxilla   13

10. First major ray of dorsal fin spinelike,
    caudal fin, at most, shallowly concave *Tinca tinca*, page 140
    First major ray of dorsal fin not
    spinelike, caudal fin forked   11

11. Gill rakers on lower limb of first arch
    > 7, predorsal scales difficult to count 12
    Gill rakers on lower limb of first arch,
    < 7 predorsal scales easy to count   *Notropis amblops*, page 133

12. Snout projecting little beyond a
    somewhat oblique mouth, premaxillary
    frenum usually absent   *Rhinichthys atratulus*, page 136
    Snout projecting well beyond a
    ventral mouth, premaxillary
    frenum usually present   *R. cataractae*, page 137

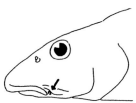 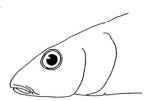

Figure 71. Snouts of *Rhinichthys atratulus* (right) and *R. cataractae* (left).

13. Lateral line scales < 50   *Semotilus corporalis*, page 139
    Lateral line scales > 50   14

14. Black spot at dorsal origin, no irregular
    shaped black blotches on sides   *S. atromaculatus*, page 138
    No black spot at dorsal origin, irregular
    shaped black blotches on sides   *Margariscus margarita*,
    page 132

15. Distance from anal origin to caudal
    base > 2.5 times in distance
    from snout to anal origin   *Ctenopharyngodon idella*,
    page 128

    Distance from anal origin to caudal
    base < 2.5 times in distance from
    snout to anal origin   16

16. Anal rays < 8   17
    Anal rays > 7   19

17. Lateral line scales < 40   *Notropis bifrenatus*, page 134
    Lateral line scales > 40   18

18. Mouth more ventral than terminal,
    lateral line outlined in black   *Pimephales notatus*, page 135
    Mouth more terminal than ventral,
    lateral line not outlined in black   *P. promelas*, page 136

19. Mouth inferior, usually 8 anal rays   *Notropis hudsonius*, page 134
    Mouth terminal, usually > 8 anal rays   20

20. Dorsal origin about over pelvic origin,
    9 anal rays   *Luxilus cornutus*, page 131
    Dorsal origin distinctly behind pelvic
    origin, 10 anal rays   *Notropis rubellus*, page 135

Campostoma anomalum (Rafinesque, 1820), central stoneroller

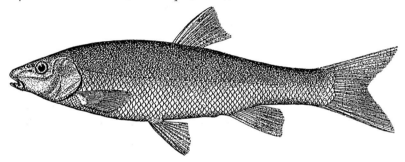

Figure 72. *Campostoma anomalum*, from Evermann and Kendall (1892), plate XVI.

This introduced species is widely distributed in freshwaters of the eastern half of North America. First reported in Connecticut by Whitworth *et al.* (1968). Intensive sampling in the Byram River drainage basin in 1987 and 1988 showed that the population sampled in 1965 and 1967 did not survive, although more than one age class was present in the 1960s. Sexual maturity is reached in 1-3 years and they spawn in spring in riffles. Breeding males have many nuptial tubercles on much of their bodies and orange and black in their fins. Specimens attain lengths of 15-20 cm and consume a variety of invertebrates.

Carassius auratus (Linnaeus, 1758), goldfish

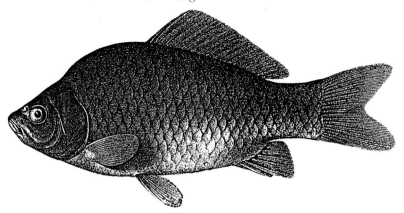

Figure 73. *Carassius auratus*, from Storer (1855), figure 1, plate 21.

Numerous populations of this introduced species, native to the freshwaters of Asia, have been transported to most of the drainage basins of North America. First reported in Connecticut by Linsley (1844b). Although populations have been established in most drainage basins of the state, most of the known populations that have maintained themselves for a long time period are associated with a few smaller rivers and ponds. Sexual maturity is reached in 1-3 years and eggs are broadcast on vegetation from spring to early summer. Lengths of 25-30 cm are attained and they feed on a variety of invertebrates.

Ctenopharyngodon idella (Valenciennes, 1844), grass carp

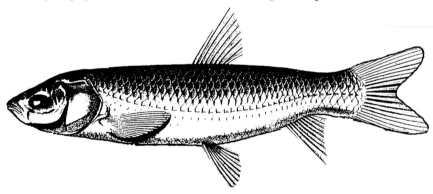

Figure 74. *Ctenopharyngodon idella*, from Steindachner (1866), plate 18, figure 1.

This species is native to eastern Asia and was first introduced into the freshwaters of North America in the early 1960s for research in aquatic plant control. Populations are now established in the lower Mississippi River, and have been legally and illegally stocked throughout North America. First reported in Connecticut in the 1980s (R. Orciari and T. Barry, DEP), and specimens have been introduced into ponds in most drainage basins of the state; none of the known populations are self sustaining. As of 1988, all further specimens introduced into the freshwaters of this state must be incapable of reproduction. This is the only species of fish that lives within the freshwaters of Connecticut that is known to be able to survive on a diet primarily of plant materials. They are also able to digest animal proteins, and when plants are unavailable, grow and reproduce on a diet of invertebrates. Lengths of 5-55 cm have been reported from specimens growing in this state. Sexual maturity is reached in 2-4 years and spawning takes place in spring in waters of high velocity. Eggs are broadcast and no care given them or young.

Cyprinus carpio Linnaeus, 1758, common carp

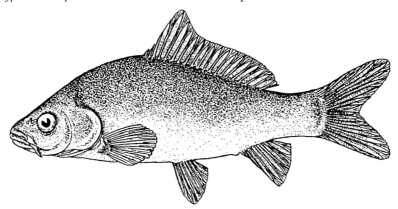

Figure 75. *Cyprinus carpio*, from Whitworth *et al.* (1968), page 57.

This Asiatic species has been widely introduced throughout the freshwaters of North America. First reported in Connecticut by Linsley (1844b). The stock introduced in ponds near the Hudson River in New York (DeKay 1842) was probably the source. Populations are present in most drainage basins of the state, although large populations are usually associated with larger streams and a few lakes. Sexual maturity is reached in 3-5 years and spawning takes place in spring. Eggs are broadcast in shallow vegetated areas and no care is given eggs or young. Lengths of 70-100 cm are often attained and they feed on a variety of invertebrates.

Danio rerio (Hamilton, 1822), zebra danio

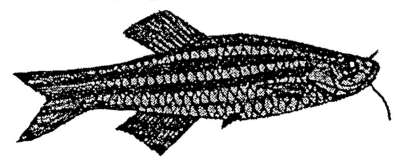

Figure 76. *Danio rerio*, from F. Day (1878), plate CLI, figure 4.

This introduced species is found in the freshwaters of Pakistan, Nepal, Bangladesh and along the southeast cost of India. The individuals (2-4 cm) that we captured (1985) in the Thames River drainage basin were probably recently introduced by home aquarists and would not be able to establish a viable population in this state.

Exoglossum maxillingua (Lesueur, 1817), cutlips minnow

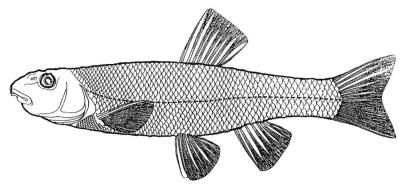

Figure 77. *Exoglossum maxillingua*, from Cope (1869a), plate XI, figure 1.

This native species is found in the freshwaters of part of the mid-Atlantic and northeast sections of North America. First reported in Connecticut by Webster (1942); Connecticut was not included in the range described by Jordan, Evermann, and Clark (1930). Populations are found in the Hudson and Housatonic drainage basins and coastal basins west of the Housatonic River. Only drainage basins of the Housatonic River below the fall line at Falls Village, Connecticut, have populations. There are no known populations in drainage basins of either the Housatonic or Hudson Rivers in Massachusetts. One individual was obtained from one location in a tributary of the Farmington River in 1988 (Hagstrom, DEP). That specimen, or population, was probably introduced. Sexual maturity is reached in 1-2 years and spawning occurs in spring. Lengths of 15-25 cm are often attained and they feed on a variety of invertebrates.

Leuciscus idus (Linnaeus, 1758), ide

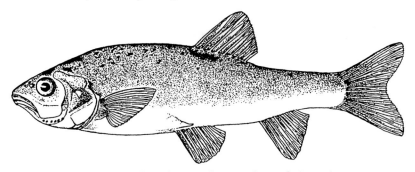

Figure 78. *Leuciscus idus*, from Whitworth *et al.* (1968), page 59.

This Eurasian species has been widely introduced into the freshwaters of North America. First reported from one pond in an eastern coastal drainage basin in Connecticut (Whitworth *et al.* 1968). That population was subsequently eradicated (Chuck Phillips, DEP). Sexual maturity is reached in 3-4 years and eggs are broadcast over vegetation in spring. Males develop nuptial tubercles. Lengths of 25-30 cm are attained and a variety of invertebrates and small fishes are consumed.

Luxilus cornutus (Mitchill, 1817), common shiner

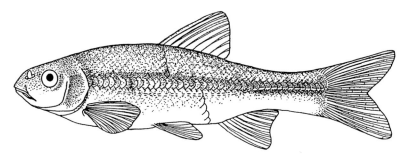

Figure 79. *Luxilus cornutus*, from Whitworth *et al.* (1968), page 62.

This native species is widely distributed in the freshwaters of North America east of the Rocky Mountains. First reported in Connecticut by Storer (1842b). Populations, often large, are typically found in intermediate to small streams in all drainage basins of the state. Sexual maturity is reached in 1-2 years and breeding males have nuptial tubercles, red fins and scattered reddish pigments on their bodies. Spawning takes place in spring and eggs are broadcast in riffle areas or over the nests of sea lamprey or fallfish. No care is give eggs or young. Lengths of 10-20 cm are attained and a variety of invertebrates are consumed.

Margariscus margarita Cope, 1868, pearl dace

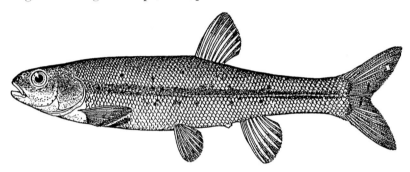

Figure 80. *Margariscus margarita*, from Kendall (1902), page 360.

This introduced species is widely distributed throughout much of north central North America. First reported in Connecticut by Whitworth *et al.* (1968). Extensive sampling in that area (Byram River drainage basin) in 1987 and 1988 revealed no specimens were present. Sexual maturity is reached in about 2 years. Males develop nuptial tubercles on the head and females often develop tubercles on the pectoral fins. Both sexes intensify their colors during the spawning season. Males defend territories in riffles, but nests are not constructed. Eggs are deposited in spring. Lengths of 8-12 cm are attained and they feed on a variety of invertebrates.

Notemigonus crysoleucas (Mitchill, 1814), golden shiner

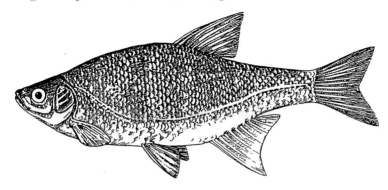

Figure 81. *Notemigonus crysoleucas*, from Whitworth et al. (1968), page 60.

This native species is widely distributed in the freshwaters of North America. First reported in Connecticut by DeKay (1842). Populations, often large, are found in all drainage basins of the state. Although viable populations are usually associated with larger rivers and lakes and ponds, individuals may be collected in any body of water. Sexual maturity is reached in 1-3 years and spawning takes place in late spring through early summer. Eggs are broadcast over vegetation and no care is given them or young. Lengths of 25-45 cm are often attained in lakes and ponds. They consume a variety of invertebrates.

Notropis amblops (Rafinesque, 1820), bigeye chub

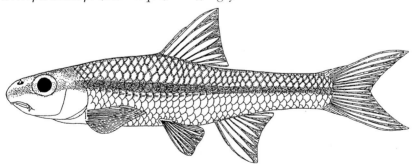

Figure 82. *Notropis amblops*, from Trautman (1957), figure 63.

This introduced species is distributed throughout the freshwaters of central North America. First reported in Connecticut from a collection we obtained (1987) in Mopus Brook, a tributary of the Hudson River in western Connecticut. That individual (3 cm), or the population, was probably only

recently introduced and subsequent samples have yielded no other specimens. Sexual maturity is reached in 1-2 years. Males develop nuptial tubercles. Eggs are broadcast in riffle areas. Lengths of 6-8 cm are attained and a
variety of invertebrates are consumed.

Notropis bifrenatus (Cope, 1869), bridle shiner

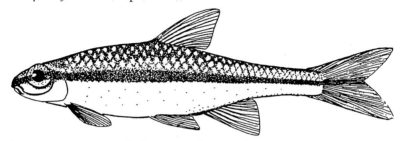

**Figure 83. *Notropis bifrenatus*, from Whitworth *et al.* (1968), page
61.**

This native species is distributed in freshwaters of the eastern quarter of
North America. Both the species description (Cope 1869a) and range, that
included Connecticut (Cope 1869b), were published in the same year. We
have no indication of where specimens were collected in Connecticut.
Populations, often associated with standing bodies of water and slower moving portions of streams, have been found in all drainage basins of the state.
However, there seem to be fewer individuals in a population, and fewer populations sampled in recent years (compared to the 1960s and 70s). Sexual
maturity is usually reached in 1 year and spawning occurs in spring.
Breeding males are bright yellow below the lateral band and all colors are
intensified. Lengths of 4-6 cm are attained and they feed on a variety of
invertebrates.

Notropis hudsonius (Clinton, 1824), spottail shiner

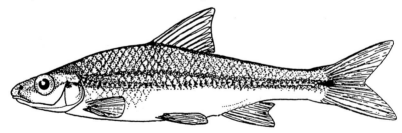

Figure 84. *Notropis hudsonius*, from Whitworth *et al.* (1968), page 63.

This native species is widely distributed in the freshwaters of much of
eastern North America. Connecticut was not included in the range listed by

Jordan, Evermann, and Clark (1930). It was first reported here by Webster (1942). Populations, often large, are found in the major rivers and a few lakes of all drainage basins of the state. Sexual maturity is reached in 1-2 years. Spawning often takes place in higher velocity areas of tributaries of major watercourses near that watercourse. Eggs are broadcast and no care given them or the young. Spawning males develop nuptial tubercles. Lengths of 10-15 cm are attained and they consume a variety of invertebrates.

Notropis rubellus (Agassiz, 1850), rosyface shiner

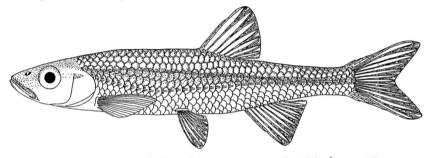

Figure 85. *Notropis rubellus*, from Trautman (1957), figure 78.

This introduced species is widely distributed in the freshwaters of eastern North America. First reported in Connecticut by Whitworth and Schmidt (1971). Not collected in that area (Connecticut River) since. Sexual maturity is reached in 1-2 years and males develop nuptial tubercles and intensified color during the spawning season. Eggs are broadcast in riffle areas in spring through early summer. Lengths of 6-8 cm are attained and a variety of invertebrates consumed.

Pimephales notatus (Rafinesque, 1820), bluntnose minnow

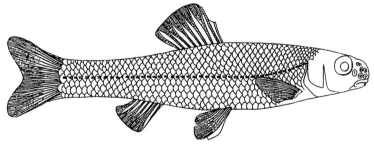

Figure 86. *Pimephales notatus*, from Cope (1869a), plate XIII, figure 5.

This introduced species is widely distributed in the freshwaters of eastern North America. First reported in Connecticut by Whitworth *et al.* (1968). Additional specimens have not been captured in that area (Byram

River) since. A small stream in the Housatonic River drainage basin has had a viable population for a few years (M. Humphries, DEP). That population was probably the source for other populations that have become established in other watercourses in the Housatonic River drainage basin. Sexual maturity is reached in 1 year and spawning occurs in spring. Eggs are attached to the underside of rocks and are cared for until they hatch. Lengths of 4-8 cm are attained and they feed on a variety of invertebrates.

Pimephales promelas Rafinesque, 1820, fathead minnow

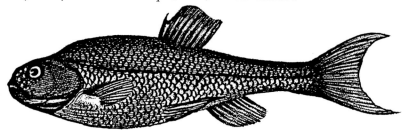

Figure 87. *Pimephales promelas*, from Kirtland (1840b), plate XXVII, figure 2.

This introduced species is widely distributed in the freshwaters of North America. First reported in Connecticut by Whitworth *et al.* (1968). Specimens have not been recaptured in that area of the Connecticut River. Since 1986, specimens have been captured in many areas of all of the major and some of the coastal drainage basins of Connecticut. Some of those populations, especially in the Housatonic River drainage basin, seem to be viable (N. Hagstrom, DEP). Sexual maturity is attained in 1 year and spawning occurs in spring and early summer. Eggs are deposited under many substrates and are cared for until they hatch. Lengths of 4-8 cm are often attained and they consume a variety of invertebrates.

Rhinichthys atratulus (Hermann, 1804), blacknose dace

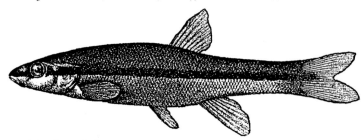

Figure 88. *Rhinichthys atratulus*, from Storer (1855), figure 4, plate 21.

This native species is widely distributed in freshwaters throughout much of North America east of the Rocky Mountains. First reported in this state by DeKay (1842). Populations, often large, are typically found in the smaller streams of all drainage basins of the state. Sexual maturity is reached in 1 year and spawning occurs in spring in riffle areas. Males develop pads between the rays of their pelvic fins during the spawning season. Additionally, they have reddish orange pelvic and pectoral fins and develop orange pigments on their sides. Lengths of 5-8 cm are attained and they consume a variety of invertebrates.

Rhinichthys cataractae (Valenciennes, 1842), longnose dace

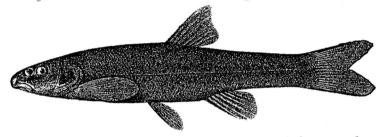

Figure 89. *Rhinichthys cataractae*, from Storer (1855), figure 1, plate 22.

This native species is widely distributed in freshwaters throughout much of North America east of the Rocky Mountains. First reported in this state by Ayres (1843b). Populations, often large, are typically found in the medium sized streams in all drainage basins of the state. Sexual maturity is reached in 1-2 years and spawning occurs in spring in riffles. Males develop reddish orange upper lips during the breeding season. Lengths of 8-14 cm are attained and they consume a variety of invertebrates.

Scardinius erythrophthalmus (Linnaeus, 1758), rudd

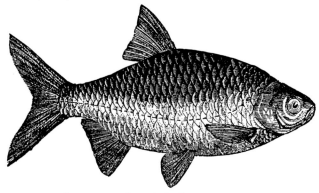

Figure 90. *Scardinius erythrophthalmus*, from Goodrich *et al*. (1881), page 476.

This introduced species is distributed from Great Britain eastward throughout much of northern and central Europe and Asia. Populations have been introduced in some drainage basins in North America since the 1900s. Although specimens have not been reported from Connecticut, they have been obtained (4-10 cm) in both New York and Massachusetts. Pharyngeal teeth are 3,5-5,3 as contrasted to 0,5-5,0 for *Notemigonus crysoleucas*. Sexual maturity is reached in 2-3 years. Spawning takes place in early summer over vegetation in lakes and slow moving areas of rivers. Adults reach lengths of 20-30 cm and consume a variety of plant and animal foods.

Semotilus atromaculatus (Mitchill, 1818), creek chub

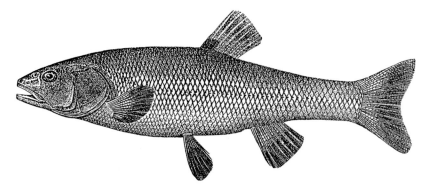

Figure 91. *Semotilus atromaculatus*, from H.W. Smith (1890b), plate XXVII.

This native species is widely distributed in the freshwaters of North America east of the Rocky Mountains. First reported in Connecticut by Linsley (1844b). Populations, often large, are typically found in the smaller streams of all coastal basins from New Haven and west, in the Housatonic and Hudson River drainage basins, and in part of the Farmington River drainage basin. The few scattered populations in some of the lower Connecticut River drainage basins, and in a few scattered Thames River drainage basins, were undoubtedly introduced. Sexual maturity is reached in 1-2 years and spawning occurs in spring. Males develop red pigments in the pelvic and pectoral fins and along the sides during the spawning season. Males construct nests by depositing stones on top of each other to form piles in riffle areas. Eggs are broadcast on these in spring. Lengths of 10-15 cm are often attained and they consume a variety of invertebrates and small fishes.

Semotilus corporalis (Mitchill, 1817), fallfish

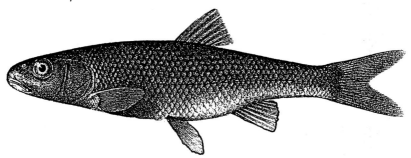

Figure 92. *Semotilus corporalis*, from Storer (1855), figure 2, plate 22.

This native species is distributed in part of northeastern North America. First reported in Connecticut by Ayres (1843a). Populations, often large, are typically found in medium sized streams in all drainage basins of the state. Sexual maturity is reached in 1-2 years and spawning occurs in spring. Males develop reddish and yellow pigment on their fins and sides during the spawning season. They construct nests, which consist of cone-shaped piles of pebbles, in riffles or near the shores in streams. Lengths of 30-40 cm are attained in larger watercourses and they consume a variety of invertebrates and small fish.

Tinca tinca (Linnaeus, 1758), tench

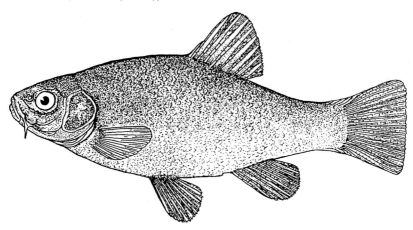

Figure 93. *Tinca tinca*, from Whitworth *et al.* (1968), page 71.

This European species has been widely introduced into the freshwaters of North America, but most populations have not survived. First reported in Connecticut by Webster (1942), however, the survey party did not obtain any specimens and included the species based on reliable reports. Specimens were subsequently collected and preserved (James Moulton and John Orintas, DEP). No specimens have been obtained for over fifteen years. Sexual maturity is reached in 3-4 years and spawning occurs in spring and early summer in shallow weedy areas. Lengths of 30-50 cm are attained and they consume a variety of invertebrates.

Family Cyprinodontidae; killifishes

Twenty-nine genera with about 268 species (marine and freshwater) are distributed throughout the world. Six species have been collected in the freshwaters of Connecticut. Most species in Connecticut not only are sexually dimorphic, but the juvenile fish also look different. Males in some species intensify their colors during the spawning season, which often extends from spring to mid-summer. Eggs are usually broadcast over vegetation and no care is given them or the young. All age classes usually travel in large schools.

Key to the species of Cyprinodontidae

1. Jaw teeth tricuspid   *Cyprinodon variegatus*, page 142
    Jaw teeth conical   2

2. Mandibular pores absent; jaw teeth
   uniserial   *Lucania parva*, page 147
   Mandibular pores present, jaw teeth
   multiserial   3

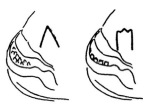

Figure 94. **Lateral views of a head showing jaw teeth conical and multiserial (left), and tricuspid and uniserial (right).**

3. Scales in lateral series > 40   *Fundulus diaphanus*, page 143
   Scales in lateral series < 39   4

4. Dorsal rays < 9   *F. luciae*, page 145
   Dorsal rays > 9   5

5. Eye length contained > 0.5 times in
   snout length, predorsal area scaleless,
   head length > 3.5 times in standard
   length, dorsal rays < 14   *F. heteroclitus*, page 144
   Eye length contained < 0.5 times in
   snout length, predorsal area scaled,
   head length < 3.5 times in standard
   length, dorsal rays > 13   *F. majalis*, page 146

Cyprinodon variegatus Lacepede, 1803, sheepshead minnow

Figure 95. *Cyprinodon variegatus*, from Whitworth *et al.* (1968), page 84.

This marine species is distributed along the east coast of North America from Massachusetts to Mexico. Populations containing many age classes and spawning adults are regularly found from spring through late fall in freshwaters near saltwaters of all watercourses in Connecticut that drain into Long Island Sound (Whitworth *et al.* 1975). There is a possibility that some populations may be anadromous, *i.e.*, have to spawn in freshwaters. Sexual maturity is reached in 1 year and lengths of 4-8 cm are attained (females larger). They feed on a variety of invertebrates.

Fundulus diaphanus (Lesueur, 1817), banded killifish

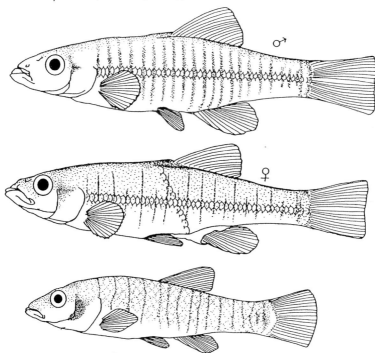

Figure 96. *Fundulus diaphanus*, **from Whitworth *et al*. (1968), page 85.**

This native species is widely distributed in freshwaters of eastern North America, and in saltwaters along the Atlantic coast. First reported in Connecticut by Linsley (1844b). Freshwater populations are commonly found in lakes and ponds in most drainage basins of the state; occasionally in streams. Saltwater populations are often present in the estuarine areas of many streams. This species was widely introduced as a forage fish in the lakes and ponds of Connecticut in the late 1800s and early 1900s. Sexual maturity is reached in 1 year and lengths of 6-10 cm are often attained. They feed on a variety of invertebrates.

Fundulus heteroclitus (Linnaeus, 1766), mummichog

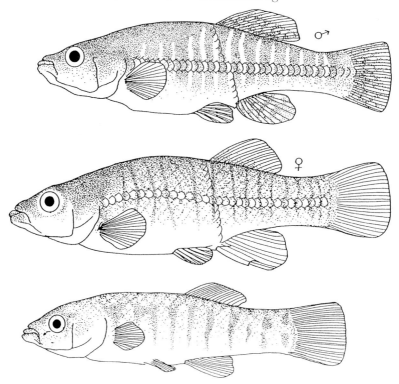

Figure 97. *Fundulus heteroclitus*, from Whitworth *et al.* (1968), page 87.

This marine species is found along the Atlantic coast from Maine to Florida, with freshwater populations reported in Virginia and New York. Large populations containing many age classes and spawning adults are regularly found from late spring to early fall in freshwaters near the mouths of all watercourses in Connecticut that empty into Long Island Sound (Whitworth *et al.* 1968). Sexual maturity is reached in 1-2 years and lengths of 8-14 cm are attained. They feed on a variety of invertebrates and small fishes.

Fundulus luciae (Baird, 1855), spotfin killifish

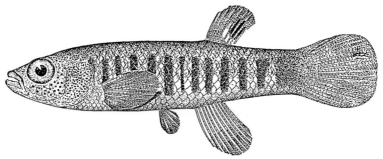

Figure 98. *Fundulus luciae*, from H.W. Smith (1890a), plate XVIII.

This marine species is distributed along the Atlantic coast from Connecticut to Georgia, and Fowler (1913) found this species in the freshwaters of Chincoteague Island, Virginia. Individuals were collected in the freshwaters of Connecticut (Thomson, Weed, and Taruski 1971). Since no other known specimens have been collected in the freshwaters or saltwaters of Connecticut, those specimens were probably strays from the usual range of this species in the mid-Atlantic states. Sexual maturity is reached in 1 year and lengths of 2-4 cm are attained. They feed on a variety of invertebrates.

Fundulus majalis (Walbaum, 1792), striped killifish

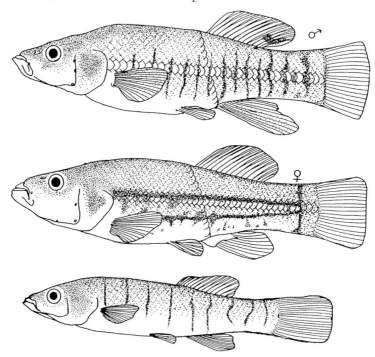

Figure 99. *Fundulus majalis*, from Whitworth *et al.* (1968), page 88.

This marine species is distributed along the Atlantic coast from Massachusetts to Florida. Populations containing many age classes are regularly found from spring to early fall in freshwaters near saltwaters of all watercourses in Connecticut that drain into Long Island Sound (Marcy 1976a, Whitworth *et al.* 1975). Sexual maturity is reached in 1-2 years and lengths of 10-18 cm are attained. They feed on a variety of invertebrates and small fishes.

Lucania parva (Baird and Girard, 1855), rainwater killifish

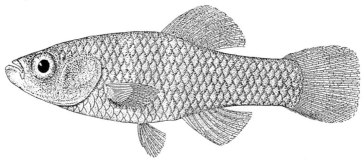

Figure 100. *Lucania parva*, from Evermann and Kendall (1892), plate XXV.

This marine species is found along the east coast of North America from Massachusetts to Texas. Individuals occasionally enter freshwaters near saltwaters of most watercourses in Connecticut that drain into Long Island Sound (Whitworth *et al.* 1975). Sexual maturity is reached in 1 year and lengths of 4-7 cm are attained. They feed on a variety of invertebrates.

Family Engraulidae, anchovies

Sixteen genera with about 140 species (mostly marine) are distributed worldwide in the Atlantic, Indian, and Pacific Oceans. Several South American species are restricted to freshwaters and some marine species occasionally enter freshwater. One species has been collected in the freshwaters of Connecticut.

Anchoa mitchilli (Valenciennes, 1848), bay anchovy

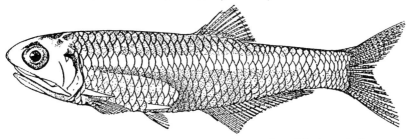

Figure 101. *Anchoa mitchilli*, from Bigelow and Welsh (1924), figure 51.

This marine species is found along the east coast of North America from Maine to Mexico. Large populations containing all age classes regularly enter from spring through fall, occasionally at other times, freshwaters near saltwaters of all watercourses in Connecticut that drain into Long Island Sound (Marcy 1976a, Whitworth *et al.* 1975). Sexual maturity is reached in 1 year and lengths of 6-12 cm are often attained. Pelagic eggs are broadcast in Long Island Sound from spring through late summer. Thus, young fish are often found in freshwaters throughout late spring to late summer. All age classes travel in large schools and feed on a variety of invertebrates.

Family Esocidae, pikes

One genus with five species is distributed in the freshwaters of the northern hemisphere. Four species have been collected in the freshwaters of Connecticut. Most species travel in small groups, or live a solitary life and are associated with shallow areas with either submerged or emergent vegetation. Larger individuals migrate into deeper waters during the fall and winter. Spawning occurs in spring in shallow weedy areas and eggs are broadcast over vegetation. No care is provided for eggs or young. Most species have insatiable appetites and will swallow fish their own size. Hybridization between redfin and chain pickerel and chain pickerel and northern pike have probably occurred in many waterbodies.

Key to the species of Esocidae

1. Cheeks and opercles completely
   scaled   2
   Cheeks partly or fully scaled,
   opercles with lower half naked   3

2. Snout length contained < 2.4
   times in head length   *Esox niger*, page 150
   Snout length contained > 2.4
   times in head length   *E. americanus*, page 149

3. Upper half of both cheeks and
   opercles scaled   *E. masquinongy*, page 150
   Cheeks wholly scaled and half   *E. lucius*, page 149
   of opercles scaled

Esox americanus Gmelin, 1758, redfin pickerel

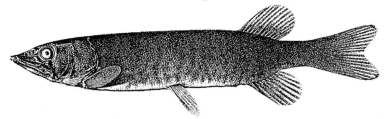

Figure 102. *Esox americanus*, from Storer (1858), figure 2, plate 24.

This native species is widely distributed in North America. First reported in the Connecticut River in Connecticut by Ayres (1843a). Although populations are found in most drainage basins in Connecticut, most of them are associated with small streams with no, or few, mechanical barriers between them and Long Island Sound. Sexual maturity is reached in 1-2 years and lengths of 25-35 cm are often attained. They feed on a variety of invertebrates and small fishes.

Esox lucius Linnaeus, 1758, northern pike

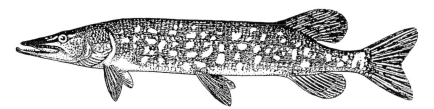

Figure 103. *Esox lucius*, from Whitworth *et al.* (1968), page 50.

This introduced species is widely distributed in the freshwaters of northern North America. First reported in Connecticut by Ayres (1851-1854). Those individuals probably migrated south from populations introduced into the Connecticut River in Massachusetts. Populations are now established in drainage basins in both the Housatonic and Connecticut Rivers. Recently, populations have been introduced into drainage basins in the Thames River. Sexual maturity is reached in 1-2 years and lengths of 70-80 cm are often attained. They feed on a variety of fishes, invertebrates, and miscellaneous items.

Esox masquinongy Mitchill, 1824; muskellunge

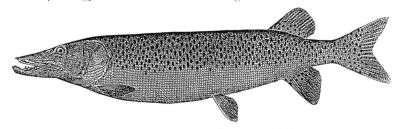

Figure 104. *Esox masquinongy*, from H.W. Smith (1890b), plate XLI.

This introduced species is discontinuously distributed throughout north-central North America. First reported in Connecticut by Ayres (1851-1854). Specimens were subsequently collected in that drainage basin (Anonymous 1875b, 1898, 1902), and in the Thames River drainage basin. However, no viable populations have been documented. Sexual maturity is reached in 2-4 years and lengths in excess of 90 cm are often attained. They feed on a variety of fishes and invertebrates.

Esox niger Lesueur, 1818, chain pickerel

Figure 105. *Esox niger*, from Whitworth, Berrien, and Keller (1968), page 51.

This native species is widely distributed in the freshwaters of eastern North America. First reported in Connecticut by DeKay (1842). Populations are typically found in larger streams, lakes, and ponds in every drainage basin in the state. Sexual maturity is reached in 1-2 years and lengths of 45-55 cm are often attained. They feed on a variety of fishes and invertebrates.

Family Fistulariidae, cornetfishes

One genus with about four species is found in the shallow waters of tropical seas. One species has been collected in the freshwaters of Connecticut.

Fistularia petimba Lacepede, 1803, red cornetfish

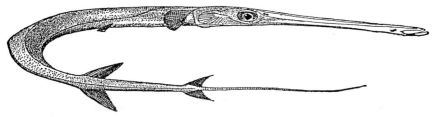

Figure 106. *Fistularia petimba*, from Weber and DeBeaufort (1922), figure 4.

This marine species is distributed in the warm waters of the western Atlantic. Individuals occasionally stray north and enter freshwaters near the mouths of the rivers of Connecticut (P. Howell-Heller, DEP) and New York (C.L. Smith 1985) that drain into Long Island Sound. Lengths of 10-15 cm are attained and they feed on a variety of invertebrates.

Family Gadidae, cods

Twenty-one genera with about 55 species (marine, with one freshwater) are distributed in the Arctic, Atlantic, and Pacific Oceans; the freshwater species has a holarctic distribution). Seven species have been collected in the freshwaters of Connecticut.

Key to the species of Gadidae

1. More than one dorsal fin   2
   One dorsal fin   *Enchelyopus cimbrius*, page 152

2. Barbel absent on chin   *Merluccius bilinearis*, page 153
   Barbel present on chin   3

3. Three dorsal fins   *Microgadus tomcod*, page 153
   Two dorsal fins   4
4. Pelvic fins lacking long filaments   *Lota lota*, page 152
   Pelvic fins with 2 long filaments   5

5. First dorsal fin with 1 or 2
   elongated filamentous rays   6
   First dorsal fin with no
   elongated filamentous rays   *Urophycis regia*, page 154
6. Lateral line scales usually > 125,
   maxilla usually does not
   extend beyond eye   *U. chuss*, page 155
   Lateral line scales usually < 124,

maxilla usually extends
beyond eye   *U. tenuis*, page 155

Enchelyopus cimbrius (Linnaeus, 1766), fourbeard rockling

Figure 107. *Enchelyopus cimbrius*, from Storer (1858), figure 1, plate 29.

This marine species is distributed in North America along the Atlantic coast from Newfoundland to southern New England, and further offshore to North Carolina. Individuals occasionally enter freshwaters near the mouths of Connecticut rivers that drain into Long Island Sound (C. Fontneau, Omni Analysis). Adults often reach lengths of 15-25 cm, and feed on a variety of invertebrates.

Lota lota (Linnaeus, 1758), burbot

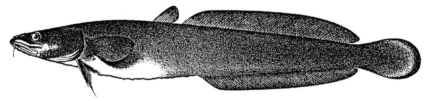

Figure 108. *Lota lota*, from Storer (1858), figure 4, plate 28.

This introduced species is widely distributed in the freshwaters of the northern hemisphere. First reported in Connecticut by Linsley (1844b). Although specimens have been obtained from two drainage basins in recent years, the only viable population is in the Hollenbeck River drainage basin. Sexual maturity is probably reached in 2-3 years in Connecticut and spawning takes place in the stream in late winter-early spring. Lengths of 15-30 cm are attained and they consume a variety of invertebrates and small fishes.

Merluccius bilinearis (Mitchill, 1814), silver hake

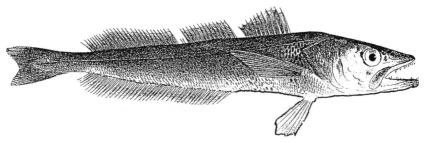

Figure 109. *Merluccius bilinearis*, from DeKay (1842), figure 148.

This marine species is distributed along the east coast of North America from Newfoundland to the Bahamas. During fall individuals occasionally enter freshwaters near the mouths of all Connecticut rivers that drain into Long Island Sound (Whitworth and Schmidt 1971). Adults often reach lengths in excess of 40 cm, and feed on a variety of fishes and invertebrates.

Microgadus tomcod (Walbaum, 1792), Atlantic tomcod

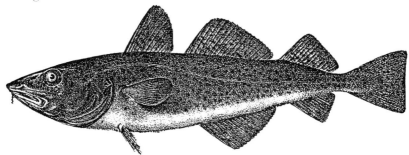

Figure 110. *Microgadus tomcod*, from Storer (1858), figure 4, plate 27.

This marine species is distributed along the Atlantic coast from Newfoundland to Virginia. Populations containing all age classes, and spawning adults, are commonly found from fall to spring, often at other times of year, in freshwaters near the mouths of all rivers in Connecticut that drain into Long Island Sound (Marcy 1976a, Whitworth *et al.* 1975). There may be anadromous populations found in some rivers because an anadromous population was documented in the Saugatuck River. Anonymous (1930) and Booth (1967) postulated that some populations in Connecticut might have had an anadromous component. Spawning occurs in late fall and winter, often in the upper end of estuaries. Adults reach lengths of 20-30 cm, and feed on a variety of invertebrates and fishes.

Urophycis chuss (Walbaum, 1792), red hake

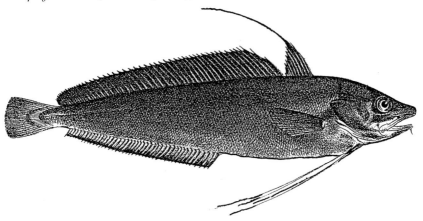

Figure 111. *Urophycis chuss*, from DeKay (1842), figure 150.

This marine species is distributed along the Atlantic coast of North America from Nova Scotia to Virginia. Individuals occasionally enter freshwaters near the mouths of all Connecticut watercourses that drain into Long Island Sound (Whitworth and Schmidt 1971). Adults often reach lengths of 40-50 cm, and feed on a variety of invertebrates and fishes.

Urophycis regia (Walbaum, 1792), spotted hake

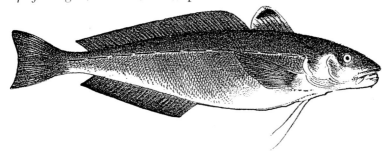

Figure 112. *Urophycis regia*, from DeKay (1842), figure 149.

This marine species is distributed along the Atlantic coast from southern New England to Florida. Individuals occasionally enter freshwaters near the mouths of all Connecticut rivers that empty into Long Island Sound (P. Howell-Heller, DEP). Lengths of 30-40 cm, are often attained and they feed on a variety of fishes and invertebrates.

Urophycis tenuis (Mitchill, 1814), white hake.

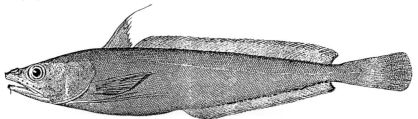

Figure 113. *Urophycis tenuis*, from Goode and Bean (1895), figure 312.

This marine species is distributed along the Atlantic coast from Newfoundland to North Carolina. Individuals occasionally enter freshwaters near the mouths of all rivers of Connecticut that empty into Long Island Sound (D. Tolderlund, U.S. Coast Guard Academy). Lengths of 60-70 are often attained and they feed on a variety of fishes and invertebrates.

Family Gasterosteidae, sticklebacks

Five genera with about 7 species (marine and freshwater) are found in the waters of the northern hemisphere. Five species have been collected in the freshwaters of Connecticut. Although a few freshwater populations were documented for *Apeltes quadracus*, there may be distinct freshwater populations of both *Pungitius pungitius* and *Gasterosteus aculeatus*. Additionally, more research may reveal that all of those species may have anadromous populations besides the saltwater and freshwater populations.

Spawning usually occurs from spring through at least midsummer, and most species reach sexual maturity in 1 year. The coloration of males often intensifies during spawning and they select and defend a territory in vegetation. They build a nest of plant materials that are held together with a kidney secretion. Females enter the nest and lay their eggs after elaborate courtship activities. Males then chase the females from the nest and guard the eggs until they hatch. Males often care for the young for a short time.

Key to the species of Gasterosteidae

1. Pelvic bones not joined   *Apeltes quadracus*, this page
   Pelvic bones joined   2

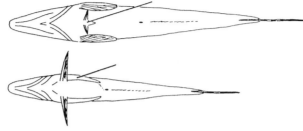

***Figure 114.* Pelvic bones joined (upper) and not joined (lower).**

2. Caudal peduncle without a
   lateral keel   *Culaea inconstans*, page 157
   Caudal peduncle with a lateral
   keel   3

3. Seven-11 dorsal spines   *Pungitius pungitius*, page 158
   Zero to 4 dorsal spines   4

4. Twenty-eight or more bony plates
   on a side   *Gasterosteus aculeatus*, page 157
   Five or 6 bony plates on a side   *G. wheatlandi*, page 158

Apeltes quadracus (Mitchill, 1815), fourspine stickleback

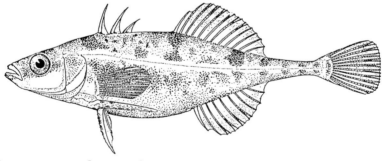

Figure 115. *Apeltes quadracus*, from Jordan and Evermann (1896-1900), figure 322.

    This marine species is distributed along the Atlantic coast from Nova Scotia to Virginia. Some populations are restricted to freshwaters. First reported in Connecticut by Ayres (1843b). Populations containing many age classes and spawning adults are regularly found throughout most of the year in freshwaters near the mouths of all watercourses in Connecticut that drain into Long Island Sound. There are also a few populations that are restricted to freshwater (Whitworth *et al.* 1968). Adults reach lengths of 4-6 cm, and feed on a variety of invertebrates.

Culaea inconstans (Kirtland, 1841), brook stickleback

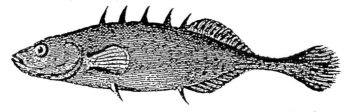

Figure 116. *Culaea inconstans*, from Kirtland (1840a), plate II, figure 1.

This introduced species in widely distributed in the freshwaters of northern North America. First reported in Connecticut by Behnke and Wetzel (1960). None have been documented in that drainage basin (Connecticut River) since Whitworth *et al.* (1968). Lengths of 6-8 cm are reached and they feed on a variety of invertebrates.

Gasterosteus aculeatus Linnaeus, 1758, threespine stickleback

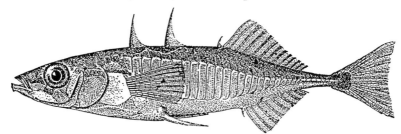

Figure 117. *Gasterosteus aculeatus*, from DeKay (1842), figure 8.

This species has marine populations along the eastern, southern, and western coasts of North America. There are also freshwater populations along both coasts and in the Great Lakes region of North America. Only saltwater populations are known in Connecticut. Populations containing many age classes, and occasionally spawning adults, are commonly captured throughout most of the year in some years, and occasionally in others, in freshwaters near the mouths of rivers that drain into Long Island Sound (Whitworth *et al.* 1975). Adults often reach lengths of 6-8 cm, and feed on a variety of invertebrates and small fishes.

Gasterosteus wheatlandi Putnam, 1867, blackspotted stickleback

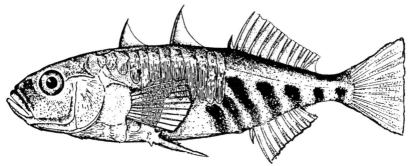

Figure 118. *Gasterosteus wheatlandi*, from Thomson *et al.* (1971), figure 64.

This marine species is distributed along the Atlantic coast from Newfoundland to New York. Individuals occasionally enter freshwaters near the mouths of all rivers in Connecticut that empty into Long Island Sound (Thomson *et al.* 1971). Adults reach lengths of 5-8 cm, and feed on a variety of invertebrates and small fishes.

Pungitius pungitius (Linnaeus, 1758), ninespine stickleback

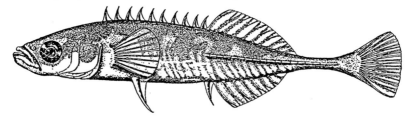

Figure 119. *Pungitius pungitius*, from Bigelow and Welsh (1924), figure 72.

This species is distributed in both freshwaters and saltwaters in the northern hemisphere. Only saltwater populations are known to inhabit Connecticut waters. Populations containing many age classes and often spawning adults are commonly found throughout most of the year in some years, and occasionally in others, in all rivers in Connecticut that drain into Long Island Sound (Whitworth *et al.* 1968). Adults reach lengths of 4-6 cm, and feed on a variety of invertebrates.

Family Gobiidae, gobies

Two hundred genera with about 1500 species (mostly marine, some freshwater) are distributed throughout the world. One species has been collected in the freshwaters of Connecticut.

Gobiosoma bosc (Lacepede, 1900), naked goby

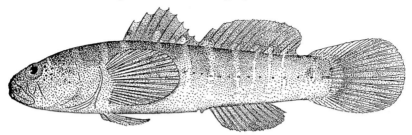

Figure 120. *Gobiosoma bosc*, from Hildebrand and Cable (1940), figure 30.

This marine species is distributed along the Atlantic coast from Massachusetts to Florida. Some adults and juveniles during spring and summer, typically enter freshwaters near the mouths of all the rivers of Connecticut that drain into Long Island Sound (Whitworth and Schmidt 1971). Lengths of 4-7 cm are often attained and they feed on a variety of invertebrates and small fishes.

Family Ictaluridae, bullhead catfishes

Nine genera with about 50 species are distributed in the freshwaters of North America. Five species have been collected in the freshwaters of Connecticut. All species found in Connecticut have poison glands near the bases of the dorsal and pectoral spines. Secretions from these glands, introduced in wounds inflicted by the spines, may cause temporary pain. Spawning occurs from spring through early summer, depending on the species. Nests are constructed by cleaning the substrate in a small area, often below vegetation or debris. Some species utilize depressions in the substrate, or bank, or hollow logs for nests. Both sexes usually participate in clearing the nest and fanning the eggs. Eggs are laid in masses. Usually, one or both parents guard the young for a short time. Young especially, and often other age classes travel in schools.

The population dynamics of this family in some watercourses in Connecticut are very interesting. For example, in the Connecticut River from Enfield south, populations of brown bullhead were most abundant until the middle 1960s, and white catfish predominated from then until the present. However, since the middle 1980s, channel catfish populations have been rapidly expanding (R. Jacobs, DEP).

Key to the species of Ictaluridae
1. Caudal fin deeply forked   2
    Caudal fin not deeply forked   3

2. Anal rays, 18-25, relative head
    size large   *Ameiurus catus*, in part, page 161
    Anal rays, 25-29, relative head
    size small   *Ictalurus punctatus*, page 163

3. Serrae on posterior edge of pectoral
    spines weak or absent   *Ameiurus melas*, page 161
    Serrae on posterior edge of pectoral
    spines moderate to strong   4

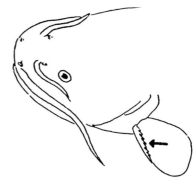

Figure 121. Pectoral spines with weak (left) and strong (right) serrae.

4. Chin barbels whitish, anal rays
    usually > 24, anterior anal rays little
    longer than posterior rays   *A. natalis*, page 162
    Chin barbels dusky to black, anal rays
    usually < 24, anterior anal
    rays much longer than posterior rays   5

5. Chin barbels pale, relative head
    size large   *A. catus*, in part, page 161
    Chin barbels dark, relative head
    size small   *A. nebulosus*, page 162

Ameiurus catus (Linnaeus, 1758), white catfish

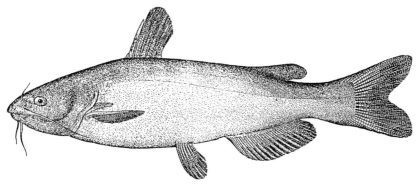

Figure 122. *Ameiurus catus*, from H.W. Smith (1891), plate XLV.

This introduced species is widely distributed in fresh and brackish waters in eastern North America. First reported in Connecticut by Behnke and Wetzel (1960). Populations are now established in lakes, ponds, and larger watercourses of most drainage basins of Connecticut. Sexual maturity is reached in 2-4 years and lengths of 50-60 cm are often attained. They feed on a variety of invertebrates and fishes.

Ameiurus melas (Rafinesque, 1820), black bullhead

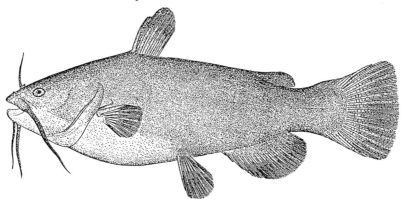

Figure 123. *Ameiurus melas*, from Evermann and Kendall (1892), plate XI.

This introduced species is widely distributed in the freshwaters of North America. First reported in Connecticut by Behnke and Wetzel (1960). Although specimens have been collected in two other locations, there is no evidence that any of them represent established populations. Sexual maturity is reached in 2-3 years and lengths of 30-40 cm are attained. They feed on a variety of invertebrates and fishes.

Ameiurus natalis (Lesueur, 1819), yellow bullhead

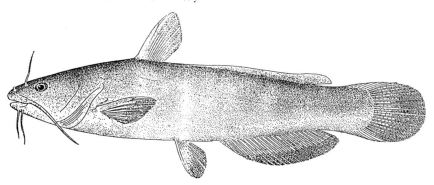

Figure 124. *Ameiurus natalis*, from Evermann and Kendall (1892), plate XII.

This introduced species is widely distributed in the freshwaters of North America. First reported in Connecticut by Whitworth, Minta, and Orciari (1980). A few populations are established in all of the major drainage basins of Connecticut (R. Jacobs, DEP). Sexual maturity is reached in 2-3 years and lengths of 30-40 cm are attained. They feed on a variety of invertebrates and fishes.

Ameiurus nebulosus (Lesueur, 1819), brown bullhead

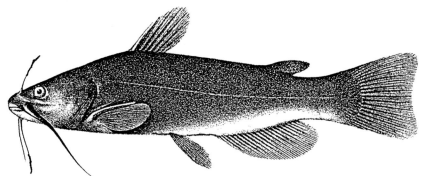

Figure 125. *Ameiurus nebulosus*, from Storer (1855), figure 3, plate 20.

This native species is widely distributed in the freshwaters of North America. First reported in Connecticut by DeKay (1842). Populations are found in all of the drainage basins of Connecticut, mainly in lakes, ponds, and larger rivers. Individuals may be found in any body of water. Sexual maturity is reached in 2-3 years and lengths of 30-40 cm are attained. They consume a variety of invertebrates and small fishes.

Ictalurus punctatus (Rafinesque, 1818), channel catfish

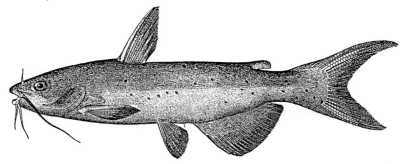

Figure 126. *Ictalurus punctatus*, from Evermann and Kendall (1892), plate XIII.

This introduced species is widely distributed in the freshwaters of North America. First reported in Connecticut by Behnke and Wetzel (1960). Within the last ten years this species has become one of the dominant ictalurids in the Connecticut River (W. Hyatt and R. Jacobs, DEP). Individuals have been collected in the Housatonic River and will probably show up soon in lakes and ponds in all drainage basins of the state. Sexual maturity is reached in 2-4 years and lengths of 50-60 cm are attained. They consume a variety of invertebrates, fishes, and miscellaneous items.

Family Labridae, wrasses

Fifty-seven genera with about 500 species (marine) are found in the Atlantic, Indian, and Pacific Oceans. Two species have been collected in the freshwaters of Connecticut.

Key to the species of Labridae
1. Opercles mostly naked, < 18
    dorsal spines   *Tautoga onitis*, page 164
    Opercles mostly scaled, > 17
    dorsal spines   *Tautogolabrus adspersus*, page 164

Tautoga onitis (Linnaeus, 1758), tautog

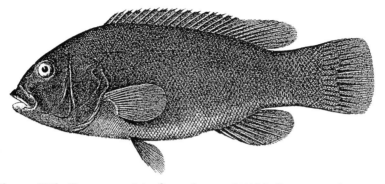

Figure 127. *Tautoga onitis*, from Storer (1855), figure 2, plate 20.

This marine species is distributed along the Atlantic coast from Nova Scotia to South Carolina. Individuals occasionally enter freshwaters near the mouths of all Connecticut rivers that drain into Long Island Sound (Whitworth and Schmidt 1971). Adults often reach lengths in excess of 40 cm, and feed on a variety of invertebrates.

Tautogolabrus adspersus (Walbaum, 1792), cunner

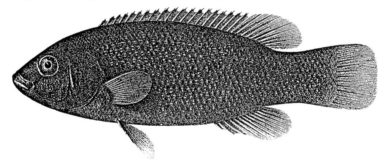

Figure 128. *Tautogolabrus adspersus*, from Storer (1855), figure 1, plate 20.

This marine species is distributed along the Atlantic coast of North America from Labrador to Virginia. Individuals occasionally enter freshwater near the mouths of all of the rivers in Connecticut that drain into Long Island Sound (Whitworth *et al.* 1975). Adults often reach lengths of 15-20 cm, and feed on a variety of invertebrates and small fishes.

Family Lophiidae, goosefishes

Four genera with about 25 species are found in the Arctic, Atlantic, Indian, and Pacific Oceans. One species has been collected in the freshwaters of Connecticut.

Lophius americanus Valenciennes, 1837, goosefish

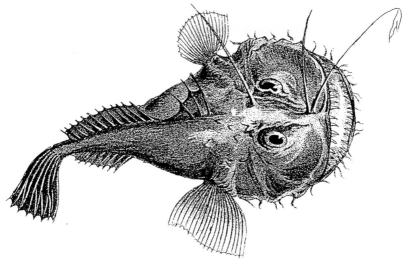

***Figure 129. Lophius americanus*, from DeKay (1842), figure 87.**

This marine species is found along the Atlantic coast of North America from Newfoundland to North Carolina. Individuals occasionally enter freshwaters near the mouths of all rivers of Connecticut that drain into Long Island Sound (P. Howell-Heller, DEP). Adults often reach lengths in excess of 60 cm, and feed on a variety of invertebrates and small fishes.

Family Loricariidae, suckermouth catfishes

About 70 genera containing a minimum of 550 species are found in freshwaters from Costa Rica and South America. One species has been collected in the freshwaters of Connecticut, although others have probably been introduced also. Since so many new species have been described in this family (Boeseman 1968), and the geographic origin of the individuals was not known, this species could not be identified. Therefore, a typical loricariid is illustrated. The individuals (4-8 cm) we collected in a drainage basin of the Thames River would not be able to live long enough to establish viable populations.

Figure 130. Hypostomus plecostomus (Linnaeus, 1776), suckermouth catfish, from Shaw (1804), plate 101.

Family Moronidae, temperate basses

One genus with 6 species (marine, freshwater, and anadromous) is found in North America and in marine waters off Europe, North America, and North Africa. Two species have been collected in the freshwaters of Connecticut. Both species often travel in large schools, which are sometimes segregated by age classes.

Key to the species of Moronidae

1. Dorsal fins separate, teeth on
   basihyal, sides striped   *Morone saxatilis*, page 168
   Dorsal fins joined by a membrane,
   no teeth on basihyal,
   sides not striped   *M. americana*, page 167

Morone americana (Gmelin, 1789), white perch

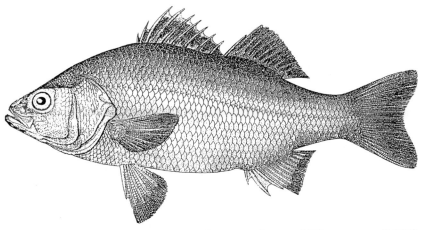

Figure 131. ***Morone americana*,** **from Jordan and Eigenmann (1888), plate LXVII.**

This species is distributed along the Atlantic coast and in freshwaters from Nova Scotia to Florida. First reported in Connecticut by Linsley (1844b), who reported only saltwater populations. This species probably entered the freshwaters of Connecticut as an anadromous species and subsequently developed a gene pool that had to live in freshwaters. Since the early 1900s, that stock has been transported to all drainage basins of the state. An anadromous population, as well as a saltwater population, has been documented in the Thames River drainage basin. Sexual maturity is reached in 2-4 years. Spawning occurs in spring and eggs are broadcast and adhere to the substrate, usually vegetation or rocks. Adults often reach lengths of 25-35 cm, and feed on a variety of invertebrates and small fishes.

Morone saxatilis (Walbaum, 1792), striped bass

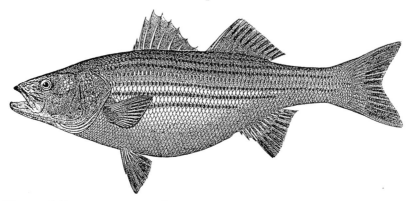

Figure 132. *Morone saxatilis*, from Jordan and Eigenmann (1888), plate LXIX.

This marine species is distributed along the Atlantic coast of North America from Nova Scotia to Florida. Populations have been introduced along the Pacific coast of North America. One freshwater population is found near the Atlantic coast and many freshwater populations have been introduced throughout North America. This species is anadromous in some rivers from the Hudson River southward. Populations containing many age classes, but never spawning adults, are often found in freshwaters near the mouths of all rivers of Connecticut that empty into Long Island Sound. Although specimens can be found at any time of year, greater numbers are often found in spring and fall (Merriman 1941, Marcy 1976a, Whitworth *et al.* 1975, Warner and Kynard 1986, Kynard and Warner 1987). Adults often reach lengths in excess of 70 cm, and feed on a variety of fishes and larger invertebrates.

Family Mugilidae, mullets

Thirteen genera with 95 species (mostly marine, some freshwater) are distributed worldwide. Two marine species have been collected in the freshwaters of Connecticut.

Key to the species of Mugilidae
1. Eleven spines and rays in the anal fin,
   few scales on the 2nd dorsal fin   *Mugil cephalus*, page 169
   Twelve spines and rays in the anal fin,
   many scales on the 2nd dorsal fin   *M. curema*, page 169

Mugil cephalus Linnaeus, 1758, striped mullet

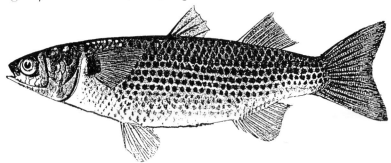

Figure 133. *Mugil cephalus*, from DeKay (1842), figure 42.

This marine species is distributed worldwide, centered on the tropics. Populations are found as far north as Nova Scotia on the east coast of North America. Linsley (1844b) reported them present only in saltwaters. Individuals occasionally enter freshwaters near saltwaters (D. Tolderlund, U.S. Coast Guard Academy). Lengths of 20-40 cm are reached in other areas of their range and they feed on a variety of plant and animal foods that are often found in the detritus.

Mugil curema Valenciennes, 1836, white mullet

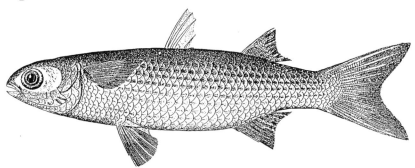

Figure 134. *Mugil curema*, from Smith (1891), plate LI.

This marine species is distributed along the east coast of North America from Massachusetts to Brazil, and along the Pacific coast from California to Chile. During summer and fall individuals occasionally enter freshwaters near the mouths of all watercourses in Connecticut that drain into Long Island Sound (Whitworth and Marsh 1980). Lengths of 15-25 cm are reached and they feed on a variety of plant and animal foods that are often found in the detritus.

Family Ophidiidae, cusk-eels

Forty-eight genera with about 164 species (mostly marine) are found in the Atlantic, Indian, and Pacific Oceans. One species has been collected in the freshwaters of Connecticut.

Ophidion marginatum (DeKay, 1842), striped cusk-eel

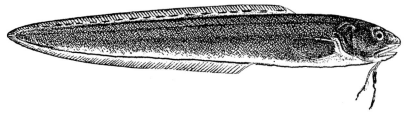

Figure 135. *Ophidion marginatum*, from DeKay (1842), figure 169.

This marine species is distributed along the Atlantic coast from Massachusetts to South America, more commonly found in warmer waters. Individuals occasionally enter freshwaters near the mouths of rivers in Connecticut that drain into Long Island Sound (C. Fontneau, Omni Analysis). Lengths of about 2 cm have been reported in freshwaters and a variety of invertebrates are consumed.

Family Osmeridae, smelts

Six genera with about 10 species (anadromous, marine, and freshwater) are distributed in the northern hemisphere. One anadromous species and its landlocked form have been collected in the freshwaters of Connecticut.

Osmerus mordax (Mitchill, 1814), rainbow smelt

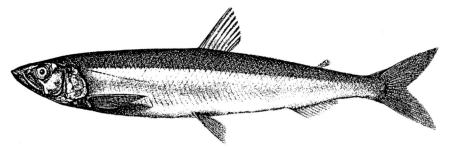

Figure 136. *Osmerus mordax*, from Storer (1858), figure 4, plate 25.

This anadromous species is distributed along the Atlantic coast from Nova Scotia to Florida. First reported in Connecticut by DeKay (1842). Anadromous populations were documented for the Thames and Connecticut River drainage basins and landlocked populations have been introduced into some lakes in Connecticut; however, individuals may be collected in freshwaters near the mouths of any watercourse in Connecticut that drains into Long Island Sound (Whitworth *et al.* 1975).

This species may be similar to white perch in that both saltwater and freshwater populations have developed from an anadromous form. No saltwater populations have been documented, although eggs have been found attached to the substrate in saltwaters. Spawning occurs in late winter-early spring. Males develop nuptial tubercles and large groups of fish spawn, usually at night. Eggs are broadcast and adhere to whatever they strike. No care is given the eggs or young. Adults then return to the ocean. Sexual maturity is reached in 1-3 years and lengths of 15-25 cm (anadromous) and 10-15 cm (freshwater) are attained. They feed on a variety of invertebrates and small fishes.

Family Percidae, perches

Nine genera with about 160 species are distributed in the freshwaters of the northern hemisphere, mostly in North America. Four species have been collected in the freshwaters of Connecticut.

Key to the species of Percidae

1. Preopercle strongly serrate, maxilla
    usually extends past the middle of eye   2
    Preopercle entire or weakly serrate,
    maxilla usually does not
    extend past the middle of eye   3

2. Canine teeth absent   *Perca flavescens*, page 173
    Canine teeth present   *Stizostedion vitreum*, page 174

3. Least depth between lateral line and
    first dorsal base contained < 4 times
    in depth below lateral line   *Etheostoma olmstedi*, page 172
    Least depth between lateral line and
    first dorsal base contained > 4 times
    in depth below lateral line   *E. fusiforme*, page 172

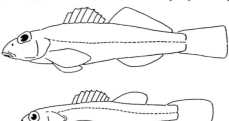

Figure 137. **Position of lateral line in *Etheostoma fusiforme* (right) and *E. olmstedi* (left).**

Etheostoma fusiforme (Girard, 1854), swamp darter

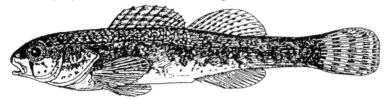

Figure 138. Etheostoma fusiforme, from Whitworth et al. (1968), page 113.

This native species is found in coastal freshwaters from Maine to North Carolina. Connecticut was first reported within the range by Jordan and Evermann (1896). Except for a few populations in coastal drainages between the Connecticut and Thames Rivers, all populations are in streams, lakes, and ponds east of the Thames and Quinebaug Rivers (Schmidt and Whitworth 1979). Populations are usually associated with vegetation. Sexual maturity is reached in 1 year. Spawning occurs in spring and eggs are deposited over vegetation. Lengths of 3-6 cm are often attained and they feed on a variety of invertebrates.

Etheostoma olmstedi Storer,1842, tessellated darter

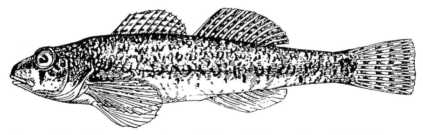

Figure 139. Etheostoma olmstedi, from Whitworth et al. (1968), page 114.

This native species is found in freshwaters of eastern North America from the St. Lawrence River in southern Canada to rivers in the northern parts of Florida. First reported in Connecticut by Storer (1842a); it was described from specimens collected near Hartford, Connecticut, by Charles H. Olmsted, President of the Hartford Natural History Society. Populations, often large, are found in all drainage basins of Connecticut. Most are associated with streams, however, lake and pond populations are occasionally encountered.

Males develop pads on the pectoral fins during the spawning season and their color intensifies. Males select territories, often under rocks. After the female lays her eggs, she leaves the nest area and the males cares for the eggs. Lengths of 7-13 cm are often attained and they feed on a variety of invertebrates.

Perca flavescens (Mitchill, 1814), yellow perch

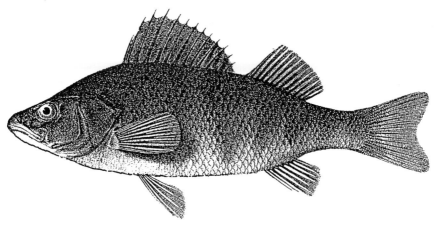

Figure 140. *Perca flavescens*, from Storer (1855), figure 1, plate 2.

This native species is widely distributed throughout the eastern half of North America. First reported in Connecticut by Ayres (1843a). Populations are found in all drainage basins of the state, usually associated with lakes, ponds, and larger streams. Sexual maturity is reached in 2-5 years and spawning occurs in early spring. Eggs are deposited in long ribbons bound together by a jellylike substance and are attached to plants. No care is provided the eggs. All age classes travel in large schools and consume a variety of invertebrates and fishes.

Stizostedion vitreum (Mitchill, 1818), walleye

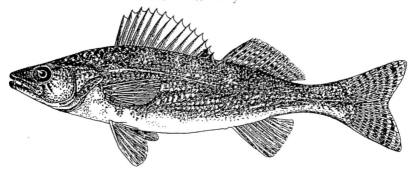

Figure 141. *Stizostedion vitreum*, from Whitworth *et al.* (1968), page 116.

This introduced species is spottily distributed throughout northern and eastern freshwaters of North America. Populations have been widely introduced outside of this range, often not successfully. First reported in Connecticut by Rice (1887). Although specimens have been introduced since then, small populations are established in only the main stem of the Connecticut and Housatonic Rivers. Populations have been introduced into a few lakes recently by the DEP. Sexual maturity is reached in 2-6 years and spawning occurs in early spring. Eggs are broadcast over rocky areas and no parental care is given the eggs or young. Lengths in excess of 50 cm are often attained and they feed on a variety of fishes and invertebrates.

Family Percopsidae, trout-perches

One genus with two species is found in freshwaters of northern North America. One species has been collected in the freshwaters of Connecticut

Percopsis omiscomaycus (Walbaum, 1792), trout-perch

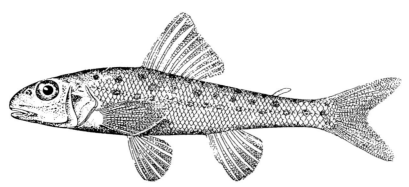

Figure 142. *Percopsis omiscomaycus*, from Jordan and Evermann (1896-1900), figure 329.

This introduced species is widely distributed in the freshwaters of northern North America. Only reported from Connecticut in 1879 by specimens obtained from the Housatonic River drainage basin and deposited in the zoology museum at Harvard. Specimens were also obtained from the Housatonic River in Massachusetts (McCabe 1942). No other specimens have been collected in that drainage basin. Adults reach lengths of 12-18 cm and feed on a variety of invertebrates and small fishes.

Family Petromyzontidae, lampreys

Six genera with about 40 species (most freshwater, some anadromous) are found worldwide, mostly in the northern hemisphere. Two species (one anadromous, one freshwater) live all or part of their lives in the freshwaters of Connecticut. Adult lampreys may be either parasitic or nonparasitic, and one species of each life style lives in Connecticut. Juvenile (ammocoetes) and adult lampreys are identified using structures of the mouth and number of myomeres between the last gill opening and the anus. Past identifications of the species in this family in southern New England are difficult to evaluate. For example, Linsley (1844b) identified *Lampetra appendix* from the Housatonic River and sent specimens to Dr. Storer in Massachusetts, who agreed with him. He also reported that Dr. Ayres had a new species of lamprey from a stream near Hartford. I have not been able to find a reference to that specimen. However, the only species that has verified specimens from any drainage basin of the state until the middle 1900s is *Petromyzon marinus*.

Both species spawn in spring. Nests are constructed in gravel areas and eggs are deposited and covered. After spawning, adults die. Young (ammocoetes) burrow in the stream bottom and obtain food by filtering it from the water and substrate. Adults and young differ in appearance and after a few years in the bottom of the stream the young transform into the adult form and assume adult feeding habits.

Key to the species of Petromyzontidae

1. Mouth not hoodlike, no fine
   papillae around the edge of the
   mouth   2
   Mouth hoodlike, fine papillae
   around the edge of the mouth   3

2. Mouth with many large teeth   *Petromyzon marinus*, page 177
   Mouth with scattered weak teeth   *Lampetra appendix*, page 177

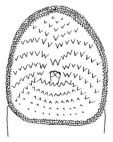

Figure 143. **Ventral view of mouth of adult *Petromyzon marinus* (right) and *Lampetra appendix* (left).**

3. Nonpigmented post-nostril area smaller than the nostril itself, melanophores on upper lip developed throughout, melanophores on caudal peduncle well developed throughout the region   *Petromyzon marinus*, page 177

   Nonpigmented post-nostril area about twice the size of nostril, melanophores on lower half of upper lip poorly developed, melanophores absent or poorly developed on lower margin of caudal peduncle   *Lampetra appendix*, page 177

Figure 144. **Dorsal view of head of juvenile (ammocoete), *Petromyzon marinus* (right) and *Lampetra appendix* (left).**

Lampetra appendix (DeKay, 1842), American brook lamprey

Figure 145. *Lampetra appendix*, from DeKay (1842), figure 211.

This introduced species is discontinuously distributed throughout the central and eastern areas of North America. Only known in Connecticut from one stream (Kettle Brook, a small tributary that enters the Connecticut River in Windsor Locks). That population has been known since the middle 1950s (Russell Hunter, formerly with the DEP and the University of Connecticut). Interestingly, a State Fisheries Hatchery was located on this brook for a period of time in the early 1900s. And this species may have been inadvertently introduced to the hatchery with a shipment of fish brought to the hatchery from out of state. This species transforms in fall and spawns the following spring, thus has a short adult life. Lengths of 15-25 cm are attained.

Petromyzon marinus Linnaeus, 1758, sea lamprey

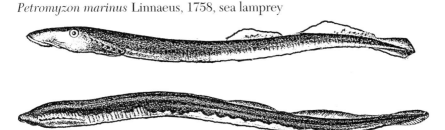

Figure 146. *Petromyzon marinus*, from DeKay (1842), adult (upper), figure 247, ammocoete (lower), figure 248.

This anadromous species is found along the Atlantic coasts of Europe (Ireland to the Baltic Sea) and North America (Labrador to Florida); some populations landlocked in freshwaters, *e.g.*, Lake Michigan. First reported from Connecticut by Linsley (1844b). Populations were probably established in all watercourses that had access to the ocean prior to the building of dams. Many populations have been documented in drainage basins of the Connecticut River, some populations in drainage basins of the central and western coastal rivers, and one population in a drainage basin of the Housatonic River.

Ammocoetes transform at age 5 years, migrate to Long Island Sound, and probably spend 1.5 years as parasites. We have little documentation of which species they utilize and where they live in saltwaters. As they mature sexually, they migrate to freshwaters, usually arriving in late winter to early spring. They then migrate upstream and complete the cycle by spawning and dying.

Family Pholidae, gunnels

Four genera with about 13 species are found in the north Atlantic and Pacific Oceans. One species has been collected in the freshwaters of Connecticut.

Pholis gunnellus (Linnaeus, 1758), rock gunnel

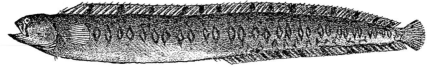

Figure 147. *Pholis gunnellus*, from DeKay (1842), figure 36.

This marine species is distributed along both sides of the Atlantic Ocean. It is found along the coast of North America from Labrador to Delaware. Individuals occasionally enter freshwaters near the mouths of all rivers of Connecticut that drain into Long Island Sound (P. Howell-Heller, DEP). Adults often reach lengths of 15-25 cm, and feed on a variety of invertebrates.

Family Pleuronectidae, righteye flounders

Forty-one genera with about 100 species (marine) are found in the Arctic, Atlantic, Indian, and Pacific Oceans; some populations may enter freshwaters. Two species have been collected in the freshwaters of Connecticut.

Key to the species of Pleuronectidae

1. Lateral line strongly curved
   over pectoral fins   *Pleuronectes ferrugineus*, page 179
   Lateral line not strongly curved
   over pectoral fins   *P. americanus*, page 179

Pleuronectes americanus Walbaum, 1792, winter flounder

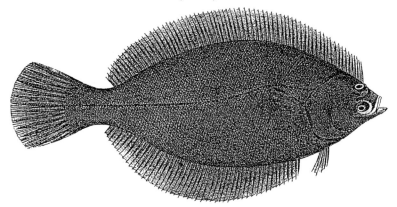

Figure 148. *Pleuronectes americanus*, from DeKay (1842), figure 153.

This marine species is distributed along the east coast of North America from Labrador to Georgia. Many juveniles (2-5 cm) during the summer months enter freshwaters, from their estuarine spawning grounds, near saltwaters of all watercourses of Connecticut that drain into Long Island Sound. Individuals from any age class occasionally enter at any time of the year (Whitworth and Schmidt 1971). Adults often reach lengths of 30-40 cm, and feed on a variety of invertebrates.

Pleuronectes ferrugineus (Storer, 1839), yellowtail flounder

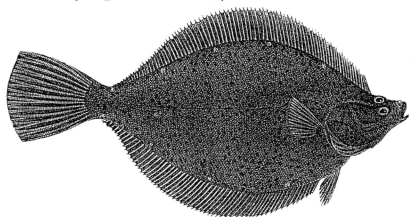

Figure 149. *Pleuronectes ferrugineus*, from DeKay (1842), figure 155.

This marine species is distributed along the Atlantic coast from Newfoundland and Labrador to Virginia. Individuals occasionally enter freshwaters near the mouths of all rivers of Connecticut that enter Long Island Sound (P. Howell-Heller, DEP). Adults often reach lengths of 35-45 cm and feed on a variety of invertebrates.

Family Poeciliidae, livebearers

Twenty-two genera with about 150 species (mostly freshwater, some marine) are distributed in North, Central, and South America. Three species have been collected in the freshwaters of Connecticut, although more have probably been introduced. Only one of them, *Gambusia affinis*, is native to North America and has been able to survive in one pond in Connecticut over the winter.

Gambusia affinis (Baird and Girard, 1853), western mosquitofish

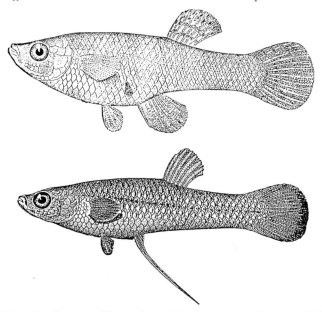

Figure 150. Gambusia affinis, from Evermann and Kendall (1892), plate XXV (female), and Hildebrand (1918), page 4 (male).

This introduced species is widely distributed in the freshwaters of North America. Although Steinmetz and Boehm (1980) reported the first population that overwintered in Connecticut (a pond on the campus of Southern Connecticut State University, New Haven), this species was probably introduced many times during the 1930s and 40s for mosquito control. Because this species cannot survive cold winters, that population will eventually perish. Sexual maturity is reached in 1 year. The anterior four to six anal rays of the male are modified into a grooved structure that is called the gonopodium. Males swim next to females, insert the gonopodium into the vent of the female, and transfer sperm along the groove to the female. Females are often only fertilized once and store a sperm supply. Young probably are born from June through September only. Males rarely live more than one year and females rarely live more than 2 or 3 years. Adults reach lengths of 3-7 cm, and feed on a variety of small invertebrates.

Poecilia reticulata Peters, 1859, guppy

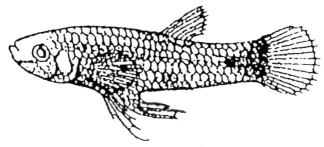

Figure 151. *Poecilia reticulata*, from Filippi (1869), figure 6.

This introduced species is found in the freshwaters of Venezuela, Guianas, Barbados, and Trinidad. Although it has probably been introduced many times in most drainage basins of the state, none of the individuals introduced should be able to establish viable populations. We captured individuals (1-4 cm) of both sexes.

Poeciliopsis sp

Figure 152. *Poeciliopsis* sp, courtesy of R. Jack Schultz.

There are at least 3 species and some all female forms of this genus, that are distributed in the freshwaters of Pacific coast drainage basins of Mexico, that could have been introduced (Schultz 1969). We captured a few individuals (2-4 cm) in some of the drainage basins of the Thames River. None of the introduced specimens should be able to establish viable populations.

Family Pomatomidae, bluefishes

Two genera with 3 species (marine) are distributed in the Atlantic, Indian, and Pacific Oceans. One species has been collected in the freshwaters of Connecticut.

Pomatomus saltatrix (Linnaeus, 1766), bluefish

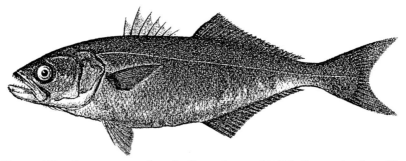

Figure 153. *Pomatomus saltatrix*, from Storer (1853), figure 1, plate 15.

This marine species is distributed throughout the warm and temperate seas of the world. Populations are found along the east coasts of North and South America from Nova Scotia to the southern coast of Argentina. Large populations of juveniles during the summer months regularly enter freshwaters near the mouths of all rivers of Connecticut that empty into Long Island Sound. They often enter at 5 cm, in early summer, and leave at 15 cm, in fall. Other age classes enter occasionally during the summer and early fall (Whitworth and Schmidt 1971). Adults often reach lengths in excess of 60 cm, and feed on a variety of fishes.

Family Rajidae, skates

Fourteen genera with about 190 species are found in all oceans. One species has been collected in the freshwaters of Connecticut.

Raja erinacea (Mitchill, 1825), little skate

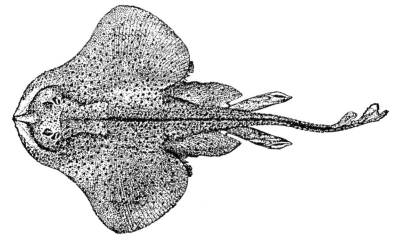

Figure 154. *Raja erinacea*, from Jordan and Evermann (1896-1900), figure 29.

This marine species is found along the Atlantic coast of North America from Nova Scotia to Florida. Individuals occasionally enter freshwaters near the mouths of all rivers of Connecticut that drain into Long Island Sound (P. Howell-Heller, DEP). Adults often reach lengths of 40-50 cm, and feed on a variety of invertebrates and fishes.

Family Salmonidae, trouts

Ten genera with about 68 species (most freshwater, some anadromous) are distributed worldwide, mainly in the northern hemisphere. Twelve species have been collected in the freshwaters of Connecticut. Young salmonids often have color patterns different from adults. These consist of a series of dark blotches of various shapes and sizes on their dorsum and sides (often called parr marks). Additionally, the young of anadromous forms have a stage between the parr and adult called a smolt. This is usually a silvery stage that, in color, resembles the adult.

Both juveniles and adults are included in the key for those species that have at least one viable population in the freshwaters of the state. Species that do not have at least one viable population are usually only included in the key to adults. Because external characteristics are extremely variable within each stage, and because hybrids and other species that are not included in the keys may be present, some specimens may be difficult to identify.

Various hybrids between selected members of this family have been made to obtain "superior" fishes by the DEP and by interested individuals and organizations, *e.g.*, the "tiger" (progeny of female brown trout and male brook trout), and the "splake" (progeny of male brook trout and female lake trout). Although the former is considered infertile, the latter produces a moderate number of fertile individuals that produce fertile progeny.

Salmonids usually make an upstream movement to spawn in fall and early winter. Females usually build redds (nests) in riffles by clearing areas with their caudal peduncle. After the eggs are laid and covered, adults leave. Young hatch in the spring.

Key to the species of Salmonidae

1. > 17 rays in dorsal fin   *Thymallus arcticus*, page 194
   < 17 rays in dorsal fin   2

2. Specimen > 10-12 cm   3
   Specimen < 10 cm (if specimens
   are near 10 cm, follow both options)   13

3. Maxilla does not extend to middle
   of the eye   *Prosopium cylindraceum*,
   page 190

   Maxilla extends to at least the
   middle of the eye   4

4. Anal rays > 12   5
   Anal rays < 13   7

5. Distinct black spots on back and
   caudal fin   6
   No distinct black spots on back
   and caudal fin   *Oncorhynchus kisutch*, page 187

6. 3 small black spots on both lobes
   of caudal fin   *O. tshawytscha*, page 190
   Spots only on upper lobe of
   caudal fin   *O. nerka*, page 189

7. Color pattern of light spots on
   a dark background   8
   Color pattern of dark spots on
   a light background   10

8. Pyloric caeca > 90, caudal fin

usually deeply forked, sides
usually do not have spots   *Salvelinus namaycush*, page 193
Pyloric caeca < 90, caudal fin
usually little forked, sides usually
have red or pink spots   9

9. Dorsal rays usually > 9, anal rays

Figure 155. **Ventral view of viscera showing pyloric caeca.**

usually > 8   *S. fontinalis*, page 193
Dorsal rays usually < 10, anal rays
usually < 9   *S. alpinus*, page 192

10. Maxilla extends only to posterior
    margin of eye, or slightly
    beyond   *Salmo salar*, page 191
    Maxilla extends well beyond
    posterior margin of eye   11

11. Basibranchial teeth present, yellow
    orange to red orange line on each
    side of throat along inner
    border of dentary bone   *Oncorhynchus clarki*, page 187
    Basibranchial teeth absent, no
    colored lines on each side of throat
    along inner side of dentary bone   12

12. Few or no spots on caudal fin, pale
    halos surround spots on sides   *Salmo trutta*, page 192
    Many spots on caudal fin, no pale
    halos surround spots on sides   *Oncorhynchus mykiss*, page 188

13. Maxilla extends to at least the
    middle of the eye   14
    Maxilla does not extend past the
    middle of the eye   *Prosopium cylindraceum*,
                                             page 190

14. Anal rays > 12   15

Anal rays < 12   16

15. Parr marks short, oval shaped and
    only extend a little below lateral line,
    adipose fin without melanophores   *Oncorhynchus nerka*, page 189
    Parr marks elongated and extend
    about as far below the lateral line
    as they extend above, adipose
    fin with melanophores   *O. kisutch*, page 187

16. Adipose fin with dark border,
    combined width of all parr marks
    < combined space between
    all parr marks   *O. mykiss*, page 188
    Adipose fin without dark border,
    combined width of parr marks
    equal to or > combined width
    of all parr marks = to or >
    combined space between all
    parr marks   17

17. Shortest caudal ray < 0.5 of longest
    caudal ray   *Salmo salar*, page 191
    Shortest caudal ray > 0.5 of
    longest caudal ray   18

18. Tip of chin with dark pigment,
    adipose fin clear, in life, below
    border, few dark spots below
    lateral line, usually < 10 parr marks   *Salvelinus fontinalis*, page 193
    Tip of chin with no dark pigment,
    adipose fin orange, in life, many
    dark spots below lateral line,
    usually > 10 parr marks   *Salmo trutta*, page 192

Oncorhynchus clarki (Richardson, 1836), cutthroat trout

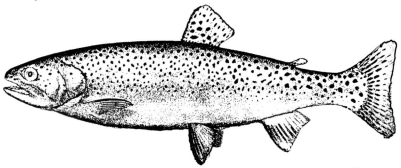

Figure 156. *Oncorhynchus clarki*, from Smith and Kendall (1921), figure 3.

This introduced species has anadromous and freshwater populations distributed along the Pacific coast of North America from California and north. Freshwater populations are established in most drainage basins from the Mississippi River westward. Although many individuals have been introduced into the freshwaters of Connecticut since the late 1800s, none of them have established viable populations. Sexual maturity is reached in 2-4 years and lengths of 25-35 cm are often attained. They consume a variety of invertebrates and small fishes.

Oncorhynchus kisutch (Walbaum, 1792), coho salmon

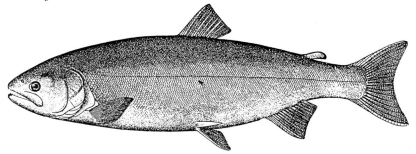

Figure 157. *Oncorhynchus kisutch*, from Bean (1889), figure 3, plate XLVI.

This introduced species has anadromous populations on both sides of the Pacific Ocean; some populations have been landlocked. Populations have been introduced into all drainage basins of Connecticut since the late 1800s. The DEP introduced a population into the Thames River Drainage Basin in the late 1960s and early 1970s. There are no known established populations. Adults attain lengths of 50-60 cm, and feed on a variety of fishes. Sexual maturity is attained in 2-4 years.

Oncorhynchus mykiss (Walbaum, 1792), rainbow trout

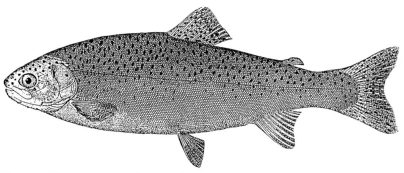

Figure 158. Oncorhynchus mykiss, from L. Stone (1896), plate 85.

This introduced species has anadromous and freshwater populations on both sides of the Pacific Ocean; in North America from Alaska to Mexico. Freshwater populations have been introduced throughout the world, both as a sport and a food fish. Populations were probably first introduced into the freshwaters of Connecticut during the 1870s from eggs obtained from Seth Green in nearby New York (Green 1874 and 1882). He probably obtained his eggs from the same source as the Connecticut Fish Commission, the McCloud River, California (Wales 1939). Since then, numerous freshwater and anadromous populations have been introduced into most drainage basins of the state. Only a few of these populations are able to maintain themselves. Sexual maturity is reached in 2-7 years and lengths of 40-50 cm are commonly attained. They consume a variety of aquatic insects and fishes.

Oncorhynchus nerka (Walbaum, 1792), sockeye salmon

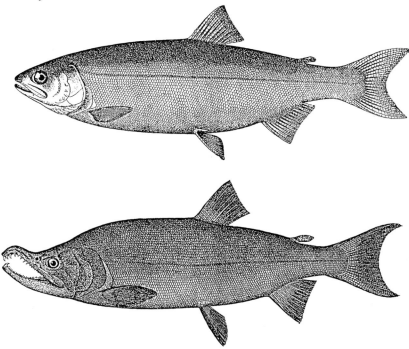

***Figure 159. Oncorhynchus nerka*, from Bean (1889), non-spawning adult (upper), figure 6, breeding male (lower), figure 7, plate XLVIII.**

This introduced species has anadromous and freshwater populations on both sides of the Pacific Ocean, in North America from Alaska to California. Populations have been introduced since the late 1800s. The population introduced into East Twin Lakes in the 1930s, as reported by Webster (1942), may be viable, although there is a strong possibility that none of the populations in this state could survive without help from humans. Sexual maturity is reached in 2-4 years and lengths of 35-45 cm are often attained. They feed on a variety of invertebrates.

Oncorhynchus tshawytscha (Walbaum, 1792), chinook salmon

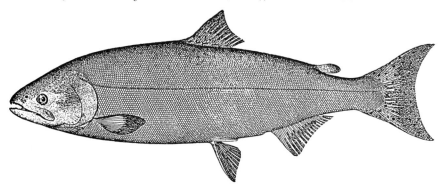

Figure 160. *Oncorhynchus tshawytscha*, from Bean (1889), figure 1, plate XLVI.

This introduced species has anadromous and freshwater populations on both sides of the Pacific; they are found in North America from Alaska to California. Both types have been introduced throughout the world, and freshwater populations have been established in many areas outside of the native range in North America. Since first introduced into the freshwaters of Connecticut in the late 1800s, no viable population have been established. Adults reach lengths in excess of 50 cm, and feed on fishes. Sexual maturity is attained in 2-5 years.

Prosopium cylindraceum (Pallas, 1784), round whitefish

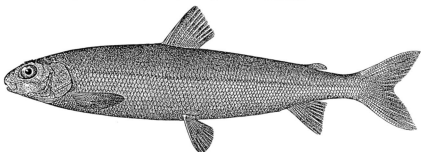

Figure 161. *Prosopium cylindraceum*, from H.W. Smith (1890a), plate XXXVI.

This introduced species is discontinuously distributed across northern North America and Europe in freshwater. Stocks were introduced into East Twin Lakes in the 1870s. Later references, *i.e.*, Bean (1885) and Anonymous (1922), were probably based on those introductions. Since then, every so often, a specimen has been obtained from that lake (John Orintas, Peter Minta, James Moulton, and Cole Wilde, DEP). Sexual maturity is reached in 2-3 years and lengths of 30-40 cm are often attained. They consume a variety of invertebrates.

Salmo salar Linnaeus, 1758, Atlantic salmon

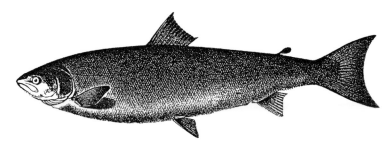

Figure 162. *Salmo salar*, from Storer (1858), figure 2, plate 25.

Anadromous and freshwater populations are found in North America from northern Quebec to Connecticut, and in Europe from Portugal to the Arctic circle. First documented in Connecticut by Linsley (1844b) although popular literature reported them earlier, *i.e.*, Pease and Niles (1819). Only anadromous populations were reported. All populations were eliminated in Connecticut prior to the middle 1800s. Both landlocked and anadromous stocks were introduced during the late 1800s; however, all efforts were unsuccessful. Anadromous stocks have been introduced, beginning in the 1960s, to the Connecticut River drainage basin in New England in an effort to restore the species to that portion of its historic range. Most individuals that have returned have been captured, transported to hatcheries, and held until sexually mature. These fish have been spawned with each other in an attempt to develop a gene pool that will successfully return to this drainage basin. Results to date are encouraging (Gephard *et al.* 1992). Some stocks also have been introduced into a few areas of the Thames River drainage basin. Beyond the restoration effort, DEP has released, and continues to release, adult Atlantic salmon into the Naugatuck and Shetucket rivers to support a recreational fishery. These adults are no longer of use to the restoration effort and would otherwise be discarded. Sexual maturity is reached in 4-9 years. Adults often reach lengths in excess of 60 cm, and feed on a variety of fishes and invertebrates.

Salmo trutta Linnaeus, 1758, brown trout

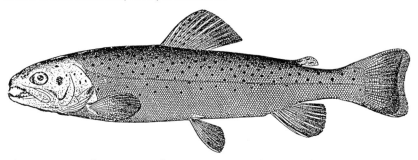

Figure 163. *Salmo trutta*, from Evermann (1891), plate XXIII.

This introduced species has anadromous and freshwater populations native to Europe and western Asia. Freshwater and anadromous populations have been widely introduced throughout the world. Since this species was first introduced in Connecticut, probably in the 1860s, many freshwater and anadromous populations have been stocked. Viable populations are found in all drainage basins of the state, especially in western Connecticut. A few anadromous specimens are still produced from the gene pools in some of the coastal streams. Sexual maturity is reached in 2-5 years. Adults of freshwater forms often reach lengths of 30-40 cm; anadromous forms are larger, and feed on a variety of invertebrates and fishes.

Salvelinus alpinus (Linnaeus, 1758), Arctic char

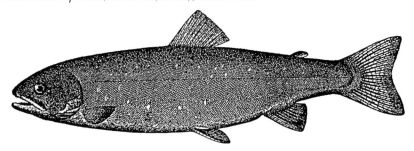

Figure 164. *Salvelinus alpinus*, from Kendall (1915-1916), figure 18.

This introduced species has anadromous and freshwater populations with a circumpolar distribution in the northern hemisphere. Although individuals have been introduced in Connecticut since the late 1800s, none of them have established viable populations. Sexual maturity is reached in 2-3 years and lengths of 20-30 cm are attained. They consume a variety of invertebrates.

Salvelinus fontinalis (Mitchill, 1814), brook trout

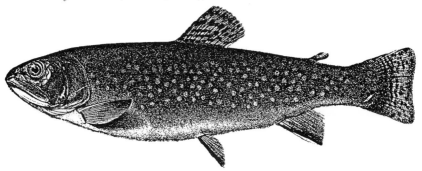

Figure 165. *Salvelinus fontinalis*, from Storer (1858), figure 3, plate 25.

This native species is found in the eastern half of North America. It has been widely introduced outside of that range. First reported in Connecticut by DeKay (1842). Populations are found in all drainage basins of the state, usually in the small to medium sized streams. Sexual maturity is reached in 1-3 years and lengths of 20-30 cm are attained. They feed on a variety of invertebrates.

Salvelinus namaycush (Walbaum, 1792), lake trout

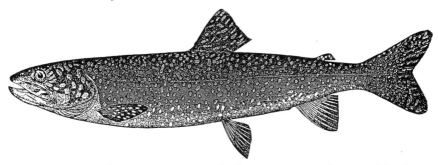

Figure 166. *Salvelinus namaycush*, from H.W. Smith (1890b), plate XXXIX.

This introduced species is found in freshwaters of the northern part of North America and has been widely introduced outside of that range. Although specimens have been introduced in Connecticut since the late 1800s (Pease 1874, Anonymous 1875a), none of them have established viable populations. Sexual maturity is reached in 3 to 9 years and lengths in excess of 60 cm are often attained. They consume a variety of fishes and invertebrates.

Thymallus arcticus (Pallas, 1776), Arctic grayling

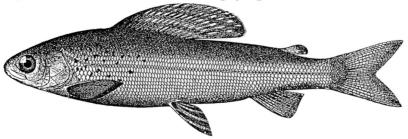

Figure 167. *Thymallus arcticus*, from Evermann (1891), plate XXII.

This introduced species is found in the colder waters of North America from Montana to Alaska. Populations have been widely introduced outside of this range. Although individuals have been introduced into the freshwaters of this state since the late 1870s (Pease 1874), none of them have established a viable population. Sexual maturity is reached in 5-8 years and spawning occurs in early spring. Lengths of 30-40 cm are attained and a variety of invertebrates are consumed.

Family Sciaenidae, drums

Fifty genera with about 210 species (mostly marine, a few freshwater) are distributed worldwide. Five marine species have been collected in the freshwaters of Connecticut.

Key to the species of Sciaenidae

1. No barbel on chin   2
   At least one barbel on chin   4

2. Dorsal rays > 29   *Leiostomus xanthurus*, page 196
   Dorsal rays < 30   3

3. Dorsal rays > 24   *Cynoscion regalis*, page 195
   Dorsal rays < 23   *Bairdiella chrysoura*, page 195

4. Single barbel on chin   *Menticirrhus saxatilis*, page 196
   More than one barbel on chin   *Micropogonias undulatus*,
                                         page 197

Bairdiella chrysoura (Lacepede, 1802), silver perch

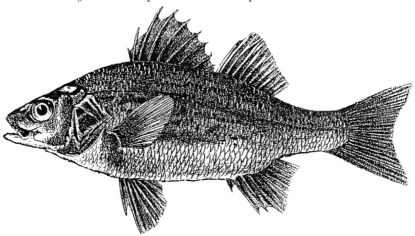

Figure 168. *Bairdiella chrysoura*, from DeKay (1842), figure 2.

This marine species is distributed along the east coast of North America from New York to Texas. Individuals occasionally enter freshwaters near the mouths of all rivers of the state that drain into Long Island Sound (Whitworth, Minta and Orciari 1980). Lengths of 15-20 cm are attained and they consume a variety of invertebrates and small fishes.

Cynoscion regalis (Bloch and Schneider, 1801), weakfish

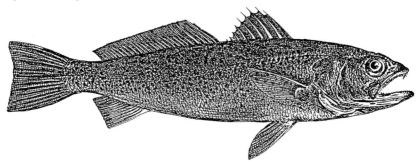

Figure 169. *Cynoscion regalis*, from DeKay (1842), figure 24.

This marine species is distributed along the Atlantic coast from Nova Scotia to Florida. Younger age classes (2-8 cm) during the summer months regularly enter freshwaters near the mouths of all rivers in Connecticut that drain into Long Island Sound (Marcy 1976a, Whitworth *et al.* 1975). They consume a variety of invertebrates and small fishes. Linsley (1844b) hypothesized that the numbers of this species utilizing freshwaters were inversely related to populations of *Pomatomus saltatrix*. Because populations of the latter have been so high for many of the last 20 years, this could explain why the populations of *C. regalis* in freshwaters have been so low.

Leiostomus xanthurus Lacepede, 1802, spot

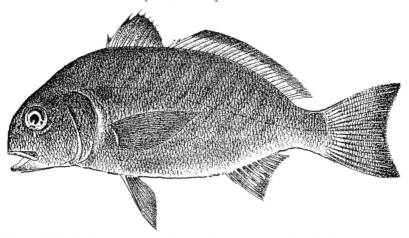

Figure 170. *Leiostomus xanthurus*, from DeKay (1842), figure 195.

This marine species is distributed along the east coast of North America from Massachusetts to Texas. Individuals often enter freshwaters near the mouths of all rivers of Connecticut that drain into Long Island Sound (Whitworth, Minta, and Orciari 1980). Lengths of 20-25 cm are often reached and they feed on a variety of invertebrates and small fishes.

Menticirrhus saxatilis (Bloch and Schneider, 1801), northern kingfish

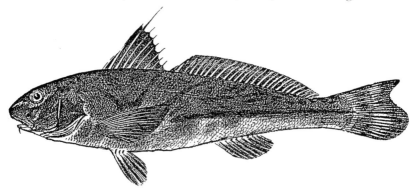

Figure 171. *Menticirrhus saxatilis*, from DeKay (1842), figure 20.

This marine species is distributed along the Atlantic coast from Maine to Florida. Juveniles (2-14 cm) during the summer months regularly enter freshwaters near the mouths of all rivers of Connecticut that drain into Long Island Sound (Whitworth, Minta, and Orciari 1980). They feed on a variety of invertebrates and small fishes.

Micropogonias undulatus (Linnaeus, 1766), Atlantic croaker

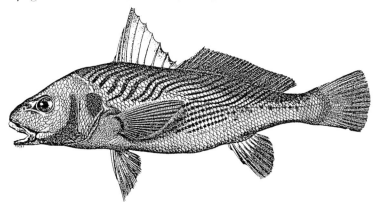

Figure 172. *Micropogonias undulatus*, from Cuvier and Valenciennes (1830), plate 119.

This marine species is distributed along the Atlantic coast from Massachusetts to Argentina, rarely north of New York. Juveniles (around 100 mm) were collected for the first time in freshwaters near the mouths of the Housatonic River in 1993 (Caromile, Kaputa, Long and Whitworth). Adults often reach lengths of 40 to 50 cm and feed on a variety of invertebrates and small fishes.

Family Scombridae, mackerels

Fifteen genera with about 48 species (marine) are distributed worldwide in tropical and subtropical seas. Two species have been collected in the freshwaters of Connecticut.

Key to the species of Scombridae

1. Dorsal spines < 13   *Scomber scombrus*, page 198
   Dorsal spines > 12   *Scomberomorus maculatus*, page 198

Scomber scombrus Linnaeus, 1758, Atlantic mackerel

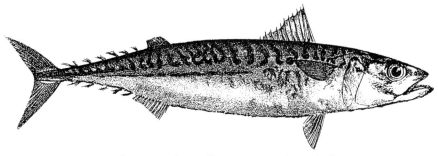

Figure 173. *Scomber scombrus*, from DeKay (1842), figure 34.

This marine species is distributed along the Atlantic coast from Labrador to North Carolina. Adults occasionally enter freshwaters near the mouths of all rivers of Connecticut that drain into Long Island Sound (Whitworth and Schmidt 1971). Adults often reach lengths of 30-35 cm, and feed on a variety of planktonic organisms.

Scomberomorus maculatus (Mitchill, 1815), Spanish mackerel

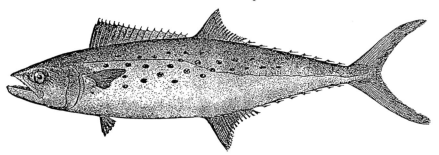

Figure 174. *Scomberomorus maculatus*, from H.W. Smith (1891), plate LI.

This marine species is distributed along the Atlantic coast from Maine to Brazil. Young specimens were captured for the first time in the lower Housatonic River (Caromile, Kaputa, Long, and Whitworth) and in the lower Thames River (D. Tolderlund, U.S. Coast Guard Academy) in 1993. The species is primarily found offshore; however, young have been reported in other estuaries. Lengths of 60-80 cm are reached and a variety of invertebrates and fishes are consumed.

Family Serranidae, sea basses

Thirty-five genera, with about 370 species, are found in all tropical and subtropical oceans. One species has been collected in the freshwaters of Connecticut.

Centropristis striata (Linnaeus, 1758), black sea bass

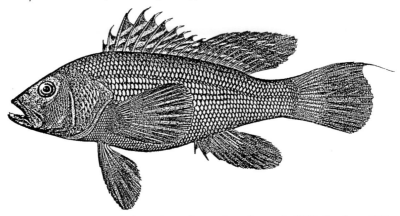

*Figure 175. **Centropristis striata**, from Goode et al. (1884), plate 162.*

This marine species is distributed along the Atlantic coast from Maine to Florida. Individuals occasionally enter freshwaters near saltwaters in all rivers in Connecticut that drain into Long Island Sound (Linsley 1844b, P. Howell-Heller, DEP). Lengths of 50-60 cm are reached and a variety of invertebrates and small fishes are consumed.

Family Soleidae, soles

Thirty-one genera with about 120 species (marine) are distributed worldwide in tropical and subtropical seas. One species has been collected in the freshwaters of Connecticut.

Trinectes maculatus (Bloch and Schneider, 1801), hogchoker

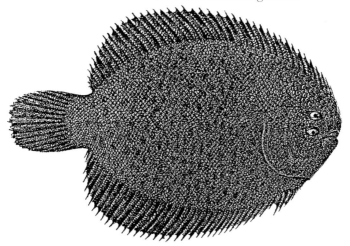

Figure 176. *Trinectes maculatus*, from Storer (1863), figure 1, plate 32.

This marine species is distributed along the east coast of North America from Nova Scotia to Panama. Large populations containing many age classes are regularly found during the summer months in freshwaters near saltwaters in all rivers in Connecticut that drain into Long Island Sound; some specimens are found over 60 kilometers from saltwaters (Whitworth *et al.* 1968). Lengths of 15-25 cm are often attained and they feed on a variety of invertebrates.

Family Sparidae, porgies

Twenty-nine genera with about 100 species are found in the Atlantic, Indian, and Pacific Oceans. Two species have been collected in the freshwaters of Connecticut.

Key to the species of Sparidae

1. Caudal fin deeply forked   *Stenotomus chrysops*, page 202

    Caudal fin shallowly forked   *Archosargus probatocephalus* , page 201

Archosargus probatocephalus (Walbaum, 1792), sheepshead

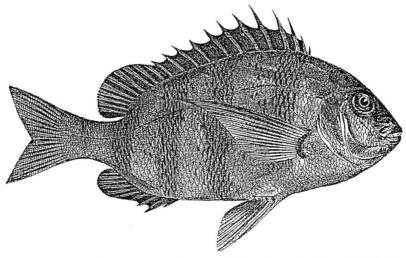

Figure 177. Archosargus probatocephalus, from DeKay (1842), figure 23.

This marine species is distributed along the Atlantic coast of North America from the Bay of Fundy to Texas, more commonly found from New York south. Although specimens have not been collected in Connecticut since Linsley (1844b), the species is included because many southern species have been collected in the saltwaters and nearby freshwaters of Connecticut in recent years, and specimens were collected in the Hudson River (C.L. Smith 1985). Lengths of 60-70 cm are reached and a variety of invertebrates and fishes are consumed.

Stenotomus chrysops (Linnaeus, 1766), scup

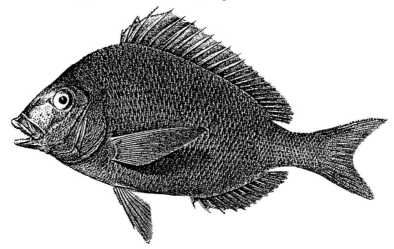

Figure 178. *Stenotomus chrysops*, from Storer (1853), figure 4, plate 10.

This marine species is distributed along the Atlantic coast from Maine to South Carolina. Individuals occasionally enter freshwaters near the mouths of rivers in Connecticut that drain into Long Island Sound (P. Howell-Heller, DEP). Lengths of 25-35 cm are attained and they feed on a variety of invertebrates.

Family Squalidae, dogfish sharks

Eighteen genera with about 70 species (marine) are distributed in the Atlantic, Indian, and Pacific Oceans. One species has been collected in the freshwaters of Connecticut.

Squalus acanthias Linnaeus, 1758, spiny dogfish

Figure 179. *Squalus acanthias*, from DeKay (1842), figure 210.

This marine species is distributed in temperate coastal waters of both sides of the Atlantic and Pacific Oceans. Individuals occasionally enter freshwaters near the mouths of all rivers of Connecticut that drain into Long Island Sound (Whitworth and Marsh 1980). Adults often reach lengths of 70-90 cm, and feed on a variety of larger invertebrates and fishes.

Family Stichaeidae, pricklebacks

About 31 genera with 60 species are found in the Arctic and northern Atlantic and Pacific Oceans; mainly Pacific. One species has been collected in the freshwaters of Connecticut.

Ulvaria subbifurcata (Storer, 1839), radiated shanny

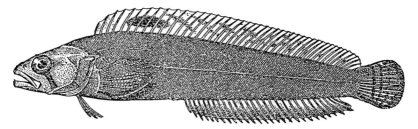

***Figure 180. Ulvaria subbifurcata*, from Bigelow and Welsh (1924), figure 184.**

This marine species is distributed along the Atlantic coast of North America from Newfoundland to southern New England. Individuals occasionally enter freshwaters near the mouths of rivers in Connecticut that drain into Long Island Sound (C. Fontneau, Omni Analysis). Adults often reach lengths of about 10 cm, and feed on a variety of invertebrates.

Family Stromateidae, butterfishes

Three genera with about 13 species (marine) are distributed in coastal waters of western Africa, southern Asia, and North and South America. One species has been collected in the freshwaters of Connecticut.

Peprilus triacanthus (Peck, 1804), butterfish

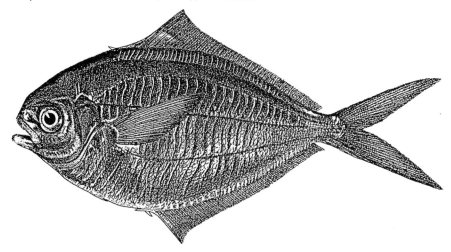

Figure 181. *Peprilus triacanthus*, from DeKay (1842), figure 80.

This marine species is distributed along the east coast of North America from Nova Scotia to Florida. Individuals occasionally enter freshwaters near the mouths of rivers in Connecticut that drain into Long Island Sound (P. Howell-Heller, DEP). Adults often reach lengths of 20-30 cm, and feed on a variety of invertebrates and fishes.

Family Syngnathidae, pipefishes

Fifty-five genera with about 230 species (mostly marine, some freshwater) are distributed throughout the world. Two species have been collected in the freshwaters of Connecticut.

Key to the species of Syngnathidae

1. Caudal fin present   *Syngnathus fuscus*, page 205
   Caudal fin absent   *Hippocampus erectus*, page 205

Hippocampus erectus Perry, 1810, lined seahorse

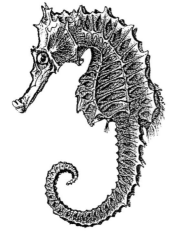

Figure 182. *Hippocampus erectus*, from Storer (1863), figure 4, plate 33.

This marine species is distributed along the Atlantic coast from Nova Scotia to South Carolina. Individuals occasionally enter freshwaters near the mouths of rivers in Connecticut that drain into Long Island Sound (C. Fontneau, Omni Analysis). Lengths of 8-14 cm are reached and a variety of planktonic organisms are consumed.

Syngnathus fuscus Storer,1839, northern pipefish

Figure 183. Syngnathus fuscus, **from Whitworth *et al.* (1968), page 96.**

This marine species is distributed along the Atlantic coast from Nova Scotia to Florida. Populations containing many age classes during the summer months regularly enter freshwaters near the mouths of all watercourses in Connecticut that enter Long Island Sound (Marcy 1976a, Whitworth *et al.* 1975). Adults often reach lengths of 15-25 cm, and feed on a variety of invertebrates and small fishes.

Family Synodontidae, lizardfishes

About 5 genera with 39 species (marine) are distributed along the shores of the Atlantic, Indian, and Pacific Oceans. One species has been collected in the freshwaters of Connecticut.

Synodus foetens (Linnaeus, 1766), inshore lizardfish

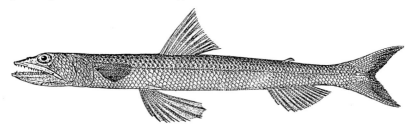

Figure 184. *Synodus foetens*, from Evermann and Kendall (1892), plate XXI.

This marine species is distributed along the Atlantic coast of North America from Massachusetts to South America. Individuals occasionally enter freshwaters near the mouths of rivers in Connecticut that empty into Long Island Sound (C. Fontneau, Omni Analysis). Lengths of 25-35 cm are often reached and they feed on variety of fishes and invertebrates.

Family Tetraodontidae, puffers

Sixteen genera with about 118 species (mostly marine) are distributed in subtropical and tropical oceans. Some species are restricted to the freshwaters of the Congo River, southern Africa, and the Guianas. Two marine species have been collected in the freshwaters in Connecticut.

Key to the species of Tetraodontidae

1. Jaw teeth divided by a suture,
   body without strong bony spines   *Sphoeroides maculatus*, page 207
   Jaw teeth not divided by a suture,
   body with strong bony spines   *Chilomycterus schoepfi*, page 207

Chilomycterus schoepfi (Walbaum, 1792), striped burrfish

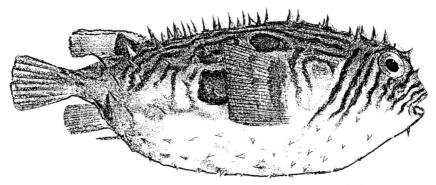

Figure 185. *Chilomycterus schoepfi*, from DeKay (1842), figure 185.

This marine species is distributed along the Atlantic coast of North America from southern New England to Florida, more common south of North Carolina. Juveniles occasionally enter freshwaters near the mouths of rivers of Connecticut that drain into Long Island Sound (Bob Sampson, formerly with the DEP). Lengths of 15-25 cm are attained and a variety of invertebrates are consumed.

Sphoeroides maculatus (Bloch & Schneider, 1801), northern puffer

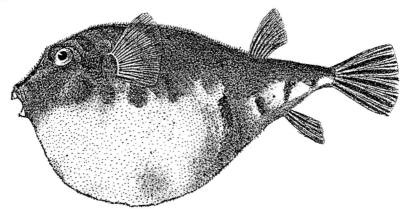

Figure 186. *Sphoeroides maculatus*, from DeKay (1842), figure 178.

This marine species is distributed along the Atlantic coast of North America from Maine to Florida. Juveniles occasionally enter freshwaters near the mouths of rivers in Connecticut that drain into Long Island Sound (P. Howell-Heller, DEP). Lengths of 15-25 cm are often attained and they feed on a variety of invertebrates.

Family Triglidae, searobins

Fourteen genera with about 86 species (marine) are distributed world wide in tropical and temperate seas. Two species have been collected in the freshwaters of Connecticut.

Key to the species of Triglidae

1. Black spot on anterior dorsal fin
   membranes, sides without dark
   longitudinal stripes, body
   elongate and slender   *Prionotus carolinus*, this page
   No black spot on anterior dorsal
   fin membranes, sides with two
   dark longitudinal stripes, body
   short and stocky   *P. evolans*, page 209

Prionotus carolinus (Linnaeus,1771), northern searobin

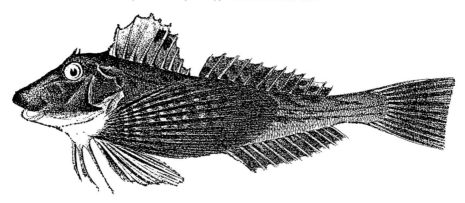

Figure 187. *Prionotus carolinus*, from DeKay (1842), figure 12.

This marine species is distributed along the Atlantic coast of North America from Nova Scotia to Florida. Some adults and juveniles during the summer months typically enter freshwaters near the mouths of rivers of Connecticut that drain into Long Island Sound (Whitworth & Marsh 1980). Lengths of 25-35 cm are commonly reached and they consume a variety of invertebrates and fishes.

Prionotus evolans (Linnaeus, 1766), striped searobin

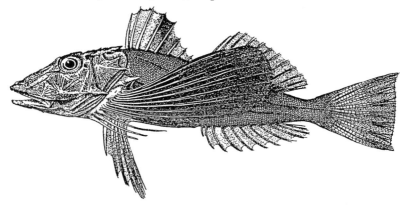

Figure 188. *Prionotus evolans*, from Goode *et al.* (1884), plate 71.

This marine species is distributed along the Atlantic coast of North America from Nova Scotia to the Carolinas. Juveniles occasionally enter freshwaters near the mouths of rivers in Connecticut that drain into Long Island Sound (P. Howell-Heller, DEP). Lengths of 35-45 cm are commonly reached and they feed on a variety of invertebrates and small fishes.

Family Umbridae, mudminnows

Three genera with about five species (freshwater) are distributed throughout the northern hemisphere. One species lives in the freshwaters of Connecticut.

Umbra limi (Kirtland,1840), central mudminnow

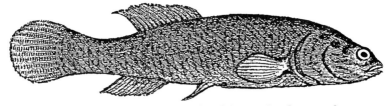

Figure 189. *Umbra limi*, from Kirtland (1840a), plate II, figure 4.

This introduced species is widely distributed in the freshwaters of middle and northern North America. First reported in Connecticut by Whitworth, Minta, and Orciari (1980). Populations, often large, are now present in the mainstem of the Connecticut River (Charles Phillips, DEP), and many of its tributaries all the way to the Massachusetts border. Sexual maturity is reached in 1-3 years. Males develop color patterns during the spawning season in early spring. Spawning takes place in the mouths of small streams entering the Connecticut River and in vegetation in the flood plain.

Eggs are broadcast over vegetation; they are adhesive, and no care is given them or the young. Lengths of 6-14 cm are reached and they feed on a variety of invertebrates.

Literature Cited

Aarrestad, P. 1992. Distribution and life history characteristics of anadromous sea lamprey (*Petromyzon marinus* L.) in the Salmon River drainage basin, Connecticut. M.S. Thesis, The University of Connecticut, Storrs, CT, 39p.

Abbott, C.C. 1871. Notes on the freshwater fishes of New Jersey. American Naturalist 4; 99-117.

Adams, J.T. 1926. New England in the republic, 1776-1850. Little, Brown and Company, Boston, MA, 438p.

Agassiz, L. 1850. Lake Superior: its physical character, vegetation, and animals, compared with those of other and similar regions. Originally published by Gould, Kendall and Lincoln, Boston, MA, 1970 reprint edition by Arno and the New York Times, New York, NY 428p.

Agassiz, L. 1854. Notes of a collection of fishes from the southern bend of the Tennessee River in the state of Alabama. American Journal of Science and Arts 67: 297-308 and 353-369.

Agassiz, L. 1855. Synopsis of the ichthyological fauna of the Pacific slope of North America, chiefly from the collections made by the U.S. Expl. Exped. under the command of Capt. C. Wilkes, with recent additions and comparisons with eastern types. American Journal of Science and Arts 69: 71-99 and 215-231.

Andrews, C.M. 1924. Connecticut's place in colonial history, an address delivered before the Connecticut Society of Colonial Wars, 28 May, 1923. Yale University Press, New Haven, CT, 49p.

Andrews, C.M. 1934. The beginnings of Connecticut, 1632-1662. Tercentenary Commission of the State of Connecticut, Yale University Press, New Haven CT, 81p.

Andrews, J.T. 1987. The late Wisconsin glaciation and deglaciation of the laurentide ice sheet. p 13-37, *in* W. Ruddiman and H.E. Wright Jr. (eds.) Volume K-3, North America and adjacent oceans during the last deglaciation. The Geological Society of America, Boulder, CO.

Anonymous. 1849. The poems of John G.C. Brainard. A new and authentic collection, with an original memoir of his life. S. Andrus and Son, Hartford, CT, 221p.

Anonymous. 1858. Note. Country Gentleman XI: 99.

Anonymous. 1867. Report of the commissioners concerning the protection of fish in the Connecticut River, Connecticut, to the General Assembly, May Session, 1867, 25p.

Anonymous. 1868. The celebration of the one hundred and fiftieth anniversary of the primitive organization of the Congregational church and Society, in Franklin, Connecticut. Tuttle, Morehouse and Taylor, New Haven, CT, 590p.

Anonymous. 1870. Fourth annual report of the commissioner concerning fisheries to the General Assembly, May Session, 1870, 37p.

Anonymous. 1871a. The freshwater bass. American Agriculturist 30:138-139.

Anonymous. 1871b. Fifth annual report of the commissioners concerning Fisheries to the General Assembly, May Session, 1871, 46p.

Anonymous. 1874. Note. Forest and Stream 2: 105.

Anonymous. 1875a. Note. Forest and Stream 4: 4.

Anonymous. 1875b. Note. Forest and Stream 5: 197.

Anonymous. 1876. Tenth annual report of the commissioners concerning Fisheries to the General Assembly, May Session, 1876, 34p.

Anonymous. 1878. The ponds suitable for black bass. American Agriculturist 37: 220.

Anonymous. 1882. Note. Bulletin of the United States Fish Commission 1: 213.

Anonymous. 1893. A memorial volume of the bicentennial celebration of the town of Windham, Connecticut. New England Printing Company, Hartford, CT, 166p.

Anonymous. 1896. Report of the state Commissioners of fisheries and game for the years 1895-1896, to his excellency the governor, and the general assembly. Hartford, CT, 94p.

Anonymous. 1897. National Cyclopedia of American biography. 4: 540. James T. White & Company, New York, NY.

Anonymous. 1898. Second biennial report of the state Commissioners of fisheries and game for the years 1897-1898, to his excellency the governor, and the general assembly. Hartford, CT, 119p.

Anonymous. 1902. Fourth biennial report of the State Commissioners of fisheries and game for the years 1901-1902, to his excellency the governor, and the general assembly. Hartford, CT, 115p.

Anonymous. 1922. Fourteenth biennial report of the State Board of fisheries and game for the years 1921-1922, to his excellency the governor, and the general assembly. Hartford, CT, 105p.

Anonymous. 1930. Eighteenth biennial report of the State Board of Fisheries and Game to his excellency, the governor, Hartford, CT, 187p.

Anonymous. 1939. History of Milford, Connecticut, 1639-1939. Braunworth and Company, Bridgeport, CT, 211p.

Anonymous. 1959. A fishery survey of the lakes and ponds of Connecticut. Report #1, State Board of Fisheries and Game, Hartford, CT, 395p.

Anonymous. 1992. Connecticut's endangered, threatened and special concern species. Connecticut Department of Environmental Protection, Hartford, CT, 15p.

Atkins, C.G. 1874. On the salmon of eastern North America and its artificial culture. Report of the United States Fish Commission for 1872-1873: 226-337.

Avery, J. 1901. History of the town of Ledyard, 1650-1900. Noyes and Davis, Norwich, CT, 334p.

Ayres, W.O. 1842. Enumeration of the fishes of Brookhaven, Long Island, with remarks upon the species observed. Boston Journal of Natural History 4: 255-264.

Ayres, W.O. 1843a. Enumeration of the fishes of Brookhaven, Long Island, with remarks upon the species observed. Boston Journal of Natural History 4: 265-292.

Ayres, W.O. 1843b. Descriptions of four species of fish from Brookhaven, Long Island, all of which are believed to be new. Boston Journal of Natural History 4: 293-302.

Ayres, W.O. 1845. An attempt to prove that *Cottus cognatus* of Richardson, *Cottus viscosus* of Haldeman, and *Uranidea quiescens* of DeKay, are one species and are identical with *Cottus gobio* of Linnaeus. Boston Journal of Natural History 5: 116-136.

Ayres, W.O. 1849. Observations on *Leuciscus pulchellus*. American Association for the Advancement of Science 2: 402-406.

Ayres, W.O. 1851-1854. Note. Proceedings Boston Society of Natural History 4: 288.

Ayres, W.O. 1863. Notes on the sebastoid fishes occurring on the coast of California. Proceedings of the Zoological Society of London for 1863: 390-402.

Bacan, E.M. 1911. The Connecticut River and the valley of the Connecticut. Putnam's Sons, New York, NY 487p.

Bailey, J.R. and J.A. Oliver. 1939. The fishes of the Connecticut Watershed. p 150-189, *in* H. E. Warfel (ed) Biological survey of the Connecticut Watershed. Survey Report 4, New Hampshire Fish and Game Department, Concord, NH.

Bailey, R.M.and G.R. Smith. 1981. Origin and geography of the fish fauna of the Laurentian Great Lakes Basin. Canadian Journal of Fisheries and Aquatic Sciences 38: 1539-1561.

Baird, S.F. 1874. Work of the U.S. Fish Commission. Transactions of the American Fisheries Society 3: 31-38.

Baker, M.C. 1971. Habitat selection in fourspine sticklebacks (*Apeltes quadracus*). American Midland Naturalist 85: 239-242.

Baldwin, E. 1838. Annals of Yale College, from its foundation, to the year 1831. Second Edition, B. and W. Noyes, New Haven, CT, 343p.

Baldwin, S.E. 1901-1903. The first century of the Connecticut Academy of Arts and Sciences. Transactions of the Connecticut Academy of Arts and Sciences 11: XIII-XXXV.

Bayles, R. M. 1889. History of Windham County, Connecticut. W.W. Preston Co., New York, NY, 1204p.

Bean, T.H. 1885. The whitefishes of North America. Transactions of the American Fisheries Society 13: 32-39.

Bean, T.H. 1889. Report on the salmon and salmon rivers of Alaska, with notes on the conditions, methods and needs of the salmon fisheries. Bulletin of the United States Fish Commission 9: 165-208.

Becker, G.C. 1983. Fishes of Wisconsin. The University of Wisconsin Press, Madison, WI, 1052p.

Beetham, N. and W.A. Niering. 1961. A pollen diagram for southeastern Connecticut. American Journal of Science 259: 69-75.

Behnke, R.J. and R.M. Wetzel. 1960. A preliminary list of the fishes found in freshwaters of Connecticut. Copeia 1960: 141-143.

Bell, M. 1985. The face of Connecticut, people, geology and the land. Bulletin 110, State Geological and Natural History of Connecticut, Hartford, CT, 196p.

Berra, T. 1981. An atlas of distribution of the freshwater fish families of the world. The University of Nebraska Press, Lincoln, NB, 197p.

Bigelow, H.B., and W.W. Welsh. 1924. Fishes of the Gulf of Maine. Part 1. Bulletin of the U.S. Bureau of Fisheries XL: 1-567.

Black, R.F. 1982. Modes of deglaciation of Connecticut: a review. p 77-100, *in* G.J. Larson and B.D. Stone (eds) Late Wisconsinan glaciation in New England. Kendall Hunt Publishing Company, Dubuque, IA.

Bloom, A.L. and M. Stuiver. 1963. Submergence of the Connecticut coast. Science 139: 332-334.

Boeseman, M. 1968. The genus *Hypostomus* Lacepede, 1803, and its Surinam representatives (Siluriformes, Loricariidae). Zoologische Verhandelingen, Number 99, 89p.

Bonnichsen, R., D. Stanford, and J.L. Fastook. 1987. Environmental change and development history of human adaptive patterns; the Paleoindian case. p 403-424, *in* W.F. Ruddiman and H.E. Wright Jr.(eds). North America and adjacent oceans during the last deglaciation. The Geology of North America, Volume K-3. The Geological Society of America, Boulder, CO.

Booth, A. 1881. Salmon and shad. Papers and Proceedings of the Connecticut Valley Historical Society, 1876-1881: 16-18.

Booth, R.A. 1967. A description of the larval stages of the tomcod, Microgadus tomcod, with comments on its spawning ecology. Ph.D. thesis, The University of Connecticut, Storrs, CT, 53p.

Borns, H.W. Jr. 1963. Preliminary report on the ages and distribution of the late Pleistocene ice in north-central Maine. American Journal of Science 261: 738-740.

Borns, H.W. Jr. 1973. Late Wisconsin fluctuations of the laurentide ice sheet in southern and eastern New England. p 37-45 *in* R.F. Black, R.B. Goldwait and H.B. Williams (eds) The Wisconsin Stage. Memoir 136, The Geological Society of America, Boulder CO.

Bothner, M.H. and E.C. Spiker. 1980. Upper Wisconsinan till recovered on the continental shelf southeast of New England. Science 210: 423-425.

Bottsell, G.A. ed. 1950. The centennial of the Sheffield Scientific School. Yale University Press, New Haven, CT, 206p.

Boyd, J. 1873. Annals and family records of Winchester, Conn., with exercises of the centennial celebration on the 16th and 17th days of August, 1871. Case, Lockwood and Brainard, Hartford, CT, 632p.

Boyle, R.H. 1969. The Hudson River, a natural and unnatural history. W.W. Norton and Company, New York, NY, 304p.

Brennan, L.A. 1974. The lower Hudson: a decade of shell middens. Archaeology of Eastern North America 2: 81-93.

Brennan, L.A. 1981. Pick-up tools, food, bones and inferences on lifeway function of shell heap sites along the lower Hudson. Archaeology of Eastern North America 9: 42-51.

Brewer, W.H. 1901-1903. The debt of this century to learned societies. Transactions of the Connecticut Academy of Arts and Sciences 11: XIVI - LIII.

Bromley, S.W. 1935. The original forest types of southern New England. Ecological Monographs 5: 61-89.

Bromley, S.W. 1945. An Indian relic area. Scientific Monthly 60: 153-154.

Brugam, R.B. 1978. Pollen indicators of land-use change in southern Connecticut. Quaternary Research 9: 349-362.

Bunker, T. 1870. On trout brooks and a hatching house. American Agriculturist 29:12.

Butler, E.L. 1948. Algonkian culture and use of maize in southern New England. Bulletin of the Archeological Society of Connecticut 22:3-39.

Butzer, K.W. 1971. Environment and archeology, an ecological approach to prehistory. 2nd edition, Adline Publishing Company, Hawthorn, NY, 703p.

Byers, D.S. 1946. The environment in the northeast. Papers of the Robert S. Peabody Foundation for Archaeology III: 3-36.

Cadigan, K.M. and P.E. Fell. 1985. Reproduction, growth, and feeding habits of *Menidia menidia* (Atherinidae) in a tidal marsh-estuarine system in southern New England. Copeia 1985: 21-26.

Camp, D.N. 1917. David Nelson Camp, recollections of a long and active life. Rumford Press, Concord, NH, 96p.

Cantor, T. 1849. Catalogue of Malayan fishes. Reprint of Journal of the Asiatic Society of Bengal XVIII, part II, by A. Asher and Company, Amsterdam, Holland, 1966.

Carlson, C. 1988. "Where's the salmon?" A reevaluation of the role of anadromous fisheries in aboriginal New England. p 47-80, *in* G. Nicholas (ed) Holocene human ecology in northeastern North America. Plenum Press, New York.

Caulkins, F.M. 1866. History of Norwich, Connecticut, from its possession by the Indians to the year 1866. Case Lockwood and Company, Hartford, CT, 704p.

Caulkins, F.M. 1895. History of New London, Connecticut, from the first survey of the coast in 1612 to 1860. H.D. Utley, New London, CT, 696p.

Ceci, L. 1975. Fish fertilizer: a native North American practice. Science 188: 26-30.

Chapin, A. B. 1853. Glastonbury for two hundred years. A centennial discourse, May 18th A.D. 1853, with an appendix containing historical and statistical papers of interest. Case, Tiffany and Co., Hartford, CT, 252p.

Chittenden, R.H. 1928. History of the Sheffield Scientific School of Yale University 1846-1922. Yale Press, New Haven Volume I, 1-298, Volume II, 299-610.

Church, S. 1851. Address, delivered at Litchfield, Conn., on the occasion of the centennial celebration. p 21-69, *in* Anonymous. Litchfield County, centennial celebration, held at Litchfield, Conn., 13th and 14th of August, 1851. Edwin Hunt, Hartford,.CT.

Clift, W. 1872. Shad culture. Transactions of the American Fisheries Society 1: 21-28.

Coffin, C.C. 1947. Ancient fish weirs along the Housatonic River. Bulletin of the Archeological Society of Connecticut 21: 35-38.

Cohen, A. 1977. Life history of the banded sunfish in Green Falls Reservoir, Connecticut. Unpublished M.S. Thesis, University of Connecticut, 21p.

Cole, J.R. 1888. History of Tolland County, Connecticut. W.W. Preston and Company, New York, NY, 922p.

Collette, B.B. 1962. The swamp darters of the subgenus *Hololepis* (Pisces, Percidae). Tulane Studies in Zoology 9: 115-211.

Comstock, J.C. 1857. Pisciculture- salmon breeding. Transactions of the Conn. state agricultural society for the year 1856. Case Tiffany and Company, Hartford, CT, 409-427.

Connally, G.G. and L.A. Sirkin. 1973. Wisconsin history of the Hudson-Champlain. p 47-69 in R.F. Black, R.B. Goldwait ,and H.B. Williams (eds) The Wisconsin stage. Memoir 136, The Geological Society of America, Boulder, CO.

Cooper, E.L. 1983. Fishes of Pennsylvania and the Northeastern United States. The Pennsylvania State University Press, University Park, PA, 243p.

Cope, E.D. 1869a. Synopsis of the Cyprinidae of Pennsylvania. Transactions of the American Philosophical Society, New Series 13: 351-410.

Cope, E.D. 1869b. On the distribution of fresh water fishes in the Allegheny region of southwestern Virginia. Journal of the Academy of Natural Sciences, Philadelphia, Series 2, 6: 207-247.

Crecco, V. and T. Savoy. 1984. Effects of fluctuations in hydrographic conditions on year-class strength of American shad (*Alosa sapidissima*) in the Connecticut River. Canadian Journal of Fisheries and Aquatic Sciences 41: 1216-1223.

Crecco, V.A. and T.F. Savoy. 1985a. Effects of biotic and abiotic factors on growth and relative survival of young American shad, *Alosa sapidissima*, in the Connecticut River. Canadian Journal of Fisheries and Aquatic Sciences 42: 1640-1648.

Crecco, V.A. and T.F. Savoy. 1985b. Density-dependent catchability and its potential causes and consequences on Connecticut River American shad *Alosa sapidissima*. Canadian Journal of Fisheries and Aquatic Sciences 42: 1649-1657.

Crecco, V., T. Savoy & W. Whitworth. 1986. Effects of density-dependent and climatic factors on American shad, *Alosa sapidissima*, recruitment: a predictive approach. Canadian Journal of Fisheries and Aquatic Sciences 43: 457-463.

Cronon, W. 1983. Changes in the land. Indians, colonists and the ecology of New England. Hill and Wang, New York, NY, 241p.

Cuvier, G. and A. Valenciennes. 1830. Histoire naturelle des poissons. Volume V, 499p. Reprinted in 1969 by A. Asher and Company, Amsterdam, Holland.

Dadswell, M.J. 1979. Biology and population characteristics of the shortnose sturgeon, *Acipenser brevirostrum* Lesueur 1818 (Osteichthes: Acipenseridae), in the Saint John River Estuary, New Brunswick, Canada. Canadian Journal of Zoology 57: 2186-2210.

Davis, M.B. 1965. Phytogeography and palynology of northeastern United States. p 377-401, H. E. Wright Jr. and D.G. Freys (eds) The Quaternary of the United States. Princeton University Press, Princeton, NJ.

Davis, M.B. 1969. Climatic changes in southern Connecticut recorded by pollen deposition at Rogers Lake. Ecology 50: 409-422.

Davis, M.B., T.E. Bradstreet, R. Stuckenrath Jr., and H.W. Borns Jr. 1975. Vegetation and associated environments during the past 14,000 years near Moulton Pond, Maine. Quaternary Research 5: 435-465.

Davis, M.B., R.W. Spear and L.C.K. Shane. 1980. Holocene climate of New England. Quaternary Research 14: 240-250.

Day, F. 1878. The fishes of India; being a natural history of the fishes known to inhabit the seas and fresh waters of India, Burma, and Ceylon. 1958 edition by Wm Dawson and Sons Ltd, London. 2 volumes. Volume 1, 778p, volume II with CXCV plates.

Day, G.M. 1953. The Indian as an ecological factor in the northeastern forest. Ecology 34: 329-346.

Decker, R.O. 1970. The New London merchants, 1645-1909; the rise and decline of a Connecticut port. Ph.D. thesis, the University of Connecticut, 354p.

Deevey, E.S. Jr. 1939. Studies on Connecticut lake sediments. I. A postglacial climatic chronology for southern New England. American Journal of Science 237: 691-724.

Deevey, E.S. Jr. 1948. On the date of the last rise of sea level in southern New England, with remarks on the Grassy Island Site. American Journal of Science 246: 329-352.

Deevey, E.S. Jr. 1949. Biogeography of the Pleistocene. Part I. Europe and North America. Bulletin of the Geological Society of America 60: 1315-1416.

DeForest, J.W. 1852. History of the Indians of Connecticut from the earliest known period to 1850. W.J. Hamersley, Hartford, CT, 509p. Reprinted in 1970 by Scholarly Press, St. Clair Shores, MI.

DeKay, J. E. 1842. Zoology of New York. Part IV. Fishes. W. & W. White and J. Visscheir, Albany, NY, 415p.

Dincauze, D.F. and M.T. Mulholland. 1977. Early and middle archaic site distributions and habitats in southern New England. Annals of the New York Academy of Sciences 288: 439-456.

Dowhan, J. J. and R. J. Craig. 1976. Rare and endangered species of Connecticut and their habitats. State Geologic and Natural History Survey, Report of Investigations. Number 6, Hartford, CT, 137p.

Dwight, S. E. 1826. Description of the eruption of Long Lake and Mud Lake, in Vermont, and of the desolation effected by the rush of waters through Barton River, and the lower country, towards Lake Memphremagog, in the summer of 1810, in a letter to the Editor. American Journal of Science and Arts 11: 39-54.

Dwight, T. 1821. Travels in New England. 4 volumes. Barbara Miller Solomon (ed). Cambridge, MA, 1969.

Eaton, A. 1831. Fish of Hudson River. American Journal of Science and Arts 20: 150-152.

Edwards, R.L. and A.S. Merrill. 1977. A reconstruction of the continental shelf areas of eastern North America for the times 9,500 B.P. and 12,500 B.P. Archaeology of Eastern North America 5: 1-43.

Elliot, C.W. 1857. The New England history, from the discovery of the continent by the Northmen, A.D. 986, to the period when the colonies declared their independence, A.D. 1776. Volume I, 479p, Volume II, 492 p. Charles Scribner, New York, NY.

Ellsworth, J.E. 1935. Simsbury, being a brief historical sketch of ancient and modern Simsbury, 1642-1935. Case, Lockwood and Brainard, Hartford, CT, 190p.

Emery, K.O., R.L. Wigley and M. Rubins. 1965. A submerged peat deposit off the Atlantic coast of the United States. Limnology and Oceanography 10 (supplement): R97-R102.

Engelhardt, F. 1937. Fulling Mill Brook, a study in industrial evolution, 1707-1937. Stephen Daye Press, Brattleboro, VT, 55p.

Evans, D.O., B.A. Henderson, N.J. Bax, T.R. Marshall, R.T. Oglesby and W.J. Christie. 1987. Concepts and methods of community ecology applied to freshwater fisheries management. Canadian Journal of Fisheries and Aquatic Sciences 44 (supplement): 448-470.

Everhart, W.H. 1966. Fishes of Maine. 3rd edition, Maine Department of Inland Fisheries and Game, Orono, ME, 96p.

Evermann, B.W. 1891. A reconnaissance of the streams and lakes of western Montana and northwestern Wyoming. Bulletin of the United States Fish Commission 11: 3-60.

Evermann, B.W. and W.C. Kendall. 1892. The fishes of Texas and the Rio Grande basin, considered chiefly with respect to their geographic distribution. Bulletin of the United States Fish Commission 12: 57-126.

Filippi, F. 1869. Note IV. *Lebistes*, nuovo genere di pesce della famiglia del Cyprinodonti. Archivio per la zoologica, l'anatomia e la fisiologia I: 69-70.

Fitting, J.E. 1968. Environmental potential and the postglacial readaptation in eastern North America. American Antiquity 33: 441-445.

Flint, R.F. 1930. The glacial geology of Connecticut. State Geologic and Natural History Survey, Bulletin Number 47, Hartford, CT, 294p.

Flint, R.F. 1933. Late-Pleistocene sequence in the Connecticut Valley. Bulletin of the Geological Society of America . 965-988.

Flint, R.F. 1953. Probable Wisconsin substages and late Wisconsin events in northeastern United States and southeastern Canada. Bulletin of the Geological Society of America 64: 897-919.

Flint, R.F. 1955. Rates of advance and retreat of the margin of the late Wisconsin ice sheet. American Journal of Science 253: 249-255.

Flint, R.F. 1956. New radiocarbon dates and late pleistocene stratigraphy. American Journal of Science 254: 265-287.

Flint, R.F. 1971. Glacial and Quaternary geology. John Wiley and Sons, New York, NY, 892p.

Forbes, S.A. 1925. The lake as a microcosm. Bulletin of the Illinois Natural History Survey 15: 527-550. Originally published in 1887 in the Bulletin of the Peoria Scientific Association.

Ford, R.I. 1981. Ethnobotany in North America: an historical phytogeographic perspective. Canadian Journal of Botany 59: 2178-2188.

Fowler, H.W. 1913. Notes on the fishes of the Chincoteague region of Virginia. Proceedings of the Academy of Natural Sciences of Philadelphia 65: 61-65.

Fowler, H.W. 1945. A study of the fishes of the southern piedmont and coastal plain. Monograph 7, Academy of Natural Sciences of Philadelphia, 408p, plus 313 figures.

Fowler, R.H. 1967. Farmington Canal. p 116-119, *in* H. Dean (ed) The heritage of Granby, its founding and history, 1786-1965. Salmon Brook Historical Society Granby, CT.

French, H.W. 1879. Art and artists in Connecticut. 1970 reprint edition, DeCapo Press, New York, NY, 176p.

Galligan, J. P. 1960. History of the Connecticut River sturgeon fishery. Connecticut Wildlife Conservation Bulletin 6, 12p.

Garman, S. 1891. Dr. H. Storer's work on the fishes. Proceedings of the Boston Society of Natural History 25: 354-357.

Garman, S. 1892. The Discoboli. Cyclopteridae, Liparopsidae, and Liparidae. Memoirs of the Museum of Comparative Zoology at Harvard College, XIV, Number 2, 93p.

Gephard, S., G. Hamley & J. Ravita. 1992. Anadromous fish enhancement and restoration. Progress Report 1991. Federal aid to sport fish restoration. F50D12, Connecticut Department of Environmental Protection, Hartford, CT, 73p.

Gill, T. 1864a. Critical remarks on the genera *Sebastes* and *Sebastodes* of Ayres. Proceedings of the Academy of Natural Sciences of Philadelphia 16: 145-147.

Gill, T. 1864b. Second contribution to the Selachology of California. Proceedings of the Academy of Natural Sciences of Philadelphia 16: 147-151.

Gill, T. 1864c. Synopsis of the Pleuronectoids of California and northwestern America. Proceedings of the Academy of Natural Sciences of Philadelphia 16: 194-198.

Gill, T. 1873. Catalogue of the fishes of the east coast of North America. Report on the condition of the sea fisheries of the south coast of New England in 1871 and 1872: 779-822.

Gill, T. 1882. Bibliography of the fishes of the Pacific coast of the United States to the end of 1879. Bulletin of the United States National Museum 11: 1-73.

Girard, C. 1852. Contributions to the natural history of the fresh water fishes of North America. I. A monograph of the cottoids. Smithsonian Contributions to Knowledge III, 80p.

Girard, C. 1856. Contributions to the ichthyology of the western coast of the United States, from specimens in the Smithsonian Institution. Proceedings of the Academy of Natural Sciences of Philadelphia 8: 131-137.

Girard, C. 1858. Fishes. Part 4, 400p, *in* Reports of explorations and surveys to ascertain the most practicable and economic route for a railroad from the Mississippi River to the Pacific Ocean. Beverly Tucker Printers, Washington, DC.

Glick, T.F. 1980. Science, technology and the urban environment; the great stink of 1858. p 122-139 *in* L.J. Bilsky (ed) Historical ecology, essays on environment and social change. Kennikat Press, Port Washington, NY.

Goldsmith, R. 1982. Recessional moraines and ice retreat in southeastern Connecticut. p 61-76 *in* G.J. Larson and B.D. Stone (eds). Late Wisconsinan glaciation of New England. Kendall Hunt Publishing Company, Dubuque, IA.

Goode, G.B. 1880. The first decade of the United States Fish Commission; its plan of work and accomplished results, scientific and economical. American Association for the Advancement of Science 29: 563-574.

Goode, G.B. 1881. Epochs in the history of fish culture. Transactions of the American Fisheries Society 10: 34-58.

Goode, G.B. 1882. Notes on the lampreys- Petromyzontidae. Bulletin of the United States Fish Commission 2: 349-354.

Goode, G.B. and T.H. Bean. 1895. Oceanic ichthyology, a treatise on the deep-sea and pelagic fishes of the world, based chiefly upon the collections made by the steamers *Blake*, *Albatross*, and *Fish Hawk* in the northwestern Atlantic, with an atlas containing 417 figures. Smithsonian / United States National Museum special bulletin, 553 p.

Goode, G. B. *et al.* 1884. Part III. The food fishes of the United States. pages 163-682, *in* Goode, G.B. (ed). The fisheries and fishery industries of the United States. Section I. Natural history of useful aquatic animals, with an atlas of two hundred and seventy seven plates. Government Printing Office, Washington, DC.

Goodkin, D. 1674. Historical collections of Indians in New England. Reprinted in Collections of the Massachusetts Historical Society for the year 1792. I: 141-227.

Goodrich, S. et al.. 1881. Johnson's natural history. Volume II. John A. Gray Press, New York, NY, 684p.

Green, S. 1874. Experiences of a practical fish culturist. Transactions of the American Fisheries Society 3: 22-24.

Green, S. 1882. Rearing of California mountain trout (Salmo irideus). Bulletin of the United States Fish Commission 1: 23.

Greenwood, P.H., D.E. Rosen, S.H. Weitzman and G.S. Meyers. 1966. Phyletic studies of teleostean fishes, with a provisional classification of living forms. Bulletin of the American Museum of Natural History 131: 339-456.

Griffin, J.G. 1965. Quaternary prehistory in the northeastern woodlands. p 655-667, in H.E. Wright Jr. and D.G. Freys (eds) The Quaternary of the United States. Princeton University Press, Princeton, NJ.

Gunter, A. 1880. An introduction to the study of fishes. Reprint edition 1963, Todays and Tommorrows Book Agency, New Dehli, 720p.

Gutherz, E. 1963. Field guide to the flatfishes of the family Bothidae in the western North Atlantic. Circular 263, United States Fish and Wildlife Service, Washington, D.C., 47p.

Hagstrom, N., M. Humphreys and W. Hyatt. 1990. A survey of Connecticut streams and rivers- Connecticut River tributaries, Scantic River, Mattabesset River, Salmon River, Coginchaug River and Eightmile River drainages. Federal aid to Sport Fish restoration F66R-2, Connecticut Department of Environmental Protection, Hartford, CT, 152p.

Hagstrom, N., M. Humphreys and W. Hyatt. 1991. A survey of Connecticut streams and rivers- central coastal and western coastal drainages. Federal aid to Sport Fish restoration F66R-3. Connecticut Department of Environmental Protection, Hartford CT, 117p.

Haime, J. 1874. The history of fish culture. Report of the commissioner for 1872 and 1873 of the United States Commission of fish and fisheries: 465-566.

Halliwell, D.B. 1979. A list of the freshwater fishes of Massachusetts. Massachusetts Division of Fisheries and Wildlife, Boston, MA, 13p.

Hallock, C. 1894. When shad were a penna-piece. Transactions of the American Fisheries Society 23: 18-20.

Hard, W. 1947. The Connecticut River. Reinhart and Company, New York, NY, 310p.

Harte, C.R. 1933. Some engineering aspects of the old Northampton Canal. Annual report of the Connecticut Society of Civil Engineers. 21-53.

Harte, C.R. 1938. Connecticut's canals. Annual report of the Connecticut Society of Civil Engineers, 118-179.

Harwood, P.L. 1932. History of eastern Connecticut- embracing the counties of Tolland, Middlesex, Windham and New London. 3 Volumes, Pioneer Historical Publishing Co., Chicago and New Haven. Vol I, 387p, Volume II, 389-844, and Volume III, 930p.

Haynes, H.W. 1889. The prehistoric archaeology of North America. p 329-368, in Winsor, J. (ed) Narrative and critical history of America. Volume I, Houghton, Mifflin and Co., Boston, MA.

Haynes, W. 1949. 1649-1949, Stonington chronology, being a year-by-year record of the American way of life in a Connecticut town. Pequot Press, Stonington, CT, 151p.

Hildebrand, S.F. 1918. Fishes in relation to mosquito control in ponds. Report of the Commissioner of fisheries for the year 1918, document 874, 15 p.

Hildebrand, S.F. and L.E. Cable. 1940. Further notes on the development and life history of some teleosts at Beaufort, N.C. Bulletin of the United States Fish Commission 48: 505-642.

Hindle, B. 1956. The pursuit of science in revolutionary America, 1735-1789. University of North Carolina Press, Raleigh, 410p.

Hoffman, M.P. 1980. Prehistoric ecological crises. p 33-42, in L.J. Bilsky (ed) Historical ecology, essays on environment and social change. Kennikat Press, Port Washington, NY.

Hollister, G.H. 1857. The history of Connecticut, from the first settlement of the colony. Volume 1, 2d edition, Case, Tiffany and Company, Hartford, CT, 612p.

Hooker, R. 1936. The colonial trade of Connecticut. Tercentenary Commission of the State of Connecticut, Yale University Press, New Haven, CT, 42p.

Hubbs, C.L. 1964. History of ichthyology in the United States after 1850. Copeia 1964: 42-60.

Hubbs, C.L. and I.C. Potter. 1971. Distribution, phylogeny and taxonomy. p 1-65, in Hardisty, M.W. and I.C. Potter (eds) The biology of lampreys. Volume 1, Academic Press, New York, NY.

Hughes, T. 1987. Ice dynamics and deglaciation models when ice sheets collapsed. p 183-220, in W.F. Ruddiman and H.E. Wright Jr. North America and adjacent oceans during the last deglaciation. The Geology of North America, Volume K-3, The Geological Society of America, Boulder, CO.

Jacobs, R.P., E.B. O'Donnell and A.P. Petrillo. 1991. Statewide largemouth bass research and management. Progress Report 1991. Dingle-Johnson Project F57R9, Connecticut Department of Environmental Protection, Hartford, CT, 51p.

Jacobson, G.L. Jr., T. Webb III, and E.C. Grimm. 1987. Patterns and rate of vegetation change during the deglaciation of eastern North America. p 227-288, in W.F. Ruddiman and H.E. Wright Jr. Volume K-3, The Geology of North America, the Geological Society of America, Boulder, CO.

Jenkins, E.H. 1925. Connecticut agriculture. p 287-425, in N.G. Osborn (ed) History of Connecticut in monographic form. Volume II, The Society of Connecticut 50: 1-16.

Johnson, G.O. 1984. Percoidei: development and relationships. p 464-498, in H.G. Moser et al. (eds) Ontogeny and systematics of fishes. Special Publication #1, American Society of Ichthyologists and Herpetologists.

Johnson, P. 1987. Changing paleoecological relationships during the late Pleistocene and Holocene in New England. Bulletin of the Archaeological Society of Connecticut 50: 1-16.

Jordan, D.S. 1877. Contributions to North American ichthyology, based primarily on the collections of the United States National Museum. II. A. Notes on Cottidae, Etheostomatidae, Percidae, Centrarchidae, Aphododevidae, Dorysomatidae and Cyprinidae, with revisions of the genera and descriptions of new or little known species. B. Synopsis of the Siluridae of the fresh waters of North America. Bulletin of the United States National Museum 10, 120p.

Jordan, D.S. 1888. The distribution of freshwater fishes. Transactions of the American Fisheries Society 17: 4-24.

Jordan, D.S. 1905. A guide to the study of fishes. Volume 1, Henry Holt and Company, New York, NY, 624p.

Jordan, D.S. 1922. Days of a man. Volume 1, 710p, Volume II, 882p, World Book Company, Yonkers-on-Hudson, New York.

Jordan, D.S. and C.H. Eigenmann. 1888. A review of the genera and species of Serranidae found in the waters of America and Europe. Bulletin of the United States Fish Commission 8: 329-441.

Jordan, D.S. and B.W. Evermann. 1896. A check list of the fishes and fishlike vertebrates of North and Middle America. United States Government Printing Office, Washington, DC. 584p.

Jordan, D.S. and B.W. Evermann. 1896-1900. The fishes of North and Middle America. Bulletin of the United States National Museum, number 47, 4 parts, 3313p.

Jordan, D.S., B.W. Evermann and H.W. Clark. 1930. Check list of the fishes and fish-like vertebrates of North and Middle America north of the northern boundary of Venezuela and Columbia. United States Government Printing Office, Washington, DC. 670p.

Josselyn, J. 1672. New Englands rarities discovered. Originally printed in London and reprinted in Boston by the Massachusetts Historical Society in 1972. 114 p.

Judd, S. 1905. The history of Hadley, Massachusetts. Haulting and Company, Springfield, MA, 504p.

Kellogg, E.C. 1857. Experiments in artificial fish breeding. Transactions of the Conn. state agricultural society for the year 1856. Case Tiffany and Co., Hartford, CT, 400-408.

Kendall, W.C. 1901. Notes on the silversides of the genus *Menidia* of the east coast of the United States, with descriptions of two new subspecies. Report of the Commissioner for fisheries for the year ending June 30, 1901, pages 241-267.

Kendall, W.C. 1902. Notes on some fresh-water fishes from Maine, with descriptions of three new species. Bulletin of the United States Fish Commission 22: 355-368.

Kendall, W.C. 1908. List of the pisces. Part1, *in* Fauna of New England. Boston Society of Natural History, Occasional Papers number 7, 152p.

Kendall, W.C. 1915-1916. The Rangely Lakes, Maine: with special reference to the habits of fishes, fish culture and angling. Bulletin of the U.S. Bureau of Fisheries 35: 485-594.

Kirtland, J. 1840a. Descriptions of four new species of fishes. Boston Journal of Natural History 3: 273-277.

Kirtland, J. 1840b. Descriptions of the fishes of the Ohio River and its tributaries. Boston Journal of Natural History 3: 338-352.

Kissel, G.W. 1974. Spawning of the anadromous alewife, *Alosa pseudoharengus* in Bride Lake, Connecticut. Transactions of the American Fisheries Society 103: 312-317.

Kner, R. 1860. Zur Familie der Characinen. III. Folge der ichthyologischen Beitrage. Denkshriften der Kaiserlichen Akademie der Wissenschaften, Mathematisch-Naturwissenschaftliche Klasse 18: 9-62.

Kynard, B. and J.P. Warner. 1987. Spring and summer movements of sub-adult striped bass, *Morone saxatilis*, in the Connecticut River. Fisheries Bulletin 86: 143-147.

Lagler, K.F. and J.R. Vallentyne. 1956. Fish scales in a sediment core from Linsley Pond, Connecticut. Science 124: 368.

Larned, E.D. 1874. History of Windham County, Connecticut. Charles Hamilton, Worcester, MA, Volume I, 580p.

Larned, E.D. 1880. History of Windham County, Connecticut. Charles Hamilton, Worcester, MA, Volume II, 600p.

Larson, F.D. and J.H. Hartshorn. 1982. Deglaciation of the southern portion of the Connecticut Valley of Massachusetts. p 115-128, *in* Larson, G.J. and D.B. Stone (eds). Late Wisconsinan glaciation of New England. Kendall Hunt Publishing Company, Dubuque, IA.

Lavine, L. 1988. Coastal adaptions in southern New England and southern New York. Archaeology of Eastern North America 16: 101-120.

Lee, D.S., C.R. Gilbert, C.H. Hocutt, R.E. Jenkins, D.E. McAllister and J.R. Stauffer Jr. *et.seq.* 1980. Atlas of North American freshwater fishes. North Carolina State Museum of Natural History, Raleigh, NC, 854p.

Leggett, W.C. 1976. The American shad (*Alosa sapidissima*), with special reference to its migration and population dynamics in the Connecticut River. p 169-225, *in* D. Merriman and L. Thorpe (eds), The Connecticut River ecological study, the impact of a nuclear power plant. American Fisheries Society Monograph number one.

Leggett, W.C. and R.A. Jones. 1971. Net avoidance behavior in American shad (*Alosa sapidissima*) as observed by ultrasonic tracking techniques. Journal of the Fisheries Research Board of Canada 28: 1167-1171.

Leopold, E.B. 1956. Two late-glacial deposits in southern Connecticut. Proceedings of the National Academy of Sciences 42: 863-867.

LeSueur, A. 1817a. Description of two new species of the genus *Gadus.*Journal of the Academy of Natural Sciences of Philadelphia, Series 1, 1: 83-85.

LeSueur, A. 1817b. A new genus of fishes, of the order Abdominales, proposed under the name of *Catostomus* and the characters of this genus, with those of its species indicated. Journal of the Academy of Natural Sciences, Philadelphia Series 1,1: 88-96 and 102-111.

Levesque, J.R. and W.R. Whitworth. 1987. Age class distribution and size of American eel (*Anguilla rostrata*) in the Shetucket/Thames River, Connecticut. Journal of Freshwater Ecology 4: 17-22.

Lewis, T.R. 1981. Near the long tidal river, readings in the historical geography of central Connecticut. University Press of America, Washington, D.C., 147p.

Lewis, W.S. 1946. The Yale Collections. Yale University Press, New Haven, CT, 54p.

Linsley, J. H. 1842. A catalogue of the Mammalia of Connecticut, arranged according to their natural families; furnished for the Yale Natural History Society. American Journal of Science and Arts 43: 345-354.

Linsley, J. H. 1843. A catalogue of the birds of Connecticut, arranged according to their natural families; prepared for the Yale Natural History Society. American Journal of Science and Arts 44: 249-274.

Linsley, J. H. 1844a. A catalogue of the reptiles of Connecticut, arranged according to their natural families; prepared for the Yale Natural History Society. American Journal of Science and Arts 46: 37-51.

Linsley, J. H. 1844b. Catalogue of the fishes of Connecticut, arranged according to the natural families; prepared for the Yale Natural History Society. American Journal of Science and Arts 47: 55-80.

Linsley, J. H. 1845. Catalogue of the shells of Connecticut. American Journal of Science and Arts 48: 271-286.

Loesch, J.G. and W.A. Lund. 1977. A contribution to the life history of the blueback herring. Transactions of the American Fisheries Society 106: 583-589.

Lougee, R.J. 1939. Geology of the Connecticut Watershed. p 131-149, in H.E. Warfel (ed). Biological survey of the Connecticut Watershed. Biological Survey 4, New Hampshire Fish and Game Department, Concord NH

Marcy, B.C. Jr. 1969. Age determinations from scales of *Alosa pseudoharengus* (Wilson) and *Alosa aestivalis* (Mitchill) in Connecticut waters. Transactions of the American Fisheries Society 98: 622-630.

Marcy, B.C. Jr. 1972. Spawning of the American shad, *Alosa sapidissima*, in the lower Connecticut River. Chesapeake Science 13: 116-119.

Marcy, B.C. Jr. 1976a. Fishes of the lower Connecticut River and the effects of the Connecticut Yankee Plant. p 61-113, in D. Merriman and L.M. Thorpe (eds) The Connecticut River ecological study; the impact of a nuclear power plant. American Fisheries Society, Monograph number 1.

Marcy, B.C. Jr. 1976b. Plankton fish eggs and larvae of the lower Connecticut River and the effects of the Connecticut Yankee Plant including entrainment. p 115-139, in D. Merriman and L. Thorpe (ed.) The Connecticut River ecological study; the impact of a nuclear power plant. American Fisheries Society, Monograph number 1.

Marcy, B.C. Jr. 1976c. Early life history studies of American shad in the lower Connecticut River and the effects of the Connecticut Yankee plant. p 141-168, in D. Merriman and L. Thorpe (eds) The Connecticut River ecological study; the impact of a nuclear power plant. American Fisheries Society, Monograph number 1.

Marcy, B.C. Jr. and F.P. Richards. 1974. Age and growth of the white perch in the lower Connecticut River. Transactions of the American Fisheries Society 103: 117-120.

Mather, F. 1896. The influence of railroads on fish culture. Transactions of the American Fisheries Society 24: 17-24.

Mayr, E. and P.D. Ashlock. 1991. Principles of systematic zoology. 2d edition, McGraw-Hill Inc., New York, NY, 475p.

McCabe, B.C. 1942. The distribution of fishes in the streams of western Massachusetts. Ph.D. Thesis, Cornell. 181p plus figures.

McDonald, M. 1887. The Connecticut and Housatonic rivers and minor tributaries of Long Island Sound. p 659-667, in G.B. Goode *et al.*, The fisheries and fishery industries of the United States. Section V, Volume 1, History and methods of the fisheries. United States Government Printing Office, Washington, DC.

McDowell, R.M. 1992. Diadromy: origins and definitions of terminology. Copeia 1992: 248-251.

McKeehan, L.W. 1947. Yale science, the first hundred years, 1701-1801. Henry Schuman, New York, NY, 82p.

Merriman, D. 1941. Studies on the striped bass (*Roccus saxatilis*) of the Atlantic coast. Fishery Bulletin 50: 1-77.

Merriman, D. 1947. Notes on the midsummer ichthyofauna of a Connecticut beach at different tide levels. Copeia 1947: 281-286.

Merriman, D. and Y. Jean. 1949. The capture of an Atlantic salmon (*Salmo salar*) in the Connecticut River. Copeia 1949; 220-221.

Merriman, D. and L.M. Thorpe (eds). 1976. The Connecticut River ecological study; the impact of a nuclear power plant. American Fisheries Society, Monograph 1, 252p.

Mickelson, D.M., L. Clayton, D.S. Fullerton and H.W. Borns Jr. 1983. The late Wisconsin glacial record of the Laurentide ice sheet in the United States. p 3-37, *in* H. E. Wright Jr. (ed) Late Quaternary environments of the United States. Volume I, Stephen Porter (ed) The late Pleistocene. University of Minnesota Press, Minneapolis, MN.

Migdalski, E.C. 1958. Anglers guide to the salt water game fishes, Atlantic and Pacific. The Ronald Press Company, New York, NY, 506p.

Migdalski, E.C. & G.S. Fichter. 1976. The fresh and saltwater fishes of the world. Alfred A. Knopf, New York, NY, 316p.

Miller, R.R. 1965. Quaternary freshwater fishes of North America. p 569-581, *in* H.E. Wright Jr. and D.G. Freys (eds) The Quaternary of the United States. Princeton University Press, Princeton, NJ.

Mitchill, S.L. 1818. The fishes of New York described and arranged. Transactions of the New York Literary and Philosophical Society I: 355-492.

Moeller, R.W. 1980. A paleo-indian site in western Connecticut. American Indian Archaeological Institute, Occasional Paper Number 2, 160p, Washington, CT.

Morton, T. 1637. New English Canaan, or New Canaan, containing abstract of New England, compiled in three books. *in* Adams, C.F. Jr. (ed). New English Canaan of Thomas Morton, with introductory matter and notes. Burt Franklin, New York, NY, 381p.

Moyle, P. 1976. Fish introductions in California: history and impact on native fishes. Biological Conservation 9: 101-118.

Mugford, P.S. 1969. Illustrated manual of Massachusetts freshwater fishes. Massachusetts Division of Fisheries and Game, Boston, MA, 127p.

Myers, G.S. 1949. Usage of anadromous, catadromous and allied terms for migratory fishes. Copeia 1949; 89-97.

Myers, G.S. 1964. A brief sketch of the history of ichthyology in America to the year 1850. Copeia 1964: 33-41.

Nelson, J.S. 1984. Fishes of the world. Second Edition, John Wiley and Sons, New York, NY, 523p.

Newman, W.S. 1977. Late Quaternary paleoenvironmental reconstruction; some contradictions from northwestern Long Island, New York. Annals of the New York Academy of Sciences 288: 545-570.

Newman, W.S., D.H. Thurber, H.S. Zeiss, A. Robcach and L. Musick. 1969. Late Quaternary geology of the Hudson River Estuary: a preliminary report. Transactions of the New York Academy of Sciences, Series II, 31(5): 548-570.

Nicholas, G.P. 1987. Rethinking the early archaic. Archaeology of Eastern North America 15: 99-124.

Nichols, J.T. 1913. A list of fishes known to have occurred within fifty miles of New York City. Proceedings of the Linnaean Society of New York 20-23: 90-106.

Oldale, R.N. and D.M. Eskenasy. 1983. Regional significance of pre-Wisconsinan till from Nantucket Island, Massachusetts. Quaternary Research 19: 302-311.

O'Leary, J. and D.G. Smith. 1987. Occurrence of the first freshwater migration of gizzard shad, *Dorosoma cepedianum*, in the Connecticut River, Massachusetts. Fishery Bulletin 85: 380-383.

Olson, A.L. 1935. Agricultural economy and the population in eighteenth century Connecticut. Tercentenary Commission of the State of Connecticut, Yale University Press, New Haven, CT, 31p.

Orcutt, S. 1882. The Indians of the Housatonic and Naugatuck Velleys. Case, Lockwood and Brainard Company, Hartford, CT, 220p.

Orcutt, S. and A. Beardsley. 1880. The history of the old town of Derby, Connecticut, 1642-1880. With biographies and genealogies. Springfield Printing Company, Springfield, MA, 844p.

Page, L. and B. Burr. 1991. A field guide to freshwater fishes. Houghton Mifflin Co., Boston, MA, 432p.

Pearcy, W.G. and S.W. Richards. 1962. Distribution and ecology of fishes of the Mystic Estuary, Connecticut. Ecology 43: 248-259.

Pease, J.I. 1874. White fish in Twin Lakes. Forest and Stream 2: 229.

Pease, J.C. and J.M. Niles. 1819. A gazetteer of the states of Connecticut and Rhode Island. W.S. Marsh, Hartford, CT, 390p.

Peters, S. 1781. General history of Connecticut, from its first settlement under George Fenweek to its latest period of amity with Great Britian prior to the revolution, including a description of the country, and many curious and interesting anecdotes, with an appendix pointing out the causes of the rebellion in America: together with the particular part taken by the people of Connecticut in its promotion. By a gentleman of the Province. To which are added additions to appendix, notes and extracts from letters verifying many important statements made by the author by S.J. McCormick, 1877. Republished in 1970 by Literature House, Upper Saddle River, NJ.

Pfeiffer, J.E. 1952. Bashan Lake: 4500 years of prehistory. Bulletin of the Archaeological Society of Connecticut 46: 45-53.

Pope, G.D. Jr. 1952. Excavation at the Charles Tyler site. Bulletin of the Archaeological Society of Connecticut 26: 3-29.

Porter, Noll 1841. Historical discourse, delivered by request before the citizens of Farmington, November 5, 1840, in commemoration of the original settlement of the ancient town in 1640. L. Skinner, Hartford, CT, 99p.

Powell, B.W. 1965. Spruce swamp: a partially drowned coastal midden in Connecticut. American Antiquity 30: 460-469.

Pracus, A.A. 1945. The South Woodstock site. Bulletin of the Archaeological Society of Connecticut 17: 1-52.

Prest, V.K. 1970. Quaternary geology of Canada. p 676-764, in R.J.W. Douglas (ed) Geology and economic minerals of Canada. Geology Survey of Canada, Economic Geology Report #1, Department of Energy, Mines and Resources, Ottawa.

Prest, V.K. 1984. The late Wisconsinan glacier complex. p 21-36, in R.J. Fulton (ed) Quaternary stratigraphy of Canada: A Canadian contribution to IGCP, project 24. Geological Survey of Canada, paper 84-10.

Rafinesque, C.S. 1817. Survey of the progress and actual state of natural sciences in the United States of America, from the beginning of this century to the present time. American Monthly Magazine and Critical Review II: 81-89.

Rafinesque, C.S. 1818. Introduction to the ichthyology of the United States. American Monthly Magazine and Critical Review II:202-203.

Rand, C. 1968. The changing landscape, Salisbury Connecticut. Oxford Press, New York, NY, 192p.

Rau, C. 1884. Prehistoric fishing in Europe and North America. Smithsonian Contributions to Knowledge 25: 1-342.

Regan, C. 1903. Descriptions de poissons nouveaux faisant partie de la collection du Musee D'Historie Naturelle de Geneve. Revue Suisse de Zoologie 2: 413-418.

Regan, C. 1909. The Asiatic fishes of the family Anabantidae. Proceedings of the Zoological Society of London, 1909: 767-787.

Rice, A.N. 1887. Occurrence of *Stizostedion vitreum* in the basin of the Connecticut. American Naturalist 21: 938-939.

Rice, A.N. 1888. *Stizostedion* in the basin of the Connecticut. American Naturalist 22: 934.

Ritchie, W.A. 1965. The archaeology of New York State. The Natural History Press, Garden City, NY, 357p.

Robins, C.R., R.M. Bailey, C.E. Bond, J.R. Brooker, E.A. Lachner, R.N. Lea and W.B. Scott. 1991. A list of common and scientific names of fishes from the United States and Canada. 5th Edition, American Fisheries Society Special Publication Number 20, 183p.

Rostlund, E. 1952. Freshwater fish and fishing in native North America. University of California Publications in Geography 9: 314p.

Russell, L.W. 1942. The Menunketisuck site, Westbrook, Connecticut. Bulletin of the Archeological Society of Connecticut 14: 3-62.

Savelle, M. 1966. A history of colonial America. Holt, Rinehart and Winston, New York, 701p.

Scarola, J.F. 1973. Freshwater fishes of New Hampshire. New Hampshire Department of Fisheries and Game, Concord, NH, 131p.

Schaefer, J.P. and J.H. Hartshorn. 1965. The Quaternary of New England, p 113-128, in H.E. Wright Jr. and D.G. Frey (eds) The Quaternary of the United States. Princeton University Press, Princeton, NJ.Schmidt, R.E. 1986. Zoogeography of the northern Appalachians. 137-159, in C.H. Hocutt and E.O. Wiley (eds) The zoogeography of North American freshwater fishes. John Wiley and Sons, New York, NY.

Schmidt, R.E. and W.R. Whitworth. 1979. Distribution and habitat of the swamp darter (*Etheostoma fusiforme*) in southern New England. American Midland Naturalist 102; 408-413.

Schultz, R.J. 1969. Hybridization, unisexuality, and polyploidy in the teleost *Poeciliopsis* (Poecillidae) and other vertebrates. American Naturalist 103: 605-619.

Scott, W.B. and E.J. Crossman. 1973. Freshwater fishes of Canada. Bulletin 184, Fisheries Research Board of Canada, Ottawa, 966p.

Scott, W.B. and M.G. Scott. 1988. Atlantic fishes of Canada. Canadian Bulletin of Fisheries and Aquatic Sciences, 219. 731p.

Sears, P.B. 1948. Forest sequence and climatic changes in northeastern North America since early Wisconsin time. Ecology 29: 326-333.

Sears, P.B. 1963. Vegetation, climate and coastal submergence in Connecticut. Science 140: 59-60.

Shaw, G. 1804. General Zoology. Volume 5, part 1, Pisces. Thomas Davison, White Friars, England, 250p.

Sirkin, L. 1982. Wisconsinan glaciation of Long Island, New York, to Block Island, Rhode Island. p 35-59, *in* G.J. Larson and B.D. Stone (eds). Late Wisconsinan glaciation of New England. Kendall Hunt Publishing Company, Dubuque, IA.

Smellie, W. 1832. The philosophy of natural history, with an introduction and various additions and alterations, intended to adapt it to the present state of knowledge by J.O. Ware. Hilliard, Gray, Little and Wilkins, Boston, MA, 327p.

Smith, C.L. 1985. The inland fishes of New York State. The New York State Department of Environmental Conservation, Albany, NY, 522p.

Smith, C.P. 1946. Housatonic, puritan river. Rinehart and Company, New York, NY, 532p.

Smith, H.W. 1890a. Notes on a collection of fishes from the lower Potomac River, Maryland. Bulletin of the United States Fish Commission 10: 63-72.

Smith, H.W. 1890b. Report on an investigation of the fisheries of Lake Ontario. Bulletin of the United States Fish Commission 10: 177-216.

Smith, H.W. 1891. Report on the fisheries of the south Atlantic states. Bulletin of the United States Fish Commission 11: 269-356.

Smith, H.W. and W.C. Kendall. 1921. Fishes of the Yellowstone National Park, with descriptions of the park waters and notes on fishing. Report of the Commissioner for fisheries for 1921, document 904, 30p.

Smith, J. 1833. Natural history of the fishes of Massachusetts, embracing a practical essay on angling. Allen and Ticknor, Boston, MA, 399p.

Smith, J.W. 1887. Gleanings from the sea: showing the pleasures, pains and penalties of life afloat, with contingencies ashore. Published by the author, Andover MA, 399p.

Springman, M.J. and B.F. Giunan. 1983. East Granby, the evolution of a Connecticut town. Phoenix Publishing, Canaan, NH, 350p.

Starr, E.C. 1926. A history of Cornwall Connecticut, a typical New England town. Tuttle, Morehouse and Taylor Co., New Haven, CT, 547p.

Steindachner, F. 1866. Ichthyologishe Mitteilungen (IX). Verhandlungen Zoologisch-Botanischen Gesellschaft 16: 761-796.

Steinmetz, C. and B. Boehm. 1980. A localized, over-wintering population of the mosquitofish, *Gambusia affinis*, in Connecticut. p 22-29 *in* P.M. Jacobs (ed) Studies of the ichthyofauna of Connecticut. Storrs Agricultural Experiment Station, Bulletin Number 457.

Steir, K. and B. Kynard. 1986. Movements of sea-run lamprey, *Petromyzon marinus*, during the spawning migration in the Connecticut River. Fisheries Bulletin 84: 749-753.

Stock, L.F. ed. 1927. Proceedings and debates of the British Parliament respecting North America. Volume II (1689-1702). Carnegie Institution, Washington, DC.

Stock, L.F. ed. 1930. Proceedings and debates of the British Parliament respecting North America. Volume III (1702-1727) Carnegie Institution Washington DC.

Stoll, N.R. *et al.* 1961. International code of zoological nomenclature adopted by the XV International Congress of Zoology. Published for the International Commission on Zoological Nomenclature, 176p.

Stone, B.D. and J.O. Peper. 1982. Topographic control of the deglaciation of eastern Massachusetts: ice lobation and the moraine incursion. p 145-166. *in* G.J. Larson and B.D. Stone (eds). Late Wisconsinan glaciation of New England. Kendall Hunt Publishing Company, Dubuque, IA.

Stone, B.W. 1974. The role of the learned societies in the growth of scientific Boston, 1780-1848. Ph.D. Thesis, Boston University, 549p.

Stone, L. 1896. The artificial propagation of salmon on the Pacific coast of the United States, with notes on the natural history of the Quinnat salmon. Bulletin of the United States Fish Commission 16: 203-235.

Storer, D.H. 1839. A report on the fishes of Massachusetts. Boston Journal of Natural History 2: 289-558.

Storer, D.H. 1842a. Description of two species of fishes. Boston Journal of Natural History 4: 58-62.

Storer, D.H. 1842b. Additional descriptions of, and observations on the fishes of Massachusetts. Boston Journal of Natural History 4: 175-190.

Storer, D.H. 1853. A history of the fishes of Massachusetts. Memoirs of the American Academy of Arts and Sciences, New Series V, part I: 49-92 and 122-168.

Storer, D.H. 1855. A history of the fishes of Massachusetts, continued. Memoirs of the American Academy of Arts and Sciences, New Series V, part II: 258-296.

Storer, D.H. 1858. A history of the fishes of Massachusetts, continued. Memoirs of the American Academy of Arts and Sciences, New Series, VI, part 11: 309-372.

Storer, D.H. 1863. A history of the fishes of Massachusetts, continued. Memoirs of the American Academy of Arts and Sciences, New Series, VIII, part II: 389-434.

Swigart, E.K. 1973. The Kirby Brook site (6-LF-2): an interim report. Bulletin of the Archeological Society of Connecticut 38: 40-53.

Swigart, E.K. 1974. The prehistory of the Indians of western Connecticut. Part I, 9000-1000 B.C. Volume I, A research report of the Shepaug Valley Archaeology Society, Washington, CT, 49p.

Swigart, E.K. 1977. The ecological placement of western Connecticut sites. Archaeology of Eastern North America 5: 61-73.

Swigart, E.K. 1987. The Woodruff rock shelter site-6LF126, an interim report-faunal analysis as a means to evaluate environment and culture. Bulletin of the Archeological Society of Connecticut 50: 43-75.

Taylor, R.J. 1979. Colonial Connecticut, a history. KTO Press, Millwood, NJ, 285p.

Teller, J.T. 1987. Proglacial lakes and the southern margin of the laurentide ice sheet. p 39-69, *in* W.F. Ruddiman and H.E. Wright Jr. (eds.) Volume K-3, North America and adjacent oceans during the last deglaciation. The Geological Society of America, Boulder, CO.

Teller, J.T. 1989. Volume and routing of late-glacial runoff from the southern Laurentide ice sheet. Quaternary Research 34: 12-33.

Thomas, M.P. 1972. Gazetteer of natural drainage areas of streams and water bodies within the state of Connecticut. Connecticut Department of Environmental Protection, Bulletin Number 1, 134p.

Thomas, P.A. 1976. Contrastive subsistence strategies and land use as factors for understanding indian-white relations in New England. Ethnohistory 23: 1-18.

Thompson, Z. 1842. History of Vermont, natural, civil and statistical , in three parts, with a map of the state and 200 engravings. Published for the author by Chauncy Goodrick, Burlington, VT, Part 1, natural, 224p, Part 2, civil, 224 p., Part 3, gazetteer, 200p.

Thomson, K.S., W.H. Weed III and A.G. Taruski. 1971. Saltwater fishes of Connecticut. Bulletin 105, State Geological and Natural History Survey of Connecticut, Hartford, CT, 165p.

Thomson, K.S., W.H. Weed III, A.G. Taruski and D.E. Simanek. 1978. Saltwater fishes of Connecticut. Bulletin 105, 2d Edition, State Geological and Natural History Survey of Connecticut, Hartford, CT, 186p.

Tolderlund, D.S. 1975. Ecological study of the Thames River Estuary (Conn.) in the vicinity of the U.S. Coast Guard Academy. U.S. Coast Guard Academy, Report RDCGA-575, 135p.

Trautman, M. 1957. The fishes of Ohio. Ohio State University Press, Columbus, OH, 683p.

Trumbull, B. 1818. A complete history of Connecticut, civil and ecclesiastical, from the emigration of its first planters, from England, in the year 1630, to the year 1764; and to the close of the Indian wars. Volume 1, 567p, Volume II, 548p. Reprint edition, 1972, Arno Press, New York, NY.

Turner, G.M. and M.W. Jacobus. 1989. Connecticut railroads, an illustrated history. The Connecticut Historical Society, Hartford, CT, 317p.

Urry, W.D. 1948. The radium content of varved clays and a possible age of the Hartford, Connecticut, deposits. American Journal of Science 246: 689-700.

Vallentyne, J.R. 1960. On fish remains in lacustrine sediments. American Journal of Science 258A: 344-349.

Vallentyne, J.R. and S. Swabey. 1955. A reinvestigation of the history of lower Linsley Pond, Connecticut. American Journal of Science 253: 313-340.

Wales, J.H. 1939. General report of investigations on the McCloud River drainage in 1939. California Fish and Game 25: 272-309.

Warner, F.W. 1972. The foods of the Connecticut Indians. Bulletin of the Archeological Society 37: 27-47.

Warner, J. and B. Kynard. 1986. Scavenger feeding by subadult striped bass, *Morone saxatilis*, below a low-head hydroelectric dam. Fisheries Bulletin 84: 220-221.

Waters, J.H. 1962. Some animals used as food by successive cultural groups in New England. Bulletin of the Archeological Society of Connecticut 31: 32-46.

Waters, J.H. 1965. Animal remains from some New England woodland sites. Bulletin of the Archeological Society of Connecticut 33:5-11.

Waters, J.H. 1967. Fish remains from southern New England archeological sites. Copeia, 1967: 244-247.

Weber, M. and L. DeBeaufort. 1922. The fishes of the Indo-Australian Archipelago. Volume IV, 410p. E.J. Brill Ltd, Leiden, Holland.

Webster, D.A. 1942. The life histories of some Connecticut fishes. p 122-227, *in* Anonymous (ed) A fishery survey of important Connecticut Lakes. State Geological and Natural History Survey, Bulletin Number 63. Hartford, CT.

Wheeler, R.A. 1966. History of the town of Stonington, county of New London, Connecticut, from its first settlement in 1649, to 1900, with a genealogical register of Stonington families. Lawrence Verry Inc., Mystic, CT, 754p.

White, A.C. 1920. The history of the town of Litchfield, Connecticut, 1720-1920. Enquirer Printer, Litchfield, CT, 360p.

Whitworth, W.R., P.L. Berrien and W.T. Keller. 1968. Freshwater fishes of Connecticut. State Geological and Natural History Survey, Bulletin Number 101, 134p.

Whitworth, W.R., D.R. Gibbons, J.H. Heuer, W.E. Johns and R.E. Schmidt. 1975. A general survey of the fishery resources of the Thames River Watershed, Connecticut. p 1-41, *in* R.L. Hames (ed) An evaluation of the fishery resources of the Thames River Watershed, Connecticut. Storrs Agricultural Experiment Station, Bulletin Number 435.

Whitworth, W.R. and P.L. Marsh. 1980. Seasonal utilization of the upper Thames Estuary, Connecticut. p 14-21, *in* P.L. Jacobson (ed) Studies of the ichthyofauna of Connecticut. Storrs Agricultural Experiment Station, Bulletin Number 457.

Whitworth, W.R., P. Minta and R. Orciari. 1980. Further additions to, and notes on the freshwater ichthyofauna of Connecticut. p 27-29, *in* P.M. Jacobson (ed) Studies of the ichthyofauna of Connecticut. Storrs Agricultural Experiment Station, Bulletin Number 457.

Whitworth, W.R. and R.E. Schmidt. 1971. Additions to "freshwater fishes of Connecticut." University of Connecticut, Occasional Papers, Biological Sciences Series 2: 1-4.

Wiegand, E.A. 1983. Rockshelters of southwestern Connecticut. Norwalk Community College Press, Norwalk, CT, 191 pages.

Williams, J.E., J.E. Johnson, D.A. Hendrickson, S. Contreras-Balderas, J.D. Williams, M. Navarro-Mendoza, D.E. McAllister and J.E. Deacan. 1989. Fishes of North America endangered, threatened, or of special concern: 1989 Fisheries 14(6): 2-20.

Williams, R. 1643. A key into the language of America: or an help to the language of the natives, in that part of America called New England. Together with brief observations of the customs, manners and worship etc of the aforesaid natives, in peace and war, in life and death. Collections of the Massachusetts Historical Society 1794: III: 203-228.

Withington, S. 1935. The first twenty years of railroads in Connecticut. Tercentenary Commission of the State of Connecticut. XLV, Yale University Press, New Haven, CT, 32p.

Wolcott, R. 1725. The poems of Roger Wolcott, *esq.* Republished in 1898 by the Club of Old Volumes, University Press, Cambridge, MA, 78 p.

Wolcott, R. 1759. A memoir for the history of Connecticut. Reprinted in Collections of the Connecticut Historical Society 3: 323-336.

Wood, G.I. 1850. The early history of the Congregational Church and the Society of North Branford. Delivered in the Congregational Church, January 6, 1850. J.H. Benham, New Haven, CT, 23p.

Wood, W. 1634. New England prospect. London 110p.

Wright, H.E. Jr. 1971. Retreat of the laurentide ice sheet from 14,000 to 9,000 years ago. Quaternary Research 1: 316-330.

Wright, H.E. Jr. 1987. Synthesis; the land south of the ice sheets. p 479-488 *in* W.F. Ruddiman and H.E. Wright Jr. (eds). The Geology of North America and adjacent oceans during the last deglaciation. Volume K-3, The Geological Society of America, Boulder, CO.

Index

Freshwater Fishes of Connecticut

Written, produced, printed and bound in Connecticut,
on Potlatch Mountie Matte recycled paper,
using vegetable inks.
Layout and typesetting composed on a
Power Macintosh 8500 in Quark XPress
using New Caledonia for text pages,
and Albertus MT for the cover.

Printed by Hitchcock Printing and Distribution Services
New Britain, Connecticut